RELIGION

THE AMERICAN CONSTITUTION AND RELIGION

RICHARD J. REGAN

The Catholic University of America Press
WASHINGTON, D.C.

Library of Congress Cataloging-in-Publication Data
Regan, Richard J.
The American Constitution and religion / Richard J. Regan.
pages cm
Includes bibliographical references and index.
ISBN 978-0-8132-2152-6 (pbk. : alk. paper)
1. Freedom of religion—United States.   2. Religion and state—United States.
3. Constitutional law—United States—Philosophy.   I. Title.
KF4783.R425 2013
342.7308'52—dc23   2013019476

CONTENTS

PREFACE

This book deals principally with Supreme Court decisions on the religious clauses of the First Amendment, in connection both with federal activity and with state and local activity via the Fourteenth Amendment. This study involves the history of the drafting of the amendments, legal analysis of the cases, and, of course, philosophical considerations. In addition, I have introduced the study with a description of the Constitution's regime principles and concluded it with a profile of Western traditions of conscience and a suggested typology of conflicts between individual conscience and public law.

The book deals summarily with a number of fundamental questions (e.g., constitutional interpretation, federalism, implied powers, and judicial review). For concise treatment of such jurisprudential questions, with bibliographies, the reader may consult Kermit L. Hall, ed., *The Oxford Companion to the Supreme Court of the United States,* 2nd ed. (New York: Oxford University Press, 2005). On theories of constitutional interpretation, the reader may consult J. Harvie Wilkerson III, *Cosmic Constitutional Theory* (New York: Oxford University Press, 2012).

I have adapted some material from previously published books and articles. I am grateful to Fordham University Press for permission regarding *Private Conscience and Public Law* (1972) and

Preface

articles in *Thought Magazine* (1979–1988), to Macmillan Company regarding *American Pluralism and the Catholic Conscience* (1963), and to *The Catholic Lawyer* regarding "The Dilemma of Religious Instruction and the Public Schools" (1964).

Richard J. Regan
Fordham University

ABBREVIATIONS

BIBLICAL

Cor.	Corinthians
Ex.	Exodus
Is.	Isaiah
Jer.	Jeremiah
Mt.	Matthew
Rom.	Romans
Tim.	Timothy
Wis.	Wisdom

OTHER

A., AA.	Article, Articles
Art.	Article
cl.	clause
C	*Commentary on the Sentences*
Q.	Question
sec.	section
ST	*Summa Theologica*

THE AMERICAN
CONSTITUTION AND
RELIGION

1

THE REGIME PRINCIPLES OF
THE CONSTITUTION

Meeting in Philadelphia from May to September 1787, the Constitutional Convention drew up an instrument of government for submission to the thirteen states. Rhode Island sent no delegates, and two important leaders of the American Revolution and future presidents of the United States were absent: Thomas Jefferson was in Paris as ambassador to France, and John Adams was in London as ambassador to Great Britain. Two fiery patriots, Patrick Henry and Richard Henry Lee, refused to attend. Nevertheless, the Convention included illustrious participants, such as Alexander Hamilton of New York, James Wilson and Gouverneur Morris of Pennsylvania, and especially James Madison of Virginia. Benjamin Franklin was present, and George Washington, the victorious commander of the army in the Revolutionary War, presided. The delegates were commercially minded, lawyer-dominated, and intent on establishing a central government with independent powers to raise taxes, regulate commerce, and govern foreign affairs.

The views of the framers of the Constitution on society and government, like the views of the framers of the Declaration of

Independence, reflected the philosophy of the British Enlightenment in general and John Locke in particular. Their religious views ran a wide gambit, from the skepticism of Franklin to the Catholicism of Daniel Carroll. Many were Deists, but most of them probably believed in the immortality of the soul and attended church services at least periodically. In fact, during the Convention's sessions in Philadelphia, the delegates occasionally attended church services, including once at a nearby Jesuit residence.

By the time of the Revolution, the colonists had laid the foundation of self-government and the framework of their legal systems. All the colonies had a bicameral legislature, the lower house of which was a popularly elected assembly that controlled the purse and participated in legislating. In New England, local officials were elected and local ordinances adopted at town meetings. Although the Crown appointed governors in the royal colonies and proprietors in the proprietary colonies, Rhode Island and Connecticut elected theirs. The governors in most colonies appointed the executive council, but Massachusetts, Rhode Island, and Connecticut voters elected theirs. The Crown—that is, the British government—appointed the judges in most colonies, but the legislatures of Rhode Island and Connecticut appointed theirs. The division of executive, legislative, and judicial powers was modeled on the British Constitution. But suffrage in the colonies was restricted. Women were excluded, and voting was in several states limited to freeholders. The colonists also adopted the principles of English law, including codes of criminal and civil law, trial by jury, and the writ of habeas corpus.

It is important to note that the framers, despite their philosophical convictions and British heritage, were engaged in practical statecraft. The pragmatic need to overcome the deficiencies of the Articles of Confederation was their driving motivation for governmental reform. The Confederation required unanimous consent of the states to regulate domestic commerce, to establish a stable currency, to collect taxes, to pay foreign debts, and to negotiate with foreign powers. The primary object of the framers was to remedy these deficiencies with a strong national government.

Four basic principles underlie the U.S. Constitution. First, the Constitution grants limited powers to the federal government, and the federal officials have only the powers the Constitution explicitly or implicitly grants. Second, the powers of the federal government derive from the consent of the people. Third, the Constitution provided for separate executive, legislative, and judicial powers, and those powers checked and balanced one another. Fourth, the Constitution provided for a federal system of government in which both the federal government and the state governments had legitimate powers.

CONSTITUTIONALISM

The expression "government of laws, not of human beings" signifies the essence of constitutionalism—that is, limited government. Law can mean customs and conventions, statutes, judicial decisions, or higher law. If we accept some or all of these as constituting a fundamental framework of government, then the word *constitution* denotes the body of rules, written and unwritten, that constitute the character of a particular government.

Unlike the kingdom of Persia, whose rulers were despots and subjects were slaves, the Greek city-states had largely unwritten constitutions that specified the roles of rulers and citizen-subjects. But the Greek city-states were internally unstable and ultimately subjugated by the Macedonians. Rome had a largely unwritten constitution embodying aristocratic and democratic elements, but it, unable by the first century B.C. to manage social and economic tensions, lapsed into rule by personal triumvirates and ultimately emperors, although subjects continued to be citizens with certain rights. Medieval Western kingdoms had custom-based constitutions, but there was no means to control the monarch's exercise of power short of rebellion, although parliaments were by the end of the thirteenth century A.D. evolving in England and elsewhere. The rise of absolute monarchies in the early modern period put an end to any institutional constitutionalism. The king claimed absolute power from God and admitted responsibility only to him.

Modern constitutionalism involved the attempts of subjects to limit the powers of kings. In England this involved the revolutions against Charles I and James II. The American colonists accepted the English settlement and developed its institutional framework and customary rights in their own evolution. But the eighteenth-century philosophy of natural rights offered by Locke was so neatly tailored to the Anglo-American tradition, the American conception of the British Constitution, and the rights of Englishmen that it deserves further consideration.

Locke's theory of knowledge was empirical and subjective. Human beings knew the sensibly perceptible phenomena of things, not the nature of things. Nevertheless, they had a self-evident idea of the law of nature. In the state of nature, all human beings were free, independent, and equal,[1] and Locke apparently thought that the indigenous inhabitants in the Americas lived in such a state. Unlike ancient and medieval philosophers, who considered human beings inclined by nature to live in an organized community, Locke postulated that human beings are by nature asocial, and they could become subject to the authority of rulers in a community only by the consent of their individual wills. The latter proposition was, for Locke, self-evident.

Nevertheless, the insecurity of the rights of individuals to their life, liberty, and property in the state of nature drives them to contract with one another to organize themselves into a society

---

1. John Locke, *Second Treatise of Government*, chap.2.

and subject themselves to rulers.[2] Although individual autonomy is the state of nature and accordingly preferable, government is necessary because the state of nature has no clear standard to define the rights of individuals or adequate power to preserve those rights. By consenting to form a society and establishing the form of government by majority decision, individuals morally oblige themselves to obey the rulers established.[3] The rulers are not parties to the contract, but trustees to define and enforce it, and so, if rulers abuse their trust, the compact is dissolved, and revolution justified.[4]

The concept of natural rights was not new with Locke. Ancient and medieval philosophers had long distinguished natural justice and naturally right order from convention, and the order of nature included an organized association of individuals with one another. Unlike those philosophers, Locke excluded sociability from his theoretical state of nature. According to him, the asocial nature of human beings was self-evident, presumably meaning an analytic proposition—that is, a proposition in which the predicate (unsociability) is contained in the definition of the subject (human being). But quite the opposite is analytically true. Human beings are rational animals, and so they as such are by nature inclined to live in cooperative association with one another in pursuit of their material well-being and especially immaterial well-being—namely, the acquisition of intellectual and moral virtue.

Locke reduced the rationality of individuals joining in an organized society and government to a calculation of necessary means to preserve one's life and secure one's rights, in effect a mutual nonaggression pact with a peacekeeping force. By restricting the function of the state to safeguarding individual rights, he eliminates from government a positive role to promote the common

2. Locke, *Second Treatise*, chap. 7.
3. Locke, *Second Treatise*, chap. 8.
4. Locke, *Second Treatise*, chap. 19.

material and immaterial good and reduces the very notion of a common good in which individuals share to the aggregation of individual goods.

The framers were not only legatees of John Locke. Their experiences as Englishmen and colonists also influenced them. They were conscious of the parliamentary struggles against the Stuarts to vindicate civil and parliamentary rights, their own struggles with royal governors, over whom they had a kind of veto power by their control of the purse, and their relatively recent struggle for independence. They accepted from these experiences the practical necessity of restraining government to limited objectives. Moreover, the framers knew that states rights were popular, and so that only a limited federal government was possible. In this context it is difficult to say how much the philosophy of Locke, albeit a theoretical framework, influenced the framers' thinking.

The preamble declares that the Constitution was being established "in order to form a more perfect union, establish justice, insure domestic tranquility, provide for the common defense, promote the general welfare, and secure the blessings of liberty." The aim of promoting the general welfare seems to indicate a broader concept of the sphere of government than Locke's, and the Supreme Court, in both *U.S. v. Butler,*[5] invalidating taxes to pay farmers to curtail agricultural production, and *Stewart Machine Co. v. Davis,*[6] validating taxes to pay unemployment compensation, affirmed the power of Congress to levy taxes for the general welfare without any specific grant of such power. The former decision held that Congress could not impose regulations on recipients invasive of the power of states to regulate agricultural production, but a later decision, *U.S. v. Darby,*[7] rejected the distinction between production and commerce. This brought regula-

---

5. *U.S. v. Butler,* 297 U.S. 1 (1936).
6. *Stewart Machine Co. v. Davis,* 301 U.S. 548 (1937).
7. *U.S. v. Darby,* 312 U.S. 100 (1941).

tions of agricultural production in connection with the power to tax within the power of Congress to regulate commerce.

Article 1, sec. 8, cl. 1 granted to Congress the power to lay and collect taxes, but Article 1, secs. 2 and 9 required that all direct taxes be apportioned on a per capita basis. Madison's notes shed no light on the distinction between direct and indirect taxes, but *Hylton v. U.S.* held in 1796 that only head and land taxes were direct taxes.[8] During the Civil War, Congress levied the first income tax, which the Supreme Court in *Springer v. U.S.* upheld as an indirect tax.[9] In 1894, Congress passed a permanent income tax, which the Supreme Court in *Pollock v. Farmers' Loan and Trust Co.* declared a direct tax and so unconstitutional.[10] Although the framers never considered the possibility of federal income taxes and would probably have denied Congress power to levy such taxes had they considered the matter, the traditional understanding of direct taxes and the unlimited constitutional power of Congress to levy indirect taxes should have sufficed to validate the income-tax law. The subsequent Sixteenth Amendment adopted in 1913, of course, settled the question.

Article 1, sec. 8, cl. 3 also granted to Congress the power to regulate commerce among the several states. The framers primarily designed the clause to enable Congress to remove barriers of interstate commerce. Through most of the nineteenth century, the constitutional issues concerning this clause involved whether state or local regulations violated it. In one case (*Gibbons v. Ogden*),[11] however, John Marshall gave broad definitions of the key words: *commerce* includes everything related to commercial intercourse; *among the several states* means all action affecting more than one state; *regulate* means complete control. Beginning in the

---

8. *Hylton v. U.S.*, 3 U.S. 171 (1796).
9. *Springer v. U.S.*, 102 U.S. 586 (1881).
10. *Pollock v. Farmers' Loan and Trust Co.*, 158 U.S. 601 (1895).
11. *Gibbons v. Ogden*, 22 U.S. 1 (1824).

late nineteenth century, Congress exercised its jurisdiction under clause to regulate railroads (the Interstate Commerce Act) and commercial combinations (the Sherman Antitrust Act). As a result of the Great Depression, the federal government assumed comprehensive management of the economy. In 1935, the Social Security Act inaugurated the welfare state. The framers, had they been legislators, might have supported the regulatory federal actions, but they would almost certainly have opposed the welfare state. Nonetheless, the general wording of the commerce clause supports its constitutionality.

Congress in 1791 passed legislation to charter the Bank of the United States for twenty years. President George Washington, over the strong objections of Thomas Jefferson, the secretary of state, signed the legislation. Congress did not recharter the bank in 1811, but a Second Bank was charted in 1816. When Maryland attempted to tax the Baltimore branch in 1818, its manager, McCulloch, refused to pay the tax, Maryland brought action against him, and the state courts ruled against the bank. McCulloch then appealed to the U.S. Supreme Court. Strict constructionists, following Jefferson, denied that Congress had power to charter national banks, since there was no express provision in the Constitution granting Congress that power. Broad constructionists, following Alexander Hamilton, the original proponent of the bank, argued for an implied congressional power.

In the landmark case of *McCulloch v. Maryland*,[12] Marshall ruled that Congress had the power to charter the bank. He admitted that Congress has only the powers enumerated in the Constitution, but argued that this includes powers implied in the enumerated powers. Unlike the Articles of Confederation, the Constitution does not exclude implied powers, and the Tenth Amendment declares only that powers not delegated to the Unit-

12. *McCulloch v. Maryland*, 17 U.S. 316 (1819).

ed States, nor prohibited to the states, are reserved to the states and the people, not that powers not *expressly* delegated are reserved to them. Congress has the power to select the means to implement its express powers to lay and collect taxes, to borrow money, to regulate commerce, to declare and conduct war, and to raise and support armies and navies. Moreover, Art. 1, sec. 8, cl.18 grants Congress the power to make all laws necessary and proper to the execution of the foregoing powers (clauses 1–17). Because clause 18 of section 8 purports to enlarge the powers of Congress, in contrast to section 9, which limits them, the word *necessary* should be interpreted to mean convenient or useful, not absolutely necessary. (Given Marshall's argument for implied powers, reliance on the so-called elastic clause [Art. 1, sec. 8, cl. 18] seems superfluous.)

The broad construction of those powers of Congress may well exceed the intentions or expectations of at least some of the framers. No framer at the Convention, according to Madison's notes, even mentioned the possibility of a federal power to tax personal income or charter a national bank, and most framers surely did not envision a federal power to tax to support unemployment compensation. But, as Justice Frankfurter once observed, the words of the Constitution that the framers wrote, not their intentions, constitute the first guidepost for interpreting it.[13]

The foregoing description of the powers of Congress makes clear that the Constitution needs to be interpreted, especially because the Constitution provides a general framework for government rather than the detailed rules of a statute. But who is to decide authoritatively whether a federal law is constitutional? *Hylton v. U.S.* indirectly addressed the question in 1796 when the Court upheld a federal tax on carriages,[14] but *Marbury v. Madison*

---

13. *Adamson v. California,* 332 U.S. 46, 64 (1947).
14. *Hylton v. U.S.,* 3 U.S. 171 (1796).

directly addressed and answered the question in 1803 when the Court invalidated the provision of a federal law regulating the Supreme Court's jurisdiction.[15]

William Marbury had been appointed justice of the peace in the District of Columbia and confirmed by the Senate, and his commission had been signed by President Adams and sealed by the outgoing secretary of state, John Marshall. The incoming secretary of state under President Jefferson, James Madison, refused to deliver the commission to Marbury. Marbury then brought an original action in the Supreme Court to order its delivery. The Judiciary Act of 1789, sec. 13, authorized the Court to issue writs of mandamus to courts and officers of the United States, and Marshall, now chief justice, interpreted, very arguably misinterpreted, the act to authorize the exercise of original jurisdiction by the Court. Marshall held that Congress could not enlarge the Court's original jurisdiction beyond the items enumerated in Art. 3, sec.2, clause 2, and that the relevant part of section 13 of the act was unconstitutional.

Marshall claimed that it was the judicial function to say what the Constitution is. The only argument he made to substantiate that claim was an appeal to the judge's oath promising to discharge judicial duties in accord with the Constitution. The Constitution does not expressly say that the Court may declare a federal law unconstitutional, although *Federalist* 78 suggests that it may. One may reasonably suppose that the Constitution allows, and the judicial function requires, the Court not to apply a federal statute deemed unconstitutional to cases before it, but that does not necessarily imply that the Court's interpretation binds the president. Indeed, that was precisely the position of President Jefferson. Nonetheless, since allowing the executive to determine the constitutionality of federal statutes in one way and the Court

---

15. *Marbury v. Madison*, 5 U.S. 137 (1803).

in another way would invite political chaos, judicial supremacy regarding interpretation of the Constitution is now commonly accepted, and so the Constitution is effectively what the Supreme Court says it is. Moreover, the legislative supremacy obtaining in many parliamentary systems means that those who write the laws also determine their constitutionality, which invites Plato's famous question: Who will watch over the guardians?

In conclusion, however much the political philosophy of John Locke was the theoretical foundation of the Constitution as an instrument of limited government, the framers tailored theory to the practical aim of statecraft—namely, to frame a powerful and practical instrument of government. The text was susceptible to broad construction, and John Marshall used judicial power to so construe the text. In *Gibbons* he gave the commerce clause a broad construction. In *McCulloch* he ascribed implied powers to Congress and invoked the elastic clause to support that position. In *Marbury* he established the Court itself as the supreme arbiter of the Constitution. Thus the Constitution, designed to confer sufficient power to meet the needs of 1787, enabled future generations to address problems that required greater federal action.

POPULAR SOVEREIGNTY

Government in Western societies involves a concept that it derives from the consent of the governed. This may mean simply that government derives from the rational and free activity of citizens seeking a common good by their organization in a body politic. It may mean that the people designate their governing personnel. It may mean that political authority resides in governments directly from the people rather than directly from God. Last, when restricted to democratic governments, it may mean that the people determine government policy either directly or through representatives, and that the people never completely transmit their power to governments and so remain the supreme political authority.

We owe to the Greeks the idea that citizens are not slaves of their rulers, although Plato and Aristotle were focused on the good or best form of government rather the derivation of political authority. This idea implies that the authority of rulers derives from the consent of the citizen-subjects. Romans of the Republic also thought that citizens were free, but they were more conscious of statutory and customary law. Cicero, for example, defined the commonwealth as an association of human beings under laws.[16]

Medieval Christian philosopher-theologians derived political authority ultimately from God, the author of nature, but they derived the ruler's authority proximately from the people. In the sixteenth century Catholic philosopher-theologians, principally Spanish, conscious of the emerging centralized monarchies and reacting against the theory of the divine right of kings, maintained an explicit transmission theory. God conferred authority immediately on the political community that human beings formed by mutual consent, and the political community transmitted its authority to the ruler they instituted. Thus they reconciled the community's derivation of authority from God and the ruler's derivation of authority from the community.

An impetus for a contract theory between governments and peoples came from Massachusetts Bay Calvinists. They espoused a twofold covenant, one between God and the elect individually and the other a theocracy between God and the elect collectively. Even when, by 1787, the Enlightenment had eroded the theological and theocratic foundations of the social covenant, the language and governmental framework of the social covenant remained embedded in the thinking of New Englanders.

Thomas Hobbes and Jean-Jacques Rousseau authored other contract theories, but American colonists preferred Locke's, because his embodied individual rights and reflected their own

---

16. Cicero, *The Commonwealth*.

experience in founding new communities and governments. Accordingly, the framers held that citizens contracted to form society and institute government for limited purposes.

But the government the framers established, like that of Locke, was not completely democratic—that is, not completely egalitarian nor completely subject to rule by the majority. The framers accepted, of course, that the body politic is the proximate source of political authority and provided for the election of the president and Congress for specified terms. The people had a voice in choosing the government, but not total control. Representatives in Congress were popularly elected, but voting was restricted by the qualifications requisite for voting for representatives of the most numerous branch of the state legislature. Slaves, of course, could not vote, nor could women, except as freeholders in some states, and most states had property qualifications on voting. Thus only adult white males could vote for representatives in Congress, and that number of eligible voters was usually further restricted by property qualifications. The state legislatures, not the people directly, elected U.S. senators. Electors chosen in the manner determined by the state legislature, not by the people directly, unless the state legislature so determined, elected the president. (The deference to state legislatures in the election of senators and the manner of choosing electors of the president represented an effort to appease those anxious to protect the interests of states.) And judges were appointed for life, not elected.

SEPARATION OF POWERS

Closely associated with the notion of government limited by nature was the notion of separate powers of government. Locke described three powers of government: legislative, executive, and federative. For him the judicial power was part of the executive power because the executive appointed the judges, and the federative power—that is, the power to declare war, conclude peace, and make treaties with foreign nations—was, subject to certain limitations, in the hands of the executive. Thus there were basically only the legislative and executive powers, since the executive power included the judicial power. Locke's principal contention was not that the two powers are completely separate, but rather that the whole legislative power should not be in the hands of the supreme executive power—namely, the king, since that would lead to tyranny and the destruction of individual liberty.

Montesquieu, in the middle of the eighteenth century, transformed Locke's position against lodging the totality of legislative power in the hands of the executive into an analysis of the natural separateness of the legislative, executive, and judicial functions of government, with a system of checks and balances to prevent any one power having undue dominance. In this respect Montesquieu admired the separate powers of the eighteenth-century British Constitution as the mirror of political liberty. So did the framers, and they modeled the separate powers in the U.S. Constitution on that of the British Constitution.

Exercise of the British legislative power required not only passage of a law by both houses of parliament (the Commons and the Lords), but also royal assent. Unlike the present British Constitution, royal assent was not a mere formality, and the king had an absolute veto power over legislation, which he often exercised. The king had supreme executive power, but his subordinate administrators, the prime minister and cabinet, held office only as long as they enjoyed the confidence of the Commons, and parliament controlled the government's purse. The judicial power was independent insofar as the judges interpreted laws and applied them to particular cases, but the executive appointed the judges, parliament could remove judges by the impeachment process, and the House of Lords was the highest appellate court. Indeed, parliament could enact legislation with the king's assent to overturn judicial decisions. Thus the British Constitution separated the legislative, executive, and judicial powers, but not completely, giving the executive an equal voice with the two houses of parliament in the legislative process, the legislature power of the purse over the executive and the power of impeachment over ministers and judges, and judges the power to interpret the laws.

The U.S. Constitution followed a similar pattern of separate powers with checks and balances, but not in every particular. It does not explicitly separate the legislative, executive, and judicial powers. Rather, the principle is implicit in the first three articles. Article I invests all the legislative power granted to the federal government in the Congress. Article II vests executive power in the president. Article III vests judicial power in the Supreme Court and the inferior courts established by Congress. The Constitution, while separating the organs of government, fuses their functions and powers. As Madison says in *Federalist* 47, the sharing in powers by which one branch of government checks and balances another was a way to restrict the exercise of governmental power and to enable each power to protect its independence.

The chief executive is a president, not a king. The president shares in legislative power by his qualified veto power, which Congress may override by two-thirds majorities in both houses of Congress. The president has the power to appoint all superior officers of the United States, ambassadors and public ministers, and judges, but only with the advice and consent of the Senate. The president has the power to negotiate treaties, but they are not valid unless the Senate ratifies them by a two-thirds majority. The president is the commander in chief of the armed forces, but Congress has the power to declare war. The principal power of Congress over the president is the power of the purse, but Congress can remove the president or any other officer of the United States, including judges, by the impeachment process. The federal courts, especially the Supreme Court, have the power over Congress by their power to interpret laws and determine their constitutionality. The federal courts have similar power regarding what statutes and the Constitution require of executive actions

Not only did the separate powers check and balance one another, but the legislative power itself was divided into a popularly elected House of Representatives and the indirectly elected Senate, and the approval of both was necessary to pass laws. The framers envisioned that the local magnates in the Senate would represent state interests and prevent precipitate or undesirable action by popular majority coalitions in the House. The popular election of Senators provided a degree of cohesion between the House and the Senate. So did the rise of national political parties, which the framers never envisioned, and so does their tight cohesion in recent decades. Nevertheless, the House and the Senate continue to check and balance one another, especially if different parties control each house. Moreover, the extra-constitutional filibuster rule is a further check on Senate action.

In one respect, the doctrine of separate powers has become an anachronism in the contemporary American polity. Congress has over the course of the twentieth century vastly expanded federal control of the economy and created the welfare state. To do that, Congress delegated to independent commissions (e.g., the Federal Communication Commission) authority to make rules, enforce them, and adjudicate particular cases. Similarly, Congress established administrative agencies with broad powers (e.g., the Social Security Administration). These independent commissions and administrative agencies have effectively become a fourth branch of government, one that for the most part operates semi-autonomously from the control of Congress and the president. Administrative personnel are responsible only to themselves, except for possible impeachment and conviction by Congress or removal by the president, who can do so only for cause in the case of independent commissions. Congress has attempted to establish power to veto administrative regulations by the resolution of one or both houses, but the Supreme Court held that this violates the constitutional requirement that laws be enacted with the participation of the president in the process (*Immigration and Naturalization Service v. Chadha*).[17] (Justice White, dissenting, argued that legislative veto provisions themselves had been enacted with the participation of the president).

The most contentious separation-of-powers issue concerns the president's power to engage U.S. armed forces in hostilities abroad without congressional authorization. The Constitution (Art. 1, sec. 8, cl. 11) reserves to Congress the power to declare war, but presidents since Jefferson (against the Barbary Coast pirates) have committed armed forces to short-term, small-scale "police actions." In the Cold War, President Truman committed U.S. forces to long-term, large-scale action in Korea, and President Lyndon Johnson did likewise in Vietnam. As a result of widespread opposition to the latter war, Congress in 1973, over President Nixon's veto, passed the War Powers Resolution. That resolution, among other things, required the president after 60–90 days of hostilities to obtain the consent of Congress for the military action if Congress had not already done so. Later presidents viewed most provisions of the resolution as unconstitutional infringement of their power as commanders in chief and claimed that the resolution did not apply to the military action they initiated. The Supreme Court never ruled on any of the cases challenging the legality of the Vietnamese war, leaving it to Congress and the president to resolve the question, and there is little reason to think that the Court will rule on the legality of any current or subsequent dispute about the president's power to engage U.S. forces in hostilities abroad.

---

17. *Immigration and Naturalization Service v. Chadha*, 462 U.S. 919 (1983).

FEDERALISM

The word derives from the Latin word *foedus* (treaty), and the Romans used the word to describe a compact of independent member states, usually for defensive military purposes. Federalism in the U.S. Constitution has a different meaning and signifies that both the United States and the state governments exercise legitimate governmental power. That is to say, the Constitution created a system of dual sovereignties, one proper to the national government and the other proper to the state governments. Accordingly, advocates of the Constitution in ratification debates were called Federalists and opponents Anti-Federalists. In exclusively national governments, on the other hand, local governments are creatures of the national government, which determines their powers. And in the case of confederate governments, the central government is the creature of fully sovereign local governments, which control the powers of the central government. Therefore, the distinctive note of a federal government is the distribution of power between the central government and local governments, which neither can unilaterally modify.

The framers adopted a system of dual—that is, divisible—sovereignty. The nineteenth-century analytic school of jurisprudence held a contrary position—namely, that sovereignty, since it means supreme authority, is by definition indivisible, and dual sovereignty impossible. (John C. Calhoun also held that sovereignty was indivisible and, since he considered the states, and not the nation, sovereign, they had the right to nullify federal legislation.) But the Constitution itself is the source of the sovereignty of both the national government and the state governments, and so the dual sovereignty, although divisible, is unified in the supreme authority of the Constitution, and Article VI explicitly states that the Constitution and treaties and laws made thereunder are the supreme law of the land. Moreover, the people are empowered to amend the Constitution, albeit by a difficult process, by the concurrence of Congress, the national legislature, by a two-thirds majority of both houses, and of the legislatures of three quarters of the states. A federal conception of the British Constitution was involved in the colonial case against parliament before the Declaration of Independence. But where the unwritten British Constitution allowed considerable latitude of interpretation of precedent and customary right, the American Constitution explicitly created a federal structure of government. This structure, as opposed to the Articles of Confederation, provided a truly national government in partnership with the states. The national government was to carry out its functions by direct jurisdiction over individuals, to exercise national powers without requiring unanimous approval of the states, as in the Continental Congress, and Article VI guaranteed the supremacy of its law. Nonetheless, the conclusion is inescapable that the federal product of the Convention was due to practical considerations, the chief of which was concern whether the states would ratify the Constitution.

The Convention initially adopted the Virginia plan, which established a national legislature in which representation in both houses was apportioned on the basis of population. The small states objected that a national legislature entirely apportioned according to population would leave their interests subordinate to those of the large states, and, worse, that it would signify that the Constitution derived from the people rather than the states. The Convention eventually agreed to the great compromise: that the Senate would comprise an equal number of members from each state; that the number of members in the House from each state would be proportional to the state's population; and that the House would originate all money bills. By declaring that the Constitution and the treaties and laws made thereunder would be the supreme law of the land, and by providing that the national government would operate directly on individuals, national supremacy was assured and the problem of dual sovereignty solved. *Federalist* 39 summed up the creation and distribution of power under the Constitution. The central government is federal in its origin from the states, national in its operations, both national and federal in the source of its legislative power (the House from the nation, the Senate from the states), federal in the extent of its powers, and federal in requiring ratification of amendments by three quarters of the states.

There are two kinds of constitutional issues involving federalism. The first regards how far the powers of the federal government reach. In the ratification debates, Anti-Federalists argued, among other things, that the powers of the federal government under the Constitution would or could be used to suppress states' rights. In response to such objections, the first Congress submitted the Tenth Amendment to the states, which promptly ratified it. That amendment provided that all powers not delegated by the Constitution to the federal government were reserved to the states and the people. But this simply states a truism: that the United States is a federal, not an exclusively national, system of government. The amendment does not say that powers not *expressly* delegated to the United States are reserved to the states and the people, and *McCulloch* held the contrary—namely, that powers implied by the enumerated powers and the elastic clause *are* delegated to the United States.

The Court, contrary to strict interpretation of the words of the amendment, invoked it from 1895 to 1936 to invalidate federal legislation regulating production (*U.S. v. E. C. Knight* [1895]),[18] employer-employee relations (*Hammer v. Dagenhart* [1918]),[19] and agriculture (*U.S. v. Butler* [1936]).[20] But that interpretation, with

18. *U.S. v. E. C. Knight*, 156 U.S. 1 (1895); see also *Carter v. Carter Coal Co.*, 298 U.S. 238 (1936).
19. *Hammer v. Dagenhart*, 247 U.S. 251 (1918).
20. *U.S. v. Butler*, 297 U.S. 1 (1936).

one short-lived exception,[21] was from 1937 consigned to the dustbin of history,[22] except to prohibit federal mandates on state governments or officials to perform specific duties.[23] The Court after the Civil War also gave state officials immunity from federal income taxes, but reversed itself in 1938.[24]

The proponents of states' rights in the last decade of the twentieth century, however, persuaded a bare majority of the Court to limit federal power under the commerce clause. Following the conservative legal scholars calling for a "new federalism," the Court in 1995 invalidated a federal law that made it a crime to possess a gun within 1,000 feet of a school (*U.S. v. Lopez*).[25] According to Chief Justice Rehnquist, the law invaded the general police power of the states because the prohibited personal behavior was not "substantially related" to interstate commerce. The same narrow majority in 2000 struck down the provision of a federal law permitting victims of gender-motivated crimes to sue their alleged attackers in federal court, since the crimes were not in any sense economic activity (*U.S. v. Morrison*).[26] If the limitation of the commerce clause in these two cases becomes precedent, Congress will need to articulate more fully the connection between a prohibited activity and commerce. In 2012, in the course of upholding the 2010 Affordable Care Act (*National Federation of Business v. Sibelius*),[27] Chief Justice Roberts added an *obiter dictum* with which the four dissenting justices concurred—namely, that Congress has no power under the commerce clause

21. *National League of Cities v. Usery,* 426 U.S. 833 (1976); overruled, *Garcia v. San Antonio Metropolitan Transit Authority,* 469 U.S. 528 (1985).

22. *National Labor Relations Board v. Jones and Laughlin,* 301 U.S. 1 (1937).

23. *New York v. U.S.,* 326 U.S. 572 (1946); *Printz v. U.S.,* 521 U.S. 898 (1997).

24. *Collector v. Day,* 78 U.S. 113 (1871, subsequently overruled by *Graves v. New York,* 306 U.S. 466 (1938).

25. *U.S. v. Lopez,* 514 U.S. 549 (1995).

26. *U.S. v. Morrison,* 529 U.S. 598 (2000).

27. *National Federation of Business v. Sibelius,* 132 S. Ct. 2566 (2012).

to compel individuals to buy services they do not want. This dictum would forbid federal regulation of the *inactivity* of individuals not engaged in commerce.

The other kind of constitutional issue involving federalism concerns whether the states have any concurrent power in the absence of federal action to legislate on matters affecting interstate commerce. Until the advent of federal regulation of the economy at the end of the nineteenth century, this was the dominant issue. The Court has uniformly held that the Commerce Clause of itself invalidates protectionist local legislation, although it may be debatable whether the local legislation is protectionist. After *Gibbons,* the question was whether the states had concurrent power over matters affecting interstate commerce in the absence of federal regulation, presupposing that the local regulation was not protectionist. Marshall had not taken a position on the question, and the Taney Court was divided between those justices who thought the federal power over interstate commerce exclusive and those who thought that the states could exercise concurrent power in all such cases.

In 1852 the Court chose a middle ground. The states have concurrent jurisdiction if the subject matter is local in nature, but not if the subject matter is national in nature—that is, requires a uniform rule (*Cooley v. Board of Wardens*).[28] The Cooley rule proved difficult to apply to modern economic situations, and so the Court ninety-one years later (1945) introduced a new rule in *Southern Pacific v. Arizona.*[29] Arizona had required that passenger trains be limited to fourteen cars and freight trains to seventy cars. Applying a balancing test to determine whether local regulation was permissible under the commerce clause, the Court held that the burden on interstate commerce outweighed the pu-

---

28. *Cooley v. Board of Wardens,* 53 U.S. 299 (1852).
29. *Southern Pacific v. Arizona,* 325 U.S. 761 (1945).

tative safety benefit of shorter trains. This is now the general rule, although the Court would be deferential to weightier safety concerns in transportation cases. Justice Scalia, among others, would recognize concurrent power in the states to regulate all matters affecting interstate commerce not involving protectionism as long as Congress has not legislated. In other words, Scalia would leave the power to negative nonprotectionist local regulations entirely in the hands of Congress.

The government of the United States might have survived without the right of the Supreme Court to decide whether a federal law is constitutional, For example, the British Constitution until recently followed the principle of parliamentary supremacy. But the American federal system could not have survived without the power of the Supreme Court to determine the constitutionality of state laws and of decisions of state courts interpreting the Constitution and federal laws. The supremacy of the federal government required federal jurisdiction over state laws and decisions in conflict with the Constitution and federal laws. Early on, the Court held state laws unconstitutional. In *Fletcher v. Peck*,[30] the Court in 1810 held that a Georgia statute revoking a land grant violated the Contract Clause (Art. 1, sec. 10, cl. 1). In 1819, the Court struck down a Maryland tax on the Second Bank of the United States (*McCulloch v. Maryland*).[31] And in 1821, the Court claimed jurisdiction to review on appeal from a state court the conviction of two lottery-ticket salesmen alleging a license to do so under a federal statute (*Cohens v. Virginia*).[32] Earlier, though, the Eleventh Amendment overturned a previous decision (*Chisholm v. Georgia*)[33] and prohibited citizens of other states and foreign citizens from instituting suits in federal courts.

30. *Fletcher v. Peck*, 10 U.S. 87 (1810).
31. *McCulloch v. Maryland*, 17 U.S. 316 (1819).
32. *Cohens v. Virginia*, 19 U.S. 264 (1821).
33. *Chisholm v. Georgia*, 2 U.S. 419 (1793).

SUMMARY

I have analyzed the four central regime principles of the Constitution. First, the Constitution reflected John Locke's notions of limited government and natural rights, but the framers drafted an instrument of government that was flexible enough to be open to the broader exercise of federal power to manage the economy and establish the welfare state. Second, the Constitution, while theoretically based on the principle of popular sovereignty—namely, the principle that government derives from the consent of the people—approached democracy gingerly in order both to establish stability and to secure ratification by the states. Third, fearful of concentrated governmental power, the framers embraced the doctrine of separate powers in which each checked and balanced the others. Fourth, the Constitution, in recognition of colonial experience and political expediency, adopted a federal structure of government with sovereignty divided between the supreme national government and the states.

2

THE FIRST AMENDMENT

AND RELIGION

※

INTERPRETING THE CONSTITUTION

Above all else, the text of the Constitution controls its interpretation, since it is the very purpose of a written constitution to define what power government officials have and how they are to exercise it, both in relation to one another and in relation to private citizens. Some provisions are so specific that they require little or no interpretation. Article 2, sec. 1, cl. 5, for example, unambiguously prescribes that the president shall have attained thirty-five years of age. Accordingly, judges faithful to their oath of office would have no choice but to apply the provision exactly as it is written in the unlikely event that they were called upon to do so.

Most provisions of the Constitution, however, are phrased in general terms. For example, we find in the clauses on religion in the First Amendment the phrases *law respecting an establishment of religion* and *free exercise of religion*. The text leaves it ultimately up to the Court to determine, interpret, and apply the phrases. Does the word *law* include administrative action? What does the word *respecting* mean? Does the indefinite article rather than the definite article modifying *establishment* signify a difference? What constitutes *establishment of religion?* What constitutes *reli-*

gion? What constitutes *exercise* of religion? Strict constructionists would have judges interpret those terms precisely as their authors understood them. Loose constructionists, on the other hand, would have judges interpret the terms in the light of contemporary community values and/or pragmatic policy considerations.

Precisely what authors of broad constitution texts understood by their terms is frequently unclear. Constitutional provisions are products of multi-member committees, passed by the multi-member houses of Congress, and ratified by multi-member state legislatures. Individual members of these bodies, especially dissenters, may have understood key terms differently, and the legislative record, especially of the Convention and the first Congress, may be ambiguous or unrevealing about the members' state of mind. As a result, it may be difficult or impossible to determine precisely what the bodies intended by the terms for specific situations. When that is the case, judges need to look elsewhere for guidance, and they then typically look to judicial precedents and pragmatic policy considerations.

It would be a misconception to think that the process of constitutional interpretation consists of "squaring" the written words of the text with a particular fact situation.[1] There is no question of the importance of the words, since they are the substance of the Constitution. But, as John Marshall said in *McCulloch*, "we must never forget that it is a *constitution* we are interpreting,"[2] since a constitution, unlike a statute, is a general framework of government designed to endure for all ages. The Constitution delineates the powers of organs of government, and such provisions cannot envision or anticipate all particular areas of application. Therefore, when there are disputes about those powers, judges will need to interpret the meaning of the text.

Historians have been able to ascertain with solid probability

1. Cf. *U.S. v. Butler*, 297 U.S. 1, 62 (1936).
2. *McCulloch v. Maryland*, 17 U.S. 316, 407 (1819).

framers' understanding of some broadly worded constitutional provisions in relation to some specific applications. (It should be noted, however, that justices often see fit, in order to justify their opinion in a case, to attribute their interpretation of a text to its framers without adequate historical evidence.) It is critically important, in my opinion, to distinguish different ways in which assertions allegedly derived from the words of a text may relate to the framers' intentions.

First, framers may have specifically contemplated and approved application of general terms to specific applications, or other actions of the framers may indicate that they would have approved such applications. Second, framers may never have contemplated application of general terms to specific applications. Third, framers may not have contemplated application of general terms to specific applications, but their other actions or the cultural milieu indicate that they would have disapproved the applications had they contemplated them. Fourth, framers may have expressly contemplated and disapproved application of a general term to specific applications.

In the first situation, since there is an explicit or implicit convergence of the words of the text with the framers' intentions, and since a constitution requires adherence to the text, their intentions should be controlling. In the other situations, the general terms diverge in varying degrees from the framers' specific intentions. The strongest case for judges interpreting general constitutional provisions in the light of community consensus and social policy is one where the framers indicated no view contrary to a specific application. The case for broad construction of a general term is weaker where other actions of the framers indicate that they would have disapproved a specific application had they contemplated it. And general terms should not be applied to specific situations where the framers explicitly contemplated and disapproved such an application.

The Constitution provides government under law, but the power of judicial review makes the Supreme Court its human oracle. The Court should, of course, strike down legislation, whether national or state, *contrary* to the framers' specific intention regarding application of a general provision of the Constitution. But what should the Court do when the particular case involves a matter *beyond* the framers' specific intentions? In cases not involving individual civil liberties claims, the Court should, in my opinion, generally defer to the legislature, especially Congress. It is not the function of the judiciary to act as a superlegislature. As dissenting Justice Stone said in *Butler* about the Court's power of judicial review, "the only check upon our ... exercise [of power] is our own sense of judicial restraint."[3]

Accordingly, regarding the establishment clause, the Court should strike down legislation *contrary* to the framers' specific intentions regarding the clause's application to a particular case, but refrain from doing so when the legislation is *beyond* the framers' specific intentions if there is a justifying secular rationale for it. (I shall later examine that test and its application to particular cases in connection with the Rutledge thesis.) Regarding the religious freedom clause, however, the Court should defer to individuals invoking it beyond the framers' specific intentions, but there may be superior countervailing public interests. (I shall also later consider such cases.)

COLONIAL AND POST-REVOLUTIONARY BACKGROUND

Before the Revolution, ten colonies had an established religion, and only Rhode Island, Pennsylvania, and Delaware did not. The Southern colonies (Maryland, Virginia, North Carolina, South Carolina, and Georgia), New Jersey, and New York

---

3. *U.S. v. Butler*, 78–79.

established the Church of England (after the Revolution, the Episcopal Church). Three New England colonies (Connecticut, Massachusetts, and New Hampshire) established the Congregational Church. Associated with the established churches were tax assessments for the support of ministers of the established religion. After the Revolution of 1688, England promulgated a Bill of Rights (1689) that granted religious freedom to Protestant dissenters, but not Catholics, Jews, or freethinkers, and the colonies followed suit. There were still in most colonies religious tests for voting and holding office and tax assessments for the support of the established religion. Even Rhode Island and Pennsylvania had religious tests for voters and officeholders. Rhode Island in 1729 disenfranchised Catholics and barred Jews from public office. Pennsylvania in 1682 required voters and officials to profess Christianity.

By 1776 physical persecution had ended and a measure of toleration obtained. The states, now independent, established new constitutions. In the South, Maryland's new constitution granted religious freedom to all Christians, authorized tax assessments for the support of the Christian religion, and required officeholders to take an oath of belief in the Christian religion. Virginia adopted a Declaration of Rights in 1776 and a Bill of Religious Freedom in 1785, which will be considered later. North Carolina's new constitution decreed religious freedom to all, but restricted holding office to Protestants. South Carolina's new constitution established the Protestant Christian religion, "tolerated" theists, exempted nonconformists from tax assessments for the support of the Episcopal Church, and restricted holding office to Protestants, and a later constitution in 1790 acknowledged the religious freedom of theists, not merely toleration, and enfranchised Catholics and others. Georgia's new constitution of 1777 granted religious freedom to all citizens and required no religious test for voting, but required that legislators be Protestant.

In the Middle Atlantic states, New York's new constitution of 1777 disestablished the Episcopal Church, granted free religious exercise, and abolished religious tests for officeholders. New Jersey's new constitution abolished compulsory Sunday church attendance and tax assessments to support the Episcopal Church, but only Protestants could be officeholders. Pennsylvania's new constitution required that officeholders be Christians and take an oath of belief in the Old and New Testaments, but a religious test of belief in God replaced the oath in 1790. Delaware's new constitution required officials to take an oath supporting government by orthodox Christians, but all religious tests were abolished in 1792.

In New England, Connecticut passed a toleration act in 1784, and dissenters were required to pay tax assessments to their churches. Massachusetts in 1780 passed a Declaration of Rights, but authorized support for the Protestant ministry and compulsory Sunday attendance at some church. New Hampshire passed a Bill of Rights, including religious freedom, in 1784, but did not give legal status to nonconformist churches and mandated tax assessments to support the Congregational Church. Connecticut did not fully disestablish the Congregational Church until 1818, Massachusetts until 1833, and New Hampshire until 1819, except for the religious test for holding office. Rhode Island in 1783 removed the prohibition against Catholics voting and holding office.

Thus there was in the post-Revolutionary period a movement toward greater religious freedom, especially for nonconforming Christians, and away from tax support of an established church except in the states of Connecticut, Massachusetts, and New Hampshire. But Catholics and Jews in many states incurred civil disabilities, especially regarding eligibility for offices. The requirement of many states that officeholders be Protestant in effect substituted a mitigated Protestant establishment for a denominational one.

Let us now consider the struggle in Virginia for religious

freedom and against religious establishment.[4] This struggle was closely associated with James Madison, who was majority leader in the House of Representatives at the time of its passage of the First Amendment, introduced the original draft of the Bill of Rights, and was chairman of the House conferees resolving differences between the House and Senate versions of the First Amendment. Dissenting in the Everson case, Justice Rutledge claimed that this controversy reveals both Madison's views on the religious clauses of the First Amendment and the historical meaning of the clauses.[5] We shall see that this is not true.

Virginia, as previously indicated, had an established church before the Revolution. But in the course of Scottish-Irish immigration and the Great Awakening, the newcomer Presbyterians and other Protestant dissenters resented the privileged position of the Church of England to which the residents of the tidewater belonged. When the Revolution made a new state constitution necessary, Virginia, under the leadership of George Mason and the young Madison in the convention of 1776, adopted a Declaration of Rights. One of the rights that the Declaration established as part of the fundamental law of Virginia was the natural right of human beings to practice religion according to the dictates of their conscience. Although this represented an advance over the principle of toleration insofar as it made freedom of religious exercise a matter of right, it left unchanged the status and privileges of the Episcopal Church, the successor of the Church of England. Madison at the convention worked for disestablishment, but realistically, if not ultimately, abandoned the fight.

When, in the fall of 1776, petitions of dissenters to end tithes to the Episcopal Church devolved on the new Virginia Assembly, that body removed the civil disabilities of dissenters and suspend-

4. Cf. Irving Brant, *James Madison* (Indianapolis and New York: Bobbs-Merrill, 1941), 1:241–50; 2:343–50.
5. *Everson v. Board of Education,* 330 U.S. 1, 15–16 (1947).

ed the general levies for the support of the Episcopal Church. The suspension was made permanent in 1779.

In the fall of 1784, the battle was renewed. The Episcopalians and Presbyterians united to seek financial support from the state, and Patrick Henry introduced a resolution that the people "pay a moderate tax ... for the support of the Christian religion or some Christian church, denomination, or communion of Christians, or some form of Christian worship."[6] This bill was intended to benefit the Christian churches and only later labeled "a Bill establishing a provision for teachers of the Christian religion."[7] Since elementary education was largely in the hands of the parishes, the bill was somewhat disguised as an educational measure. Leading the opposition, Madison defeated the proposal and succeeded in reviving and enacting Jefferson's Statute of Religious Liberty. The statute states, "No man shall be compelled to frequent or support any religious worship, place, or ministry whatsoever."[8]

Madison's victory was due to Fabian tactics, the strategic elevation of Henry, the most influential proponent of state subsidies, to the governorship, and the argument of Madison's *Memorial and Remonstrance against Religious Assessments.* Madison did not only object to Henry's bill because it aided the Christian religion, but also because the bill provided general tax support for religious institutions.[9]

Although it is difficult to conjecture Madison's views about state aid to religious institutions providing eleemosynary or secular educational functions, or whether all interaction between civil authority and organized religion should be prohibited, his later pronouncements endorse an extreme form of church-state separation. As Edward Corwin said, those pronouncements carried the

6. Brant, *James Madison,* 2:343.   7. Brant, *James Madison,* 2:346.
8. Henry Steele Commager, ed., *Documents of American History,* 5th ed. (New York: Appleton-Century-Crofts, 1949), 1:126.
9. Brant, *James Madison,* 2:350.

principle of church-state separation "to pedantic lengths."[10] In his "Essay on Monopolies,"[11] Madison opposed incorporating ecclesiastical bodies with a right to acquire property, the exemption of houses of worship from taxation, and the right of houses of Congress to choose chaplains, military chaplains, and expressed misgivings about Thanksgiving Day Proclamations, although he had issued them during his presidency.

We may reach two conclusions about the Virginia controversy over the Statute of Religious Liberty. First, the controversy sheds much light on Madison's personal views on church-state, but leaves open the central question of Madison's position as floor leader in the framing of the First Amendment. Second, the Virginia controversy was a sharp battle against discriminatory privilege and a close union of civil authority and religious activity.

DRAFTING AND RATIFYING
THE RELIGIOUS CLAUSES

Charles Pinckney of South Carolina proposed at the Convention that the Constitution prohibit a religious test for officeholders, and the Convention adopted such a provision, which became the last sentence of Art. 6, sec. 3. This is the only provision in the original Constitution about religion. The Anti-Federalists objected that the Constitution had no Bill of Rights, and some state ratifying conventions wanted an explicit statement guaranteeing religious freedom from the federal government. For example, Virginia wanted an amendment prohibiting the federal government from infringing on the free exercise of religion according to the dictates of conscience and from favoring or establishing any particular sect.

10. Edward S. Corwin, "The Supreme Court as National School Board," *Thought* 23 (1948): 671.

11. James Madison, "Essay on Monopolies," *Harper's Magazine,* March 1914, 489–95.

On June 8, 1789, Madison, as leader of the House, proposed an amendment on religion: "The civil rights of none shall be abridged on account of religious belief or worship, nor shall any national religion be established, nor shall the full and equal rights of conscience be in any manner, or on any pretext, abridged."[12] The House on July 21 referred the amendment to a select committee, and that committee on July 28 proposed the following amendment: "No religion shall be established by law, nor should the equal rights of conscience be infringed."[13]

On August 15, the House, sitting as a committee of the whole, considered the proposed amendment. To New York Congressman Sylvester's fear that the amendment might have a "tendency to abolish all religion," Madison replied that "he apprehended the meaning of the words to be that Congress should not establish a religion and enforce legal observance of it by law, nor compel men to worship God in any way contrary to their conscience."[14] To Connecticut Congressman Huntington's fear that a broad interpretation of the words would close the federal courts to suits to collect payment of assessments for established churches, Madison thought that, "if the word *national* was inserted before *religion,* it would satisfy the minds of the honorable gentlemen." Madison also expressed his belief that "the people feared one sect might obtain such preeminence, or two combine together, and establish a religion to which they would compel others to conform."[15] Congressman Gerry, an Anti-Federalist, objected to the word *national.* Indeed, he objected to the very terms *Federalists* and *Anti-Federalists,* calling the former rats, and the latter anti-rats, since he regarded the newly established "federal" government a

---

12. Joseph Gales and William Winston Seaton, eds., *The Debates and Proceedings of the Congress of the United States* (Washington, D.C: 1834), 1:434.

13. Gales and Seaton, eds., *Debates and Proceedings,* 729–31.

14. Gales and Seaton, eds., *Debates and Proceedings,* 729–31.

15. Gales and Seaton, eds., *Debates and Proceedings,* 729–31.

national government.[16] Madison withdrew his motion and commented that he did not mean to imply that the new government was national.[17]

Congressman Nathaniel Livermore of New Hampshire moved that the amendment be worded, "Congress shall make no law touching religion or infringing the rights of conscience."[18] The motion did two useful things: it used the active rather than the passive voice and so made clear who was prohibited from doing what, and it made more explicit that the amendment was a restriction on the federal legislature. But its reference to law "touching" religion was vague. The House passed the motion, 31 members voting in favor, 20 against, which, of course, was not a two-thirds majority. On August 20, Congressman Fisher Ames of Massachusetts proposed a substitute wording: "Congress shall make no law establishing religion, or to prevent the free exercise thereof or to infringe the rights of conscience."[19] The motion was passed without debate or opposition—that is, unanimously.[20]

On September 3 the Senate took up amendments to the House draft. Three proposed amendments were defeated. One would have replaced "religion, or the free exercise thereof" with "one religious sect or society in preference to others."[21] The second would have substituted "Congress shall not make any law infringing the rights of conscience or establishing any religious sect or society."[22] The third would have substituted "Congress shall make no law establishing any particular denomination or religion in preference to another, or prohibiting the free exercise thereof,

16. Gales and Seaton, eds., *Debates and Proceedings*, 729–31.
17. Gales and Seaton, eds., *Debates and Proceedings*, 729–31.
18. Gales and Seaton, eds., *Debates and Proceedings*, 729–31.
19. Gales and Seaton, eds., *Debates and Proceedings*, 766.
20. Gales and Seaton, eds., *Debates and Proceedings*, 766.
21. Anson Phelps Stokes, *Church and State in the United States* (New York: Harper, 1950), 1:546–48.
22. Stokes, *Church and State*, 1:546–48.

nor shall the rights of conscience be infringed."[23] The Senate in rejecting the foregoing proposals evidently did not want to limit the amendment to prohibiting preference of one denomination over others, and wished also to prohibit public support of several sects, which Henry had sought in Virginia in 1784.

The Senate then rejected the House wording, but afterwards accepted it with deletion of the words "nor shall the rights of conscience be infringed."[24] There is no record of why the latter words were stricken, but the Senate may have regarded them as redundant to the guarantee of the free exercise of religion or as inviting claims beyond religious ones. On September 9 the Senate accepted by a two-thirds vote revisions offered by Senator Oliver Ellsworth of Connecticut. Ellsworth's draft substituted "articles of faith or a mode of worship" for "religion," and "of religion or abridging the freedom of speech and of the press" for "thereof."[25]

On September 21 the House rejected the Senate draft and sought a conference with the Senate. The conference committee adopted the present wording of the amendment: "Congress shall make no law respecting an establishment of religion or prohibiting the free exercise thereof." (In the process, the conferees eliminated a provision that would have applied directly to state action.) On September 24 the House agreed to the committee wording, and the Senate concurred on September 25.[26]

The record of the process of ratification by the states is sparse. Only in the Virginia state senate is there any ray of light.[27] On December 12 that senate raised objections to the proposed amendment. The first was that the amendment did not prohibit violation or infringements of the rights of conscience. The second was that the amendment did not prohibit taxes for the support

23. Stokes, *Church and State*, 1:546–48.
24. Stokes, *Church and State*, 1:546–48.
25. Stokes, *Church and State*, 1:546–48.
26. Stokes, *Church and State*, 1:546–48.
27. *Journal of the Virginia Senate*, December 12, 1789 (Richmond: 1928).

of religion or its ministers, and so Congress might thereby prefer a particular denomination, which would be as dangerous as if it were established. The senate considered the amendment a departure from the one Virginia had proposed (June 27, 1788) and cited the fact that Virginia was the leader in disestablishment. But on December 15, 1791, Virginia ratified the amendment. There is no record of any debate, and so we do not know why the Virginia senate, in view of its strong objections two years before, finally accepted the amendment. Perhaps the senators decided that the amendment was the best they could obtain, or were persuaded that the amendment did prohibit taxes for the support of a particular denomination or its ministers, as the amendment was generally thought to have done. Massachusetts, Connecticut, and Georgia did not consider the amendment or any others of the Bill of Rights. Since Virginia was the requisite tenth state to ratify the Bill of Rights, they may not have thought their ratification relevant.

THE RUTLEDGE THESIS

In his dissent in the Everson case, Justice Rutledge offered the most detailed analysis of the establishment clause in any Court opinion.[28] Rutledge contended that the framers intended a complete separation of church and state. To support this contention, he appealed to the wording of the clause. First, the clause did not say merely that there shall be no establishment in the technical sense, but rather that there shall be no law *respecting* an establishment of religion. But Professor Edward Corwin, a distinguished constitutional scholar, effectively rebutted this inference. The word *respecting* "is a two-edged sword."[29] It prohibits Congress from passing any law *disfavoring* an establishment of religion as well as any law *favoring* one. The word was adopted as much to

28. *Everson v. Board of Education*, 33ff.
29. Corwin, "The Supreme Court as National School Board," 671.

protect the existing state establishments as to prevent a national one.

Rutledge argued from the use of the indefinite article *an* rather than the definite article *the* before *establishment,* and especially from the reference to religion rather than church, that the establishment clause should be read broadly and not technically. But this attempt to find significance in such verbal differences obscures the first Congress' unity of thought on the establishment clause. The framing of the First Amendment, previously recounted at length, bears the imprint of the framers' fundamental agreement and manifests the absence of a sharp ideological conflict, such as the one that transpired in Virginia a few years before. Rutledge admits that, "by contrast with the Virginia history, the congressional debates on the Amendment reveal only sparse discussion."[30]

Joseph Story, a professor of law at the newly established Harvard Law School and later a Supreme Court justice, wrote one of the earliest commentaries on the Constitution and the Bill of Rights. According to him, the purpose of the establishment clause was to exclude contention among religious sects for ascendancy—that is, preferential status and subsidies for a particular sect.[31] He is right that the framers wanted to preclude preference of a particular sect, but the Senate debate makes clear that it also wanted the amendment to exclude congressional preference for any combination of sects, as Henry had sought to do in Virginia in 1784. The framers intended to exclude congressional support for religious institutions as such and religious activities in general, but there is no indication that they wanted a complete separation of church and state, much less a separation of religion from organized society. They also wanted to deny to Congress power

---

30. *Everson v. Board of Education,* 42.

31. Joseph Story, *Commentaries on the Constitution,* ed. M. Bigelow (Boston: Little, Brown, and Co., 1891), 2:634.

to disestablish the then-existing established churches in several states.

At the time of the amendment, most citizens were religious, chiefly Protestant, and there were very few agnostics or atheists, at least vocal ones. There were many Deists among professional and educated elites, but they, although denying revealed religion, recognized the existence of God and dependence on him. Accordingly, there would have been no political reason to prohibit Congress from favoring religion over unbelief, provided its action did not prefer one or more religious denominations, and there is nothing at all in the record that indicates a specific intention of the framers to do so by the establishment clause.

While the framers, in my opinion, did not intend by the establishment clause to prohibit Congress from favoring religion over unbelief without preference of one or more denominational sects, time has, as Justice Reed observed, "brought about the acceptance of a broader meaning" beyond the specific intentions of the framers—namely, that Congress may not do so.[32] Vast changes in the religious and political consciousness of American society have introduced a broader understanding of religious establishment. Even so, as Justice Douglas said, accommodation of governmental authority, of course without preference of particular sects, to religious activities related to specific civic secular interests may be constitutional.[33] This broader, but circumscribed view of the establishment clause may better express the force of the establishment clause today.

The Rutledge thesis of complete separation of church and state, indeed of religion and organized society, is historically altogether unacceptable. Neither the record of the framing of the establishment clause nor the record of congressional actions supports the thesis. The same Congress that framed the First Amendment

32. *McCollum v. Board of Education*, 333 U.S. 203, 244 (1948).
33. *Zorach v. Clauson*, 343 U.S. 306 (1952).

provided for publicly supported military and legislative chaplaincies. In the course of administering the territories of the United States, the District of Columbia, and Indian affairs, later Congresses in the course of the nineteenth century bestowed grants for education provided by sectarian religious, principally Protestant, groups.

The Rutledge doctrine of separation of church and state, unlike that of the Jacobins, does not attempt to substitute a secular civic religion for sectarian religions or to suppress free exercise of the latter, but it does rest on unsound principles. First, it assumes that the reason religious and civic activities should not intersect is that religious activity is or should be simply individual and private, not also social and public. Justice Rutledge made this point quite explicit. "To say that [government appropriations for the bus transportation of parochial school children] are not for public purposes but ... for private ends is to say that they are for the support of religion and religious teaching. Conversely, *to say that they are for public purposes is to say that they are not for religious ones*" [italics added].[34] Second, the Rutledge doctrine supposes that the government's attitude toward religion should be one of indifference or mere tolerance, since religious activity is at best a civic frill or at worst a civic threat. As Justice Douglas observed in another case, "to hold that it [the government] may not [cooperate with religious authorities] would be to find in the Constitution a requirement that the government show a callous indifference to religious groups."[35] Moreover, the First Amendment guarantees a *right* to religious exercise, thus constituting it a secular value.

Human beings are social animals, as Aristotle famously said, and so their religious and civic activities necessarily intersect at times, and because religious activities are both paramount to individuals and complementary to the goals of civic activity, the

34. *Everson v. Board of Education*, 51.
35. *Zorach v. Clauson*, 314.

government's attitude toward religion should be cooperative and friendly as far as this is constitutionally permissible. The prohibition of a religious establishment is a political principle serving the right of individuals to freedom of religious exercise—that is, a means to ensure the right of individuals to choose their religion or no religion. The often cited "wall of separation" between church and state is a misleading metaphor, and those who so interpret the term literally make an end of what is a means, an absolute of what is relative.

There are many intersections of religious and civic activities in American life. Justice Reed, dissenting in *McCulloch*, observed that "religious bodies, with other groups similarly situated," have obtained incidental advantages "as a byproduct of organized society."[36] For example, among other things, he pointed out that churches are free from taxation, that the National School Lunch Act includes aid to children attending parochial schools, that the armed forces have commissioned chaplains, and that, under the Servicemen's Readjustment Act, eligible veterans may receive instruction at government expense at church-related colleges.

In any culture in which religion plays a prominent role, the same individuals constitute both civil society and religious associations, and civic and religious interaction is inevitable. The real question, therefore, is to what degree and in what manner, consonant with the principle of religious freedom and no endorsement of religion or preference of religion over unbelief, civil authority may or should in a particular case cooperate with a religious institution or activity related to a specific secular civic interest.

EARLY CASES

Before the twentieth century there were relatively few areas of interaction between the federal government and religious activity.

---

36. *McCollum v. Board of Education*, 249.

But special responsibilities for Indians on reservations, administration of the territories of the United States and of the District of Columbia, and the military services, together with the customs of Thanksgiving Day proclamations and prayer at sessions of Congress, did involve the federal government with religion. Only infrequently was the Supreme Court asked to determine whether such involvements violated the religious guarantees of the First Amendment.

In the second half of the nineteenth century there was a bitter conflict between Mormons settling in territories of the West, especially in Utah, and the federal government administering the territories. Between 1870 and 1890, 573 Mormons were convicted of the federal crime of bigamy or unlawful cohabitation.[37] In the first of the cases involving this conflict to reach the full Supreme Court, a Mormon named George Reynolds was convicted of bigamy. On appeal, Reynolds claimed that he should have been acquitted because he sincerely believed that the tenets of his religion commanded the practice of polygamy. A unanimous Court ruled against Reynolds (*Reynolds v. U.S.*).[38] Chief Justice Waite acknowledged that Reynolds was a member of the Mormon church, that "it was the duty of male members of said church, circumstances permitting, to practice polygamy," and that the failure or refusal of male members to do so when circumstances permitted would be punished by damnation in the life to come.[39] The issue thus joined was whether the federal statute forbidding bigamy, as applied to Mormons, violated the First Amendment's guarantee of freedom of religious exercise.

Against Reynolds' claim, the Court cited the preamble to the Virginian Statute of Religious Liberty, in which its drafter, Jef-

---

37. Thomas F. O'Dea, *The Mormons* (Chicago: University of Chicago Press, 1957), 111.

38. *Reynolds v. U.S.*, 98 U.S. 145 (1878).

39. *Reynolds v. U.S.*, 161.

ferson, conceded that the government might rightfully "interfere when [religious] principles break out into overact acts against peace and public order."[40] Moreover, after the United States had adopted the Constitution and the Bill of Rights, Jefferson in his letter to the Danbury Baptist Association interpreted the religious clauses of the First Amendment to establish a "wall of separation" between church and state. (This was the first citation of the phrase in a Court opinion.)

But the Court noted that Jefferson in the same letter expressed his conviction that there was "no natural right in opposition to ... social duties."[41] Since, according to Waite, Jefferson was the "acknowledged leader" of advocates of the amendment, the Court argued the Danbury statement "may be accepted almost as an authoritative declaration of the scope and effect of the amendment."[42] Accordingly, "Congress was deprived of all legislative power over mere opinion but was left free to reach actions ... in violation of social duties or subversive of good order."[43] The Court then pointed to the long legal tradition against the practice of bigamy, particularly indicating that all the colonies had laws against bigamy, and that the same Virginia legislature that had enacted the Statute of Religious Liberty also passed a statute against bigamy that included a death penalty.

Considering the public interest served by the legislation against bigamy, the Court observed with a flourish of racial superiority that the practice had always been "odious among northern and western nations of Europe and, until the establishment of the Mormon church, was almost exclusively a feature of life of Asiatic and African peoples."[44] Marriage was not only a "sacred obligation," but also a contract subject to regulation by law.[45] Society was built on the foundation of marriage and the family, and the

40. *Reynolds v. U.S.*, 163.
42. *Reynolds v. U.S.*, 164.
44. *Reynolds v. U.S.*, 164.

41. *Reynolds v. U.S.*, 164.
43. *Reynolds v. U.S.*, 164.
45. *Reynolds v. U.S.*, 165.

principles of government are related to the kind of marital unions prevailing. Citing a Professor Lieber in a very rare judicial use of sociological data at the time, the Court argued that polygamy was patriarchal and fettered people in "statutory despotism," while monogamy led in the opposite direction, that of democracy.[46] The Court conceded that an exceptional colony of polygamists might exist for a time without disturbing the social conditions of the majority, but held that its suppression for the general welfare was within the legitimate scope of every civil government to determine.

The remaining question was whether those who practiced polygamy as a religious duty were entitled by the First Amendment to an exemption from the operation of the federal statute prohibiting it. The Court ruled that to make such an exception would introduce a new element into criminal law regarding actions, which, unlike beliefs, the government may regulate. To permit an exception for Mormons would make their religious doctrines superior to the law of the land and "permit every citizen to become a law unto himself."[47] The Court bolstered its argument by asking rhetorically whether religious beliefs would be thought to excuse those who performed human sacrifices in their rites or wives attempting to immolate themselves upon the funeral pyres of their husbands.

In a postscript little noted by commentators on the case, the Court on a petition for a rehearing vacated the sentence of the trial court.[48] The Court held that the trial court erred in imposing imprisonment at hard labor. This action suggests an element of sympathy for the Mormon offenders.

Eleven years after *Reynolds*, the Court faced a different conflict between Mormons practicing polygamy and federal law (*Davis v.*

---

46. *Reynolds v. U.S.*, 166.　　　　47. *Reynolds v. U.S.*, 167.
48. *Reynolds v. U.S.*, 168–69, note.

Beason).[49] This time the issue involved the right of Mormons to vote in the Territory of Idaho. Davis, a Mormon, was indicted for conspiracy to obstruct the administration of the laws of the territory by seeking to register as a voter and taking the legally prescribed oath in spite of the fact that he knowingly belonged to an organization prohibited by the oath. The oath required voters in the territory to disavow, among other things, the practice of bigamy or polygamy, and membership in any organization "which teaches, advises, counsels, or encourages its members, devotees, or any other person to commit the crime of bigamy or polygamy ... as a duty."[50] In a collateral attack on the indictment, Davis sought a writ of habeas corpus to obtain his freedom. He argued principally that the territorial requirements for voting and the companion oath, since they in effect proscribed membership in the Mormon Church, constituted an establishment of religion prohibited by the First Amendment.

Justice Field, speaking for another unanimous Court, noted that the issue posed by the petition was a narrow one—namely, an issue of jurisdiction. Therefore, the Court considered only whether, if the allegations were taken to be true, an offense had been committed for which the territorial court had jurisdiction to try the defendant. The Court did not weigh arguments against the oath on the basis of rights to speech or assembly, nor did it appeal to the doctrine of estoppel to preclude Davis from challenging the legality of the oath in view of his presumed perjury. Rather, the Court reviewed only the legality of Idaho's restriction of the right to vote to those who would promise not to teach or counsel the practice of polygamy, as applied to Mormons like Davis.

On that point the Court thought that there could not be any "serious discussion or difference of opinion."[51] Bigamy and polyg-

---

49. *Davis v. Beason*, 133 U.S. 333 (1890).
50. *Davis v. Beason*, 334.   51. *Davis v. Beason*, 341.

amy are declared crimes "by the laws of all civilized and Christian countries," by the laws of the United States, and by the laws of Idaho. Further, the Court argued that bigamy and polygamy "tend to destroy the purity of the marriage relation, to disturb the peace of families, to degrade woman, and to debase man."[52] If bigamy and polygamy were crimes, "then to teach, advise, and counsel their practice" would aid in their commission, and such activities were thus "themselves criminal and proper subjects of punishment, as aiding and abetting crime are in all other cases."[53]

Moreover, the First Amendment was never intended "as a protection against legislation for the punishment of acts inimical to the peace, good order, and morals of society,"[54] and there have been religious sects that, as part of their tenets, denied the existence of any marriage tie or required human sacrifices on special occasions. Should a sect of either kind attempt to carry out its doctrines, the Court did not doubt that "swift punishment would follow," and that "no heed would be given" to the religious motivations of the wrongdoers.[55]

The Mormons' claims of religious conscience in these cases were to a positive religious duty with respect to the practice of polygamy, since the Mormon religion at that time prescribed plural marriage as a religious duty for its male members. The prescription was not absolute, since "circumstances" might not permit its fulfillment, and one authority estimates that never more than 15 percent of Mormons actually practiced it.[56] Unlike a negative injunction of conscience, where the failure to follow the injunction in matters considered important would be incompatible with a responsible individual's moral integrity, a positive prescription of conscience is intrinsically dependent on the circumstances necessary for its fulfillment. In the case of Mormons like Reynolds,

---

52. *Davis v. Beason,* 341.
54. *Davis v. Beason,* 342.
56. O'Dea, *The Mormons,* 246.

53. *Davis v. Beason,* 341.
55. *Davis v. Beason,* 343.

the practice of polygamy was obviously contingent on the availability and consent of potential spouses. One expert has concluded that only 8 percent of Mormon families in Utah practiced polygamy in the last decade of the nineteenth century.[57] The relative scarcity of women and the poverty of new immigrants probably operated to restrict the practice as much as the opposition of the federal government.

But the religious duty of Mormons to practice polygamy was quite specific. Unlike their duty to preach Mormonism, where the prescription is general and the means unspecified except for a requirement to engage in missionary activity for a period of time, the duty of Mormons to practice polygamy was specific in the conduct prescribed, and its performance, if possible, was regarded as essential to their religious and moral integrity. The moral obligation thus imposed on Mormons by their religious consciences was of a moderately high order. From the viewpoint of the coercion effected by the federal restrictive legislation on the Mormons to forgo what they regarded as a religious duty, the moral plight of Reynolds was worse than that of Davis. The former was imprisoned for the practice of polygamy, while the latter, if he were not to take the oath, would have lost only the right to vote.

The public interest against the practice of polygamy was based primarily on the moral effects of the practice on those involved, including children. The Court in these cases thought the public interest to be serious and did not see how an exception could be made for Mormons without undermining the institution of monogamous marriage in the territories. Justice Field indicated briefly that he and the Court thought that polygamy undermined the ideal of personal union in marriage, reduced women to the status of chattels, and exacerbated the potential for conflict within families. The latter is plausible, as there is evidence that the

57. O'Dea, *The Mormons*, 246–47.

practice of polygamy by Mormons created considerable strains in the families.[58]

In 1899 the Court unanimously upheld the validity of a contract between the District of Columbia and Providence Hospital, a hospital controlled and operated by the Catholic Sisters of Charity (*Bradford v. Roberts*).[59] The District agreed to pay money to the hospital to help finance the construction of an isolation ward for the treatment of contagious diseases, and the hospital promised to reserve two-thirds of the ward for poor patients sent and supported by the District. On the basis of the establishment clause, Bradford sued to enjoin payment to the hospital. Justice Peckham, speaking for the Court, rejected his contention:[60] "If we were to assume ... that, under this appropriation, an agreement with a religious corporation of the tenor of this agreement would be invalid, as resulting indirectly in ... an act respecting the establishment of religion, we are unable to see that ... the corporation is of the kind described."

The Bradford decision rested essentially on the Court's contention that the hospital was not really sectarian. This contention is rather disingenuous and unrealistic, but perhaps the Court was simply striving to give expression to the crucial fact that the contract was concretely related to a significant civic interest, and the benefit to the religious corporation was consequently only incidental. At any rate, the Court did not see in the establishment clause any absolute separation of church and state.

In 1908 the Court unanimously approved the use of federal funds, which were due under a treaty to a group of Indians, for the support of Catholic schools (*Quick Bear v. Leupp*).[61]

When the United States entered World War I in 1917, Con-

---

58. O'Dea, *The Mormons*, 246–47.
59. *Bradford v. Roberts*, 175 U.S. 291 (1899).
60. *Bradford v. Roberts*, 297.
61. *Quick Bear v. Leupp*, 210 U.S. 50 (1908).

gress enacted a draft law with exemptions from combat for conscientious objectors to war affiliated with religious sects or organizations. The exemption was challenged in part as a religious establishment, but the Court upheld the exemption (*Arver v. U.S.*).[62] We shall consider the statutory and judicial history of conscientious objectors to war in a later chapter.

In 1925 the Court struck down an Oregon statute that obliged all children to attend public schools (*Pierce v. Society of Sisters*).[63] The Sisters objected to the statute as a deprivation of their property rights. Justice McReynolds, speaking for a unanimous Court, explained why the statute was unconstitutional:[64] "The child is not the mere creature of the state; those who nurture him and direct his destiny have the right, coupled with the high duty, to recognize and prepare him for additional obligations." The Pierce decision, to be sure, established only the general right of parents to send their children to schools of their own choice. While most today would agree with the correctness of the decision, they would not agree that the government is obliged to support private schools or their patrons.

In 1930 the Supreme Court for the first time passed on the question of whether state funds may be used to benefit pupils attending sectarian educational institutions (*Cochran v. Louisiana*).[65] The case did not come before the Court on the basis of a direct appeal to the religious establishment clause, since the First Amendment itself obviously applied only to the national government, not the states. Rather, Cochran contended that the state in providing free textbooks in secular subjects to parochial school pupils spent money for a private, not a public, use. Nonetheless, the church-state issue was implicitly involved. Chief Jus-

62. *Arver v. U.S.*, 245 U.S. 366 (1918).
63. *Pierce v. Society of Sisters*, 268 U.S. 510 (1925).
64. *Pierce v. Society of Sisters*, 535.
65. *Cochran v. Louisiana*, 281 U.S. 340 (1930).

tice Hughes, speaking for a unanimous Court, rejected Cochran's claim. According to Hughes, the appropriations were made for the specific purpose of providing books for the use of the school children of the state, free of cost to them, for their benefit and that of the state. The schools are not the beneficiaries of the appropriations. They obtain nothing from them, nor are they relieved of any obligation because of them. The school children and the state alone are the beneficiaries.[66]

The Cochran decision rests on the principle that the parochial school pupils, not the sectarian institutions, were the beneficiaries of the state's purchase of textbooks. This contention, like the one in the Bradford case, is somewhat an oversimplification, but perhaps again, as in the Bradford case, the Court was basically saying that the public support was genuinely related to an important civic interest and the benefit to the private institution consequentially only incidental. In the Cochran opinion we have the seeds of the distinction decisively expressed in the Everson case between direct and indirect governmental aid to religious institutions and activities.

66. *Cochran v. Louisiana*, 374–75.

3

THE FOURTEENTH AMENDMENT
AND THE FIRST

DRAFTING THE FOURTEENTH AMENDMENT

The first session of the 39th Congress opened in Washington in December 1865.[1] Though elected with Lincoln in 1864, the Congress was serving under his successor, Andrew Johnson. The new president's conservative reconstruction policy was becoming more evident to the Radical Republicans, who had originally hoped, with initial indications of success, to win him to their cause. The rupture between the president and the Radicals was looming, but not yet definitive. The Radicals' plan for the South—to be accomplished with the president's cooperation if possible, but against his will if necessary—focused on guarantees of black rights, including suffrage.

Already in the summer of 1865, Representatives John Bingham of Ohio, George Boutwell of Massachusetts, Thaddeus Stevens

---

1. The primary sources for this section are: *The Congressional Globe,* 39th Cong., 1st sess.; and Benjamin B. Kendrick, *Journal of the Joint Committee of Fifteen on Reconstruction* (New York: Columbia University, 1914). The secondary sources are: Horace E. Flack, *The Adoption of the Fourteenth Amendment* (Gloucester, Mass.: Peter Smith, 1965); and Joseph B. James, *The Framing of the Fourteenth Amendment* (Urbana: University of Illinois Press, 1951).

of Pennsylvania, and senators Jacob Howard of Michigan and William Fessenden of Maine, all future members of the Joint Committee on Reconstruction, had endorsed an outright grant of suffrage to blacks.[2] They and other Radicals had political as well as humanitarian motives for endorsing black suffrage.

The Thirteenth Amendment freeing the slaves was ratified by the requisite twenty-third state on December 6, 1865, and certified by the secretary of state on December 18. This entitled the Southern states to increased representation in the House of Representatives. The Constitution now entitled those states to full representation of the emancipated blacks instead of three-fifths. Understandably, the anomalous prospect of increased representation for the South was distasteful to the Radicals. Worse yet was the political threat that the increased representation of the South would pose to their control of the House. By the single stroke of black suffrage, the Radicals hoped both to achieve voting rights for blacks and to assure their own ascendancy in Congress.

Unfortunately for the Radicals, they had to face the hard facts of political life. The fall elections of 1865 had indicated that the Northern and border-state electorate did not approve, or at least was not enthusiastic about, black suffrage where that issue was at stake.[3] The Radicals, therefore, were obliged to persuade the public. In the interim, however, the Radicals needed a touchstone to prevent Southern and Democratic dominance in Congress. This touchstone appeared in the form of a constitutional amendment to apportion representation in the House according to the eligible voters in each state. The twofold result would be an immediate reduction of Southern representation in the House and a powerful, but indirect spur to the South to grant blacks the suffrage.

In the early weeks of the session the members of Congress

---

2. James, *Framing of the Fourteenth Amendment*, 184.
3. James, *Framing of the Fourteenth Amendment*, 185.

wisely supported the idea of an amendment apportioning representation according to the number of qualified voters in each state. This proposal had the support of President Johnson and his supporters in the Senate. But on January 8, 1866, Representative James Blaine of Maine informed the House of the proposal's consequences for New England.[4] If representation were proportioned to the number of qualified voters, then Massachusetts and other Northeastern states with large immigrant populations would lose representation unless they enfranchised their aliens. Moreover, the proposal would give a bounty to any state that enfranchised women. And the Missouri representatives pointed out that disfranchisement of ex-Confederates, which in Missouri approached one-half of the population, would radically reduce the border state's representation in Congress.

The impact of Blaine's speech was not lost on Radical leaders, and the Joint Committee on Reconstruction on January 22 accordingly adopted his plan for revision of the original amendment. The operative clause of the proposed amendment now read, "whenever the elective franchise shall be denied or abridged in any state on account of race or color, all persons of such race or color shall be excluded from the basis of representation."[5] The House adopted it on January 31.[6] But the amendment failed in the Senate, caught in a crossfire from Senator Charles Sumner of Massachusetts and ultra-Radicals on the one side, who would settle for nothing less than an outright grant of black suffrage, and Democrats and Johnson Republicans on the other, who insisted on representation proportioned to the number of qualified voters in each state.[7]

Eventually, after the Radical leadership had Republicans ham-

---

4. *Congressional Globe*, 39th Cong., 1st sess., 141–42.
5. *Congressional Globe*, 39th Cong., 1st sess., 351.
6. *Congressional Globe*, 39th Cong., 1st sess., 538.
7. *Congressional Globe*, 39th Cong., 1st sess., 1289.

mer out all proposed revisions of the amendment in a party caucus and binding the members to the product, the Senate on June 8 passed what is now section 2 of the Fourteenth Amendment.[8] The operative clause reads, "When the right to vote ... is denied to any of the male inhabitants of such state, being twenty-one years of age and citizens of the United States, or in any way abridged, except for participation of rebellion, or other crime, the basis of representation therein shall be reduced in the proportion which the number of such male citizens shall bear to the whole number of male citizens twenty-one years of age in such state." The final wording, accepted by the House on June 13, maneuvered deftly to penalize voting discrimination against blacks by Southern states, but did not operate at all against the denial of the vote to aliens, women, or ex-Confederates.[9] And all of this was accomplished without so much as mentioning blacks or their right to vote. Despite the effort and time expended on what became section 2 of the Fourteenth Amendment, the section had a short life and little or no effect. In February 1869 Congress adopted the Fifteenth Amendment, which granted blacks the right to vote. The Fifteenth Amendment was ratified on March 30, 1870, less than two years after the ratification of the Fourteenth (July 20, 1868).

But the representation provision was only one-half of the story of the drafting of the Fourteenth Amendment. The Radicals had an equally prominent interest in guaranteeing the civil rights of blacks. They sought to do so by statute (the Civil Rights Act of 1866) and constitutional amendment.

From the first days of the 39th Congress, Radicals made clear that they were prepared to carry out their program for blacks' civil rights. On January 12, 1866, Bingham suggested a constitutional amendment to the Joint Committee that would authorize Congress to pass laws necessary and proper "to secure to all per-

---

8. *Congressional Globe*, 39th Cong., 1st sess., 3042.
9. *Congressional Globe*, 39th Cong., 1st sess., 3149.

sons equal protection in their rights of life, liberty and property."[10] This proposal was referred to the Joint Committee, which adopted the following amendment: "The Congress shall have the power to make all laws necessary and proper to secure to the citizens of each state all privileges and immunities of citizens in the several states, and to all persons in the several states equal protection in the rights of life, liberty, and property."[11]

On February 13 Bingham reported the amendment to the House. In the course of debate over several weeks,[12] on February 28, Representative Robert Hale of New York objected that the amendment seemed to grant to Congress unlimited affirmative power to enact any civil rights laws it desired.[13] In response, Bingham claimed that the amendment proposed to give Congress only the power "to enforce the Bill of Rights as it stands in the Constitution today."[14] (As will be indicated, Bingham was in error about the original Bill of Rights applying to the states; he thought that Congress lacked only the power to enforce it.) On the same day, the House voted to postpone consideration of it.[15] The House was at the time preoccupied with Johnson's veto of the Freedmen's Bureau Bill, and rewording of the amendment to meet Hale's objection would have interfered with (unsuccessful) efforts to override the veto.

In April, the Joint Committee decided to combine four proposed amendments into one, with section 5 granting Congress the power to enforce them, and turned its attention on April 21 to what would become section 1 of the Fourteenth Amendment.[16] In the meantime, Bingham had discovered that the Bill of Rights

---

10. Kendrick, *Journal of the Joint Committee of Fifteen on Reconstruction*, 46.

11. Kendrick, *Journal of the Joint Committee of Fifteen on Reconstruction*, 51.

12. *Congressional Globe,* 39th Cong., 1st sess., 813.

13. *Congressional Globe,* 39th Cong., 1st sess., 1088.

14. *Congressional Globe,* 39th Cong., 1st sess., 1088.

15. *Congressional Globe,* 39th Cong., 1st sess., 1095.

16. Kendrick, *Journal of the Joint Committee of Fifteen on Reconstruction*, 46.

restricted only the action of the federal government, as Chief Justice Marshall held in *Barron v. Baltimore*,[17] not that of the states. Bingham realized, therefore, the constitutional inadequacy of the Civil Rights Bill, which Congress passed over Johnson's veto on April 9, as well as the constitutional necessity of a broad guarantee of all basic civil rights against state action, with Congress having the power to enforce them. On Brigham's insistence, the Committee adopted his own sweeping terms: "No state shall make or enforce any law which shall abridge the privileges and immunities of citizens of the United States, nor shall any state deprive any person of life, liberty, or property without due process of law, nor deny to any person within its jurisdiction the equal protection of the laws."[18] This became section 1 of the Fourteenth Amendment. The enforcement power of Congress, which was part of his original amendment, was placed in section 5.

On May 8 Stevens reported the amendment to the House. He claimed that the provisions of section 1 are "all asserted in some form or other in our Declaration [of Independence] or organic law. But the Constitution limits only the action of Congress and is not a limitation on the states. This amendment supplies [for] that defect and allows Congress to correct unjust legislation of the states."[19] On May 10, Bingham declared that the amendment conferred on Congress new authority "to protect by national law the privileges and immunities of all citizens of the Republic and the inborn [natural] rights of every person within its jurisdiction" against abridgement or denial by state action.[20] The House later that day approved the whole amendment by a vote 128 to 37.[21]

The Senate took up the proposed amendment on May 23, with Howard reporting for the Committee in place of the ailing Fes-

---

17. *Barron v. Baltimore*, 32 U.S. 243 (1833).
18. Kendrick, *Journal of the Joint Committee of Fifteen on Reconstruction*, 106–7.
19. *Congressional Globe,* 39th Cong., 1st sess., 2459.
20. *Congressional Globe,* 39th Cong., 1st sess., 2542.
21. *Congressional Globe,* 39th Cong., 1st sess., 2549.

senden.[22] According to Howard, the privileges and immunities of citizens included the rights of citizens of the several states (Art. 4, sec. 2) and those "personal rights guaranteed and secured by the first eight amendments to the Constitution."[23] He then explicitly enumerated most of the rights contained in the Bill of Rights, but denied that suffrage was one of the privileges secured by the proposed amendment.[24] With respect to the due process and equal protection clauses of section 1, he claimed that they abolished all class legislation in the states and subjected all to the same laws and punishments.

On May 29, Howard reported Republican caucus revisions to the Senate. There was now prefixed to section 1 a definition of citizenship: "All persons born or naturalized in the United States and subject to the jurisdiction thereof are citizens of the United States and of the state in which they reside."[25] The aim of this insert was to block any attempt by the South to evade the prohibitions of section 1 by claiming that emancipated blacks were not citizens of the United States or the state. Moreover, the framers had recalled that the Dred Scott decision had declared that African-descended blacks were not and could not become citizens of the United States, that that decision was still the law of the land, and that the Thirteenth Amendment had freed the slaves, but not expressly made them citizens. The definition of United States citizenship overturned that decision.

According to Howard, the insert was "simply declaratory" of what was "the law of the land already.... It settles the great question of citizenship and removes all doubt as to what persons are or are not citizens of the United States."[26] (Howard's idea of what was already the law of the land reflected the common thinking of

22. *Congressional Globe*, 39th Cong., 1st sess., 2764.
23. *Congressional Globe*, 39th Cong., 1st sess., 2765.
24. *Congressional Globe*, 39th Cong., 1st sess., 2766.
25. *Congressional Globe*, 39th Cong., 1st sess., 2869.
26. *Congressional Globe*, 39th Cong., 1st sess., 2890.

the Radicals that the emancipation of the slaves made them citizens.) According to Fessenden, the object of the definition was "to prevent a state from saying that, although a person is a citizen of the Unites States, he is not a citizen of the state."[27]

Despite Howard's claim that the definition removed all doubt about who were citizens, the Senate had a long discussion about the definition's effect on the status of Indians.[28] The general consensus was against citizenship for the Indians, and most thought that the definition excluded Indians in the territories or reservations, since they enjoyed a quasi-jurisdiction of their own.

The aims of the already passed Civil Rights Act sheds light on what Congress intended to accomplish by section 1 of the amendment. Senator Howard declared in debate on May 30 that section 1 put the "question of citizenship and the rights of freedmen under the Civil Rights Bill beyond [reliance on] the legislative power [of Congress]."[29] And Senator Lyman Trumbull, the author of the Civil Rights Bill, asserted on August 3 that section 1 was "a reiteration of the rights as set forth in the Civil Rights Bill."[30]

No one can doubt the aims of the Civil Rights Bill. That bill made all persons born in the United States and not subject to any foreign power, excluding Indians not taxed, citizens of the United States. The bill then declared that citizens in every state and territory had their right "to make and enforce contracts, to sue, to be parties and give evidence, to inherit, purchase, lease, sell, hold, and convey real and personal property, and to full and equal benefit of all laws and proceedings for the security of persons and property."[31] An earlier version of the bill had contained a general prohibition against racial discrimination in civil rights

27. *Congressional Globe*, 39th Cong., 1st sess., 2897.
28. *Congressional Globe*, 39th Cong., 1st sess., 2890–97.
29. *Congressional Globe*, 39th Cong., 1st sess., 2896.
30. *Civic Commercial*, August 3, 1866.
31. Henry Steele Commager, ed., *Documents of American History*, 9th ed. (Englewood Cliffs, N.J.: Prentice-Hall, 1973), 2:464.

in any state or territory of the United States, but this provision was deleted on March 13 because it could be broadly interpreted to include political rights.[32]

The twofold definition of citizenship was not intended to indicate any distinction between national and state citizenship. Quite the contrary was true, and the privileges and immunities clause was designed to protect both—that is, the rights of citizens as such. The clause was designed to insure no racial discrimination by the states against fundamental rights, which included those secured against the federal government by the Bill of Rights. The Radicals conceived of these rights as natural rights. The equal protection clause was designed to bar legislation by the states regarding those rights, and the due process clause was designed to secure the rights judicially. In short, the privileges and immunity clause was the substantive clause.

The framers' subsequent statements bear out this interpretation of the privileges and immunities clause. Radicals in the November 1866 congressional election argued that section 1 guaranteed equal rights to every human being. Five years later, on March 24, 1871, Bingham, the author of section 1, claimed that "the privileges and immunities clause … is chiefly defined in the first eight amendments to the Constitution of the United States."[33] What is interesting about his statement is not that it linked the privileges and immunities clause to the Bill of Rights, since Radicals had stated that view many times during congressional debate on the clause. It is rather the word *chiefly*. Bingham seems to say that the privileges and immunities of citizens extend *beyond* the Bill of Rights. At any rate, Bingham clearly states that the clause includes the Bill of Rights. Of course, he offered this interpretation five years after the drafting of the clause during the course of a political debate concerning new civil rights legislation. Nonetheless, the statement

32. *Congressional Globe,* 39th Cong., 1st sess., 1366.
33. *Congressional Globe,* 42nd Cong., 1st sess., appendix, 84.

accurately reflects the extensive aims of the Radicals, who controlled the 39th Congress, and no one in the House (or probably anywhere else) is recorded as challenging him.

Section 5 granted to Congress power to enforce the amendment, which power had been stated at the beginning of Bingham's original proposal. The framers intended that, although they thought that the privileges and immunities of citizens consisted of objective fundamental rights, Congress, not the Court, would legally determine those rights and enforce them. But, as we shall see, the Court in 1873 determined the meaning of the privilege and immunities clause in the Slaughterhouse Cases and did so in a way contrary to the framers' intention. As we shall also see, the Court from 1890 to 1936 used the due process cause substantively to strike down state legislation held to violate freedom of contract, later to strike down state legislation held to violate criminal defendants' civil rights, and still later to strike down state legislation held to violate guarantees of the First Amendment.

Congress clearly did not envision a role for the Court to exercise judicial review of state action in those cases. The original Bingham proposal, the congressional debate, and section 5 made clear that Congress was writing a blank check to itself. But it had also unwittingly, but implicitly given a blank check to the courts, especially the Supreme Court, since it is the function of the courts to say definitively what the law is. The operative clauses of section 1 are expressed in general terms, and those terms require judicial interpretation and application to state legislation. Any *general* criticism of the Court for doing so is really an attack on the principle of judicial review of state legislation and a call for the abolition or limitation of such review. This would be to burn down the house (the regime principle of judicial supremacy) in order to roast the pig (avoid bad decisions). Objections to the exercise of judicial review of state legislation should be focused on particular decisions (e.g., the Dred Scott decision, the substantive application of the due process clause to economic legislation, the Miranda ruling, the abortion decision). Critics have every right to work to reverse or limit objectionable decisions, the principal practical way being to secure sympathetic future appointees to the Court.

Senator Howard reported to the Senate on May 23 that section 5 gave "a direct affirmative delegation of power to Congress to carry out all the principles of all the guarantees" of section 1.[34] At the time that Congress passed the Fourteenth Amendment, the Radicals construed this power generously. The Thirteenth Amendment had a similar enforcement provision, and the radicals had relied on it earlier in the session regarding the Freedmen's Bureau and Civil Rights bills. Of course, some had misgivings about the Radicals' constitutional argument, but the misgivings were not sufficient to prevent passage of the two bills.

Later Congresses were to hear often that section 5 provided a constitutional basis for various civil rights laws. In fact, the Radicals made attempts in the 40th Congress to secure black suffrage by federal statute as enforcement of the Fourteenth Amendment. Boutwell, who had been a member of the Joint Committee, defended the validity of granting black suffrage by federal statute on the basis of enforcing the privileges and immunities clause of section 1.[35] He argued that the Fourteenth Amendment obliged the states to apply all their laws equally and so to grant the vote equally to male citizens over the age of twenty-one. A majority of the Congress, however, was not persuaded that the privileges and immunities of section 1 included political rights, since the disclaimers of the Radical sponsors of the Amendment on the matter of suffrage were both clear and recent.

In the course of debate over the enactment of the Enforcement

---

34. *Congressional Globe,* 42nd Cong., 1st sess., 2766.
35. *Congressional Globe,* 40th Cong., 1st sess., 555–61.

Act of 1871, Bingham rightly claimed for himself the author-ship of section 1, with the exception of the definition of citizen-ship. As indicated, he from this position of authority defended a broad construction of the section. But he also asserted that sec-tion 5 gave Congress the power to enforce the guarantees of civil rights, not only against discriminatory action by the states, but even against the failure of the states to take appropriate action to protect those rights, whether the failure was by commission or omission.[36] Bingham's exegesis of section 5 was admittedly made during the heat of congressional debate some five years after the event, but it at least evidenced how broad was the sweep of Radi-cal aims for section 5.

As a footnote regarding section 5, one should note that the Supreme Court in the Civil Rights Cases of 1883 rejected Bing-ham's position.[37] The last of the Reconstruction Civil Rights Acts, the Civil Rights Act of 1875, made it a crime to deny any person equal rights and privileges in inns, theaters, amusement parks, and transportation facilities on the basis of color or previous condition of servitude. Congress based the act on its enforcement powers under the Thirteenth and Fourteenth Amendments. According to the Court, section 5 of the Fourteen Amendment granted Con-gress only the power to correct abuses of section 1 by the states, not to take direct and primary action against private racial discrimina-tion. The Thirteenth Amendment merely abolished slavery, and no one at the time of the amendment thought that private discrimi-nation was a badge of slavery. And so Congress had no enforce-ment power under the Thirteenth Amendment to prevent it.

The sole dissenter, the first Justice Harlan, defended the law on the basis of enforcing both amendments. On the Thirteenth, he argued that the discrimination practiced by corporations and individuals in the exercise of public or quasi-public functions was

36. *Congressional Globe*, 42nd Cong., 1st sess., appendix, 85.
37. The Civil Rights Cases, 109 U.S. 3 (1883).

a badge of slavery, and so Congress under section 2 had the power of enforcement to prevent it. On the Fourteenth, he argued, differently from Bingham, that the first sentence of section 1 defined all persons born or naturalized and subject to the jurisdiction thereof as citizens of the United States and of the state in which they reside. This, unlike the prohibitions of discriminatory action by the states, is an affirmative grant, and so Congress under section 5 had the power of enforcement to protect the rights of citizenship.

THE PRIVILEGES AND IMMUNITIES CLAUSE AND THE COURT

The Supreme Court first passed on the Fourteenth Amendment in 1873 (the Slaughterhouse Cases),[38] and in those cases reduced the privileges and immunities clause to insignificance. In 1869 the Louisiana legislature granted a monopoly to a slaughterhouse with a schedule of fees for the slaughtering of animals within three parishes (counties), including New Orleans. Butchers were required to slaughter their animals at a specified place and pay reasonable compensation to the slaughterhouse company for the use of its facilities. The butchers unsuccessfully sought an injunction in the state courts and appealed to the Supreme Court. The butchers claimed that they were deprived of their right to exercise their trade, although the statute only regulated the place where they could slaughter their animals and only deprived them of the right to do so on their own premises. They alleged that the statute violated the Constitution in four ways: (1) it created an involuntary servitude prohibited by the Thirteenth Amendment; (2) it abridged the privileges and immunities of citizens of the United States; (3) it denied them the equal protection of the laws; and (4) it deprived them of their property without due process of law.

38. The Slaughterhouse Cases, 83 U.S. 36 (1873).

Justice Miller, speaking for a bare majority of five justices, sustained the statute. On the Thirteenth Amendment, he stressed the fact that its aim was designed to put the emancipation of blacks beyond legal doubt and implied that, although the amendment could apply to others, the statute did not make the butchers peons.

On the privileges and immunities clause of the Fourteenth Amendment, Miller began with an analysis of the preceding sentence defining citizenship. By declaring that all persons born or naturalized in the United States and subject to the jurisdiction thereof are citizens of the United States, the sentence overturned the Dred Scott decision. He next notes and emphasizes the distinction the sentence made between being a citizen of the United States and being the citizen of a state. A person may be a citizen of the United States without being the citizen of a state, and residence in a state is necessary to make a citizen of the United States a citizen of that state. The succeeding sentence speaks only of the privileges and immunities of citizens of the *United States* and does not mention those of citizens of a state.

Since the first sentence of section 1 distinguishes between the two citizenships and the privileges and immunities clause protects citizens of the United States, Miller drew the conclusion that the clause did not affect the preexisting constitutional status of the privileges and immunities of citizens of the states. Before the Fourteenth Amendment, the domain of the privileges and immunities of citizens of the states rested in the power of the states, not in the power of the federal government, with the exception of the few express limitations that the Constitution imposed on the state, and there those privileges and immunities remain after the amendment. Those privileges and immunities are the fundamental rights belonging to citizens of a free government, including the right to acquire and possess property. He then asked rhetorically whether the privileges and immunities clause was intended to bring within the power of Congress the entire domain of civil rights heretofore belonging to the states. In that rhetorical question, he indicated clearly his personal view about the matter.

Miller's analysis of the privileges and immunities clause, however superficially logical, is in total variance with the facts surrounding its framing. As previously indicated, the wording of the clause was in the original Bingham-proposed amendment *before* the addition of the definition of dual citizenship. The definition of U.S. citizenship was specified, as Miller himself indicated, in order to overturn the Dred Scott decision, and the definition of state citizenship was specified in order to avoid any equivocation by the Southern states still exclusively under the control of whites. The two citizenships were complementary, not contrary to one another. Moreover, Bingham and others clearly indicated during the debates before inclusion of the definition of citizenship that the privileges and immunities of citizens of the United States in the original Bingham amendment referred to those of citizens *as such,* which were fundamental—that is, natural rights.

But Miller went on to suggest privileges and immunities that owe their existence to the federal government by reason of the Constitution or the laws made under its authority. These include the right of citizens to come to the seat of the U.S. government (Washington, D.C.), to assert any claim against it, to transact any business they may have with it, to seek its protection, to share its offices, and to engage in administering its functions. Citizens of the United States have the right of free access to its seaports, the sub-treasuries, land offices, and courts of justice. Another privilege of a citizen of the Unites States is to invoke the care and protection of the federal government over the citizen's life, liberty, and property when on the high seas or within the jurisdiction of a foreign government. The Constitution guarantees the right to assemble peacefully and petition for the redress of grievances, the privilege of the writ of habeas corpus, the right to use the navigable waters of the United States wherever they penetrate, and all rights secured to citizens by treaties with foreign nations. These privileges and immunities, of course, existed before the Fourteenth Amendment, although the citizenship clause extended them to blacks.

As to the argument that the statute deprived the butchers of their property without due process of law, Miller held that the restraint Louisiana imposed on the exercise of their trade was not a deprivation of property within the meaning of the due process clause. That is to say, the due process clause imposes no substantive restraint on the states regarding property rights. As to the argument that the statute denied the butchers equal protection of the laws, Miller held that the equal protection clause was designed to forbid the gross injustices of the Black Codes enacted in Southern states after the Civil War and was unwilling to apply it to any other case.

Justice Field, speaking for the four dissenters, interpreted the citizenship clause as making persons citizens of the United States by reason of their place of birth or the fact of naturalization, not by reason of the laws of any state or the condition of their ancestry. The citizen of a state is now also a citizen of the United States residing in that state. The fundamental rights, privileges, and immunities that belong to one as a free person and a free citizen belong now to one as a citizen of the United States and are not dependent on citizenship of any state. The Fourteenth Amendment does not confer any new privileges or immunities on citizens. It assumes that there are privileges and immunities that belong to citizens as such and establishes that they shall not be abridged by state legislation. If the privileges and immunities clause refers only to such privileges and immunities as were before the amendment's adoption specially designated in the Constitution or necessarily implied by national citizenship, the clause was a vain and idle enactment. If the privileges and immunities of the clause are restricted to those so designated or implied, no state could ever have legally interfered, and no constitutional provision was required to prohibit such interference. The Constitution and the laws of the United States are the supreme law of the land (Article 6) and always overrule any state laws contrary to them.

Congress, in the Civil Rights Act of 1866, stated some of the rights included in the privileges and immunities of citizens of the United States. The Fourteenth Amendment was adopted to obviate objections to the constitutionality of the act and extended the protection of the federal government over the common rights of all citizens of the United States. Accordingly, Congress after ratification of the amendment reenacted the act under the belief that the amendment removed all doubts about its validity.

The words *privileges and immunities* were in Article 4, sec. 2. That clause provided that "the citizens of each state shall be entitled to all the privileges and immunities of citizens of the several states" and thereby protected the fundamental rights of citizens of one state against hostile and discriminatory legislation of other states. According to Field, the privileges and immunities clause of the Fourteenth Amendment extended the federal protection that Art. 4, sec. 2, gave to the fundamental rights of citizens of different states to the fundamental rights of every citizen of the United States—that is, to the rights of citizens of the same state.

In Field's view, all state-created monopolies in any trade or manufacture are an invasion of the privileges and immunities of citizens of the United States, since they encroach upon the liberty of citizens to acquire property and pursue their business. Equality of the right to lawful pursuits throughout the country is the distinguishing privilege of citizens of the United States. The state may prescribe regulations for every pursuit and calling to promote the public health, secure good order, and advance the general prosperity, but the pursuit or calling must be open to every citizen who will conform to the regulations. Only under a free government is the inalienable right of every citizen to pursue the citizen's happiness unrestrained except by just, equal, and impartial laws.

Field is clearly right about the framers' intentions about the privileges and immunities clause of the Fourteenth Amendment. But his position that free enterprise is an absolute fundamental right is disputable. Granted that freedom to engage in a trade or business is a fundamental right, one may object that it is not an absolute right—that is, that a state government might reasonably choose to charter a monopoly under certain conditions. There may be concerns about public safety, health, and adequate supply to justify a monopoly or at least make it a reasonable choice, in which case the courts should defer to the state's legislative judgment.

THE DUE PROCESS CLAUSE
AND THE COURT

With the privileges and immunities clause effectively a dead letter as a protection of civil liberties, the Court turned its attention to the due process clause. In 1877, four years after the Slaughterhouse Cases, the Court ruled on the due process clause. The 1970 Illinois Constitution declared grain elevators to be public warehouses and gave to the Illinois legislature power to pass laws regarding them. An act of the legislature in 1871 fixed the rates warehouse owners could charge, required a license, and regulated the warehouses. Munn was convicted of operating a warehouse without a license and other unlawful practices, and he obtained Supreme Court review of an adverse decision by the Illinois Supreme Court.

In the resulting Supreme Court decision, *Munn v. Illinois,*[39] the Court upheld the statute against the due process claim. Chief

---

39. *Munn v. Illinois,* 94 U.S. 113 (1877).

Justice Waite found that the businesses regulated were affected with a public interest and so could be subjected to a greater degree of regulation than purely private property could. Since it was up to the legislature, not the Court, to determine what and how much regulation was reasonable, due process was observed. In other words, the due process clause imposed no substantive limitation on state regulations of such businesses. Dissenting Justice Field thought that only property granted by the government or dedicated by its owner to public uses should be considered property affected with a public use, and that the due process clause provided substantive protection of the rights of owners of other property from deprivation by state legislatures.

In 1887, in *Mugler v. Kansas*,[40] the Court opened the door for substantive judicial review of state regulation of business under the due process clause. The question at issue was whether the prohibition laws of Kansas could rightfully extend to the manufacture of alcoholic beverages for personal use. Although the first Justice Harlan, speaking for the full Court, ruled that they could, he stated clearly that the courts will look behind the form of laws if they purport to be an exercise of police powers. The laws must have a substantial relation to the state's police powers. Between 1877 and 1890 seven justices resigned or died, and Justice Field lived on, joined in 1888 by his nephew, Justice Brewer. In 1890, in *Chicago, Milwaukee, and St. Paul Railroad Co. v. Minnesota*,[41] the Court effectively overruled *Munn* and established a substantive standard of due process concerning business regulation. The Court struck down a statute that prohibited judicial review of the reasonableness of railroad rates established by a commission. By doing so, according to the Court, the state denied the railroads due process regarding the reasonableness of the rates.

40. *Mugler v. Kansas*, 123 U.S. 623 (1887).
41. *Chicago, Milwaukee, and St. Paul Railway Co. v. Minnesota*, 134 U.S. 418 (1890).

From 1890 through 1936 the Court applied the due process clause substantively to state economic regulations, especially over the hours and wages of employees. It upheld some and disallowed others. It upheld laws regulating the maximum hours of women (*Muller v. Oregon*)[42] and ultimately those of men (*Bunting v. Oregon*).[43] But it struck down state laws establishing minimum wages for women (*Adkins v. Children's Hospital*),[44] which a fortiori applied to state laws establishing minimum wages for men. According to the Adkins majority, wages, unlike hours, constituted the heart of the contract between employers and employees, and legislation establishing minimum wages violated the due process clause. The Court refused in 1936 to review the Adkins decision in the case of a similar New York law,[45] but did review and overrule it in 1937 in *West Coast Hotel Co. v. Parrish*.[46] The latter decision put an end to the invocation of the due process clause as a substantive protection of property and liberty of contract against state infringement.

Regarding the rights of criminal defendants under the due process clause, the Court initially invoked the clause only to guarantee a fair trial, and did not apply every particular of the Fifth Amendment to the process. In 1937, in *Palko v. Connecticut*,[47] Justice Cardozo held that the due process clause protected only rights implicit in the concept of ordered liberty against infringement by the states, rights so rooted in the traditions and conscience of the nation as to be ranked as fundamental. Later, however, the Court in 1949 incorporated the Fourth Amendment

42. *Muller v. Oregon*, 208 U.S. 412 (1908).

43. *Bunting v. Oregon*, 243 U.S. 426 (1917); *Bunting* effectively overturned *Lochner v. New York*, 198 U.S. 45 (1905), which was the high-water mark of substantive due process regarding regulation of business.

44. *Adkins v. Children's Hospital*, 261 U.S. 525 (1923).

45. *Morehead v. New York ex rel. Tipaldo*, 298 U.S. 587 (1936).

46. *West Coast Hotel Co. v. Parrish*, 300 U.S. 379 (1937).

47. *Palko v. Connecticut*, 302 U.S. 319 (1937).

into the Fourteenth via the due process clause (*Wolf v. Colorado*),[48] the Warren Court incorporated most provisions of the Fifth and Sixth Amendments,[49] and the Burger Court incorporated the cruel and unusual punishment clause of the Eighth.[50]

Regarding the First Amendment, the Court in 1925, although it upheld a conviction for advocating, advising, and teaching the doctrine of anarchy by speech and printed material, assumed that the First Amendment freedoms of speech and press were among the fundamental rights protected by the due process clause against impairment by the states (*Gitlow v. New York*).[51] The assumption became reality in succeeding cases, and so the free speech clause of the First Amendment was incorporated into the Fourteenth. *Near v. Minnesota* incorporated freedom of the press in 1931,[52] and *Dejonge v. Oregon* incorporated freedom of assembly in 1937.[53] Then the Court in 1940 incorporated the free exercise of religion clause (*Cantwell v. Connecticut*).[54] Finally, the Court in 1947 completed the process of incorporating the First Amendment into the Fourteenth by incorporating the religious establishment clause (*Everson v. Board of Education*). We shall specifically consider the latter two cases later.[55]

As we have seen, the framers of the Fourteenth Amendment intended that its privileges and immunities clause apply the protections of the Bill of Rights against abridgement by the federal government to the states, although the civil rights of blacks were their specific concern. There is no evidence that the framers had

48. *Wolf v. Colorado*, 338 U.S. 25 (1949). *Mapp v. Ohio*, 367 U.S. 643 (1961), subsequently applied the federal exclusionary rule to the states.
49. *Gideon v. Wainwright*, 372 U.S. 335 (1963); *Miranda v. Arizona*, 384 U.S. 436 (1966).
50. *Furman v. Georgia*, 408 U.S. 238 (1972).
51. *Gitlow v. New York*, 268 U.S. 652 (1925).
52. *Near v. Minnesota*, 283 U.S. 697 (1931).
53. *Dejonge v. Oregon*, 299 U.S. 353 (1937).
54. *Cantwell v. Connecticut*, 310 U.S. 296 (1940).
55. *Everson v. Board of Education*, 330 U.S. 1 (1947).

any specific intention or interest in applying the clause to guarantee the free exercise of religion or to prohibit a religious establishment, but they did use general language and generally intend that the privileges and immunities clause protect the fundamental rights of citizens against adverse state action. Thus it was no judicial usurpation for the Court to incorporate those fundamental rights into the Fourteenth Amendment. The Court has never said that there is no difference between the protections of the Bill of Rights regarding the federal government and the protections of the Bill of Rights regarding state and local governments via the Fourteenth Amendment, but they are almost identical. It would have been better had the Court invoked the privileges and immunities clause rather than use a substantive interpretation of the due process clause to do so, thereby being more in accord with the intentions of the framers, but at least the Court effectively corrected Miller's glaringly erroneous interpretation of the former clause in the Slaughterhouse Cases.

4

RELIGIOUS ESTABLISHMENT AND
GOVERNMENTAL AID TO CHURCH-
RELATED SCHOOLS

❧

INTRODUCTION

Two principles seem to be central to the relation between government and religion in Western liberal democracies. The first guarantees to individual citizens and their associations freedom of specifically religious activity or inactivity and freedom of religiously inspired secular activity or inactivity, provided that exercise of those freedoms does not threaten substantial public interests. The second requires that the government be neutral in matters of religious belief or unbelief. Because liberal democracies are liberal, they espouse religious freedom, and because they are secular, they separate the business of government from that of religion. The two principles may be concurrently relevant to the same situation, and yet sometimes seem to call for different government policy. In reality, the principles are conceptually distinct and may be considered separately.

Few Western democracies today have established religions, and where such do exist, they are established more in form than in substance. There never was an established church of the United

States, and the last individual state to have one disestablished it more than a century and a half ago. In the nineteenth and twentieth centuries, the United States and Western democracies have moved beyond constitutional separation of church and state to a position of governmental neutrality toward religious belief itself.

In my opinion, the textual and contextual evidence is overwhelming that the framers of the First Amendment intended the establishment clause only to prohibit the federal government from establishing or preferring one religious sect or several over another or others. Whatever the personal views of some of the framers, they did not intend either to prohibit individual states from establishing a religion or to prohibit the federal government from favoring religious belief without compulsion in otherwise constitutional government activities.

The Fourteenth Amendment radically altered federal-state relations, and the Supreme Court more than sixty years ago incorporated the religious establishment clause of the First Amendment into the due process clause of the Fourteenth (*Everson v. Board of Education*).[1] And the Court in that case expanded the meaning of the establishment clause so as to prohibit not only the preference of one religion over another, but also the preference of religious belief over unbelief by federal or state governments. As a result, the Court has made governmental neutrality between religious belief and unbelief constitutionally normative.

Whatever one's views of the proper role of judges interpreting general constitutional provisions beyond or even contrary to the intentions of the provision's framers, however, governmental neutrality in matters of religion is consistent with the philosophy of integral liberalism. On the one hand, governmental endorsement of religion would seem to classify nonbelievers as less than first-class citizens, or at least nonbelievers would be likely so to

1. *Everson v. Board of Education*, 330 U.S. 1 (1947).

perceive it. If so, governmental endorsement of religion would be inconsistent with the civic equality characteristic of a democratic polity, or at least likely to be so perceived by unbelievers. On the other hand, a well-ordered polity, especially a democratic polity, should accommodate the efforts of individual citizens and their voluntary associations to promote their human development, and an even-handed governmental neutrality would let them do so.

Although democratic polities may, and even should, endorse the principle of governmental neutrality toward religion, they cannot and should not be indifferent toward religious belief and practice, for several reasons. On the practical level, religions traditionally set high moral standards of personal conduct for their members, the observance of which produces law-abiding and usually socially concerned citizens. (Religious fanatics of all faiths or none, of course, do commit atrocious crimes, but such fanatics are few, and responsible religious leaders of all faiths or none condemn the acts.)

On the speculative level, organized society and its hierarchically supreme agency, the state, should facilitate citizens fully developing their human personality, including its religious dimension. For organized society and the state to deny on principle the legitimacy of a religious dimension of personal development would be to adopt a hostile rather than a neutral stance toward religion. It is, of course, true that some religious movements espouse views contrary to the personalist values essential to a rightly ordered society, and that most, if not all, religious movements will have their extremists, but the abuse of religious freedom by some individuals and groups should not justify denying others the right to use theirs properly.

It is also important to note that the principle of governmental neutrality toward religion does not, in terms, extend to issues of public morality. A common enough, and conceptually confused, view holds that democratic governments would violate the principle of neutrality if they were to enforce a code of public morals by criminal sanctions. Regulation of public morals, however, is a secular matter, and principles of prudence, not the principle of neutrality, should be normative for such regulation. Nor is the principle of governmental neutrality toward religion applicable because public morals coincide with religious codes or simply because those responsible for the regulations are religiously motivated. Prohibition in the United States in the 1920s may indeed have been bad law, but it was not bad because it coincided with fundamentalist Protestant views about drinking alcohol or because those who legislated it were motivated by those views. The wisdom of criminal sanctions for behavior deemed socially harmful stands on its own merits or demerits irrespective of its religious origins.

The term *neutrality* with respect to religion needs to be defined, since one can hardly expect it to be consistently applied if it is not. Some definitions imply hostility toward religious beliefs and activities. Two Supreme Court decisions in the late 1940s, *Everson* and *McCollum*,[2] proposed a "wall of separation" between government and religion as the constitutional norm. That phrase at best is a misleading metaphor and at worst, if literally interpreted, would rule out any linkage between government and religious activities of whatever kind and under whatever circumstances. A subsequent decision, *Zorach*,[3] used the word *accommodation* to describe constitutionally permissible relations between government and religion, but failed to specify under what conditions accommodation would be constitutionally acceptable and under what conditions it would not.

The test established a decade later in *Schempp* was more analytic.[4] The first prong of that test required that there be a secular purpose of the governmental action at issue. In the context of the

2. *McCollum v. Board of Education,* 333 U.S. 203 (1948).
3. *Zorach v. Clausen,* 343 U.S. 306 (1952).
4. *Abington School District v. Schempp,* 374 U.S. 203 (1963).

Schempp case, the Court understood purpose to mean the objective purpose—that is, the objective or objectives that the government seeks to achieve by its action. Subsequent decisions shifted the focus from the objective purpose of governmental actions to the subjective motives of the legislators. In my opinion, their motives as such are irrelevant to the resolution of constitutional questions, although what legislators say about the laws they enact or amendments they adopt may indeed be relevant to interpreting the laws or amendments.

The first prong of the Schempp test requires only that governmental actions relating to religion have a valid secular purpose. Because governmental actions purporting to serve secular purposes may also have religious effects, a second prong requires that the secular effects be primary and that the effects on religion, whether favorable or unfavorable, be secondary. The effects prong will thus determine whether an asserted secular purpose of governmental action is compatible with the establishment clause. Effects manifest purposes, and so the primary effect of governmental action relating to religion will manifest the action's primary purpose.

Like the word *purpose*, the words *primary* and *secondary* need to be defined. If *primary* is understood to mean more important and *secondary* to mean less important, then the distinction, like beauty, will be in the eye of the beholder. If the effects prong is so defined, a judge friendly to religion will be inclined to rate the secular effects as more important than the religious effects in order to justify validating governmental actions, and a judge hostile to religion will be inclined to rate the religious effects as more important than the secular effects in order to justify invalidating governmental actions. Since religious and secular effects, like apples and oranges, differ qualitatively, a judgment regarding their relative importance in a given case necessarily depends on the values of the one making the judgment.

There is, however, another way of interpreting the words *primary* and *secondary,* and that is the way in which the Court used the words in the Schempp case—namely, to indicate a line of causality. If the religious benefits or burdens are incidental byproducts of the secular effects of governmental action, then the religious effects are secondary. If, on the other hand, secular benefits are incidental byproducts of the religious effects of governmental action, then the religious effects are primary. In other words, the Schempp Court understood *primary* to mean the first, or direct, effect and *secondary* to mean the second, or indirect, effect. Some justices in later decisions shifted the meaning of primary and secondary effects to one of relative importance, which would usually come down to a question of whether there is a substantial benefit to religion.

Six years after the Schempp decision, in *Walz,*[5] the Court added a third prong to the test—namely, that the religious establishment clause requires that governmental action relating to religion must avoid excessive entanglement between government and religion. The Court made no attempt then or later to explain in any principled way when relationships between government and religion involve *excessive* entanglements. The word *excessive* appears only once in the Constitution in connection with bail and fines (the Eighth Amendment). This is an appropriate usage, since it is impossible to fix a specific amount that will be proper in all cases, and common sense and judicial precedent can apply it to particular kinds of cases. But is it a manageable, objective norm regarding interactions between government and religion? Subjective attitudes toward religion or religiously related effects will inevitably influence one's judgment, whether or not relationships between government and religion constitute excessive entanglements. If one is favorably disposed toward religion or certain religiously re-

5. *Walz v. Tax Commission,* 397 U.S. 664 (1970).

lated effects, then one is likely to find that governmental action does not involve excessive entanglement, and if one is unfavorably disposed toward religion or particular effects related to religion, then one is likely to find that governmental action does.

The Court, moreover, has given no reason that the excessive-entanglement prong should be added to the Schempp test. If a governmental action has a secular purpose and a primary effect that neither advances nor inhibits religion, then how can the relationship between government and religion involve an *excessive* entanglement between them? Take the case of military chaplains in the armed services. As I shall indicate in a subsequent chapter, this provision of chaplains, in the opinion of most commentators, satisfies both prongs of the Schempp test. But it involves a lot of entanglement between government and religion, and this involvement seems unavoidable. While the Walz Court used the lack of entanglement to argue in favor of the constitutionality of tax-exemptions for property devoted to religious uses, subsequent decisions on governmental aid to church-related elementary and secondary schools used an excessive entanglement prong to invalidate the aid. In short, the excessive entanglement prong in practice became an effective means to invalidate governmental actions that pass the Schempp test.

In the Lemon case,[6] the Court added still another dimension to the Schempp test: the political divisiveness that results from government aid to church-related elementary schools. Professional commentators have rightly tended to discount this as a constitutional norm. On the one hand, if avoidance of political strife constitutes an independent religious establishment constitutional norm, no legislation on any subject that aroused division along religious lines (e.g., gay marriage) would be valid. On the other hand, judicial invalidation of governmental actions deemed to in-

---

6. *Lemon v. Kurtzman*, 403 U.S. 602 (1971).

volve political division along religious lines is unlikely to eliminate political conflict. Proponents of the stricken governmental programs would press to secure appointments to the Court favorable to their views or even a constitutional amendment. Political divisiveness without a commitment to agree to disagree respectfully can be a threat to civic unity, but the constitution of a democratic society should not be interpreted to prohibit governmental action simply because it involves such divisiveness, nor is judicial fiat likely to put an end to the conflict. Moreover, were the mere fact of political divisiveness along religious lines to be a factor in religious establishment questions, emotive reactions rather than rational analysis would be a constitutional norm that would always put the ball in the court of opponents of governmental actions with any benefits to religion.

GOVERNMENTAL AID TO CHURCH-RELATED ELEMENTARY AND SECONDARY SCHOOLS OR THEIR PUPILS

Everson v. Board of Education was the first in this series of cases to be reviewed by the Court under the incorporated religious establishment clause. A local school board had acted in accordance with a New Jersey statute and reimbursed parents, including parents whose children attended parochial schools, for money spent in sending their children to school on local buses. A taxpayer, Everson, unsuccessfully challenged the action of the local authorities in state courts and appealed to the United States Supreme Court. There a bare majority of justices sustained the school board's action.

Both majority and minority justices agreed that the religious establishment clause comprehensively forbade every form of support or aid by government to religious activity, but disagreed about whether publicly funded transportation of parochial school children constituted governmental support of religious activity.

The majority maintained that the state's contribution of free transportation was no more than an aid to the individual child, not support of the denominational school. Justice Rutledge disagreed. The funds used were raised by taxation, and "this not only helps the children to get to school and the parents to send them. It aids them in a substantial way to get the very thing that they [the children] are sent to the particular school to secure, namely, religious training and teaching."[7] And dissenting Justice Jackson quipped that the majority, like Byron's Julia, " 'whispering I will ne'er consent,' consented."[8]

I submit that both the majority and the minority were asking the wrong question. The entire Court, by accepting the thesis of complete separation of church and state, could only debate whether complete separation permitted the government to pay for the transportation of pupils to religiously oriented elementary and secondary schools. The real question should be whether, or to what extent, civil authority may cooperate with a religiously oriented activity related to secular civic interests, both regarding education in secular subjects and facilitating parents' choice of a religious orientation in their children's education. The Everson decision was before the Court adopted the Schempp test. Were it to have been applied in *Everson*, public funds for the transportation of parochial school pupils would, in my opinion, have satisfied both prongs of the test. After *Schempp* the Court used the test of that case and upheld the government lending state-approved textbooks for secular subjects to parochial school pupils (*Board of Education v. Allen*).[9] The Court in the latter case found that the lending of the textbooks satisfied both prongs of the Schempp test.

Beginning with the Lemon decision in 1971, The Court has

7. *Everson v. Board of Education*, 45.
8. *Everson v. Board of Education*, 19.
9. *Board of Education v. Allen*, 392 U.S. 236 (1968).

stricken down many forms of governmental aid to church-related elementary schools or their patrons. At issue in *Lemon* were reimbursements by Pennsylvania to parochial schools for the salaries paid to teachers of mathematics, foreign languages, physical sciences, and physical education. At issue in a companion case, *Earley v. Di Censo*,[10] was the payment by Rhode Island of a 15-percent supplement to parochial school teachers of secular subjects. The Court declined to decide whether the primary effect of the programs was neutral with respect to religion—that is, satisfied the second prong of the Schempp test—although it conceded that their purpose was secular. The Court chose rather to conclude that the cumulative impact of the programs involved excessive entanglement between government and religion.

Despite testimony by parochial school teachers in the Rhode Island program that they did not inject religion into their teaching of secular subjects, the Court found that the program had a *potential* for the teachers to do so. The teachers were employed by religious organizations and subject to the direction and discipline of religious authorities, and the teachers worked in a system dedicated to rearing children in a particular faith. As a consequence, the Court concluded that it would be hard for the teachers to separate secular teaching from religious doctrine. A comprehensive and continuous state surveillance of the teachers would be required to insure that statutory restrictions were obeyed, and that the Fourteenth Amendment's requirements regarding the separation of church and state were observed. Such surveillance would involve excessive entanglement of church and state. Moreover, state inspection of school records and state evaluation of the religious content of the school's operations would risk governmental control of the schools and the religious organizations sponsoring the schools. In the Court's view the Pennsylvania program had

10. *Earley v. Di Censo*, 403 U.S. 602 (1971).

the added defect of providing financial aid directly to the church-related school and entailed the government's power to evaluate a church-related school's financial records in order to determine which expenditures were for religious purposes and which were for secular purposes. In the case of both programs, a broader base of entanglement was found in the potential for religious division along religious lines.

The Court explicitly admitted the secular purpose of the programs at issue in *Lemon* and the companion case, and its failure to discuss the second prong of the Schempp test seems to imply that it agreed that the primary effect of the programs could be secular. That would be so if the secular educational functions assisted were separable from the religious functions of the schools. Putting the second prong of the Schempp test aside, the Court focused on the schools' potential to introduce religious indoctrination into the teaching of secular subjects and refused to allow the states to supervise the schools' use of the funds provided for exclusively secular objectives.

Conceding the undeniably religious character of parochial schools, it is obvious that there would be a *potential* for the schools to introduce religious doctrine into their teaching of secular subjects. (By the same token, of course, there is a *potential* for public schools to introduce religious or antireligious doctrine into their teaching of secular subjects.) But whether church-related schools and their teachers introduce religious doctrines into the teaching of secular subjects is a question of fact, and teachers in the Rhode Island program testified that they did not. Nor was the Court willing to allow the states to make random visitation of classes to insure, or to require church-related school administrators to certify, that the secular instruction assisted involved no religious indoctrination. The Lemon decision effectively prohibits *any* governmental funding of secular subjects taught in church-related elementary schools. On the one hand, if such a program does not attempt to insure that the educational functions assisted are free of religious influences, it will fail to pass constitutional muster, since it does not preclude the possibility of such influences, and, on the other hand, if the program does attempt to do so, it will involve a constitutionally impermissible entanglement of church and state.

Two years later, in 1973, the Court held that tuition grants and tax credits to patrons of parochial schools were unconstitutional. In *Committee for Public Education v. Nyquist*,[11] the Court invalidated grants of fifty to a hundred dollars to low-income parents for no more than 50 percent of the tuition paid for each student to attend parochial or other private schools. The Court held that the grants to parochial school patrons contained no restrictions to guarantee that only secular educational functions would be financially benefited. Although the Court conceded that the state sought to enhance opportunities for the poor to choose a religiously oriented education, it regarded the grants as having the primary effect of advancing religion. With respect to the tax credits to middle-income parents paying tuition for the education of their children in parochial schools, the Court held that there was little difference between the tuition grants to low-income parents and the tax credits to middle-class parents. Both received the same form of encouragement and reward for sending their children to parochial schools.

In his dissents in *Lemon*[12] and *Nyquist*,[13] Justice White argued that the ultimate judgment about the effect of governmental financial aid to church-related schools depends on whether the aid supports a separate secular function. If it does, then any financial benefit to religious organizations is secondary; if it does not, then the aid subsidizes religion. Justice Powell in his opinion in

11. *Committee for Public Education v. Nyquist*, 413 U.S. 756 (1973).
12. *Lemon v. Kurtzman*, 661.
13. *Committee for Public Education v. Nyquist*, 813.

Nyquist rejected that line of analysis: "We do not think that such metaphysical judgments are either possible or necessary."[14] (Powell's distaste for metaphysical judgments did not preclude him from describing the tuition grants in *Nyquist* as having "the *direct* and *immediate* effect advancing religion [italics added].")[15] But it is difficult to see how one can distinguish primary from secondary effects without causal—that is, metaphysical—judgments. There is no point in invoking the phrase *primary secular effect* without defining precisely what constitutes one effect primary and another secondary.

Ten years later, in 1983, the Court by the narrowest margin upheld the constitutionality of a Minnesota statute that permitted taxpayers to deduct from taxable income five hundred to seven hundred dollars of expenses for tuition, textbooks, and transportation of dependents attending accredited public or nonprofit private primary or secondary schools (*Mueller v. Allen*).[16] Since public schools are tuition-free and 95 percent of private schools are church-related, parochial school patrons were the principal beneficiaries of the statute.

All members of the Court agreed that the statute had a secular purpose, but disagreed sharply on the nature of the statute's primary effect. Several of the arguments advanced by Chief Justice Rehnquist for the majority on this point were, in my opinion, superficial. One argument appealed to the fact that the set of tax deductions at issue were only one among many others (e.g., medical expenses and contributions to charity), but the breadth of allowed deductions does not of itself justify inclusion of deductions alleged to violate the establishment clause. Another argument appealed to the fact that the deductions at issue were available for the educational expenses incurred by the parents of children

14. *Committee for Public Education v. Nyquist*, 783–84, n. 39.
15. *Committee for Public Education v. Nyquist*, 783–84, n. 39.
16. *Mueller v. Allen*, 463 U.S. 388 (1983).

attending any accredited nonprofit school, including the public schools, but the cash value of such deductions for the parents of children in the public schools was trivial.

Rehnquist was more on target when he noted that, whatever benefits the tax deductions provided to religious organizations sponsoring the parochial schools, the deductions provided benefits to church-related schools only as a consequence of the choice of individual parents. In the case of direct aid to parochial schools or their teachers, the Court had deemed the distinction of secular from religious functions critical. Tuition grants, tax credits, or tax deductions to the patrons of parochial schools, however, do not need to involve oversight of the schools as long as the schools are accredited and the financial benefits to the patrons do not exceed the secular educational benefits (as they patently did not in *Nyquist* or *Mueller*). Moreover, Rehnquist rejected the argument that the statute, however neutral on its face, in practice primarily and impermissibly benefited religious institutions. According to him, whatever benefits accrued to parochial school patrons from the statute could be fairly regarded as a return for the substantial relief from potential public school burdens, which parochial school patrons provided to the state and all taxpayers.

Justice Thurgood Marshall, dissenting in *Mueller*, states forthrightly that the establishment clause prohibits any tax benefit to religious education, whether in the form of tax credits or tax deductions, since any tax benefit to parochial schools or their patrons has the direct and immediate effect of advancing religion. In other words, no part of the educational program is separable from its religious purpose. One may readily concede that doctrinal or moral catechizing is integral to elementary and secondary religious education without affirming that it is integral to gym classes or arithmetic. And one may assume that parochial school personnel are religiously motivated without assuming that the proximate, as opposed to the remote, aim of parochial school personnel teaching secular subjects is doctrinal or moral. Humanities, of course, are famously difficult to teach objectively, but public school personnel must wrestle with that problem no less than their parochial school counterparts. Indeed, unless the secular and religious functions of parochial schools can be separated, it is difficult to see how student attendance at parochial schools can be judged to satisfy the secular objectives of compulsory education laws.

Tuition tax deductions to private school patrons have one advantage over tuition grants and tax credits, although not an advantage of constitutional significance. Critics of governmental aid to private schools understandably fear that state subsidies to private schools will induce middle-class parents to transfer their children from public schools to private schools and so promote a division of elementary school pupils along class and ethnic lines. But tax deductions for private school tuitions offer only a marginal incentive to parents to send their children to private schools, since the cash value of deductions to most taxpayers is relatively small in comparison with the cost of tuition. And although parents sending their children to private, especially religiously oriented, schools are of course concerned about the expense, economic considerations are not the chief reason they do so. But perhaps the majority in *Mueller* stumbled onto a way of accommodating the public interest in private schools without risking substantial damage to the public interest in public schools.

In two cases in the 1970s (*Meek v. Pittenger* and *Wolman v. Walter*),[17] the Court struck down the lending of globes, maps, and visual equipment to parochial schools, but *Mitchell v. Helms* in 2000 overruled those decisions and upheld the lending of secular educational materials to parochial schools.[18]

17. *Meek v. Pittenger*, 421 U.S. 349 (1975); *Wolman v. Walter*, 433 U.S. 229 (1977).
18. *Mitchell v. Helms*, 530 U.S. 793 (2000).

The Court applied the Lemon logic in full measure in two 1985 decisions. In *Grand Rapids v. Ball*,[19] the Michigan school district had adopted two programs in which classes for nonpublic, principally parochial school students were taught by teachers hired by the public school system, but conducted in nonpublic school classrooms. One program, a shared-time program, offered classes during the regular school day to supplement the core curriculum required by Michigan for accreditation. Included were remedial and enrichment classes in mathematics and reading and classes in art, music, and physical education. Shared-time teachers were full-time employees of the public school system. The program required that all religious symbols be removed from the parochial school classrooms during instruction under the program. The second program, a community education program, offered classes in arts and crafts, home economics, Spanish, gymnastics, drama, and humanities. Community education teachers were part-time employees of the public school system, and almost all were full-time employees of the nonpublic schools where the classes were held.

Justice Brennan and four other justices struck down both programs as violations of the establishment clause. Chief Justice Burger and Justice O'Connor concurred in the holding on the community education program, but dissented from the holding on the shared-time program. Justices Rehnquist and White dissented from the holdings on both programs.

Brennan noted summarily that the legislative purpose of the programs was secular, indeed praiseworthy, but the primary effect religious. He gave three reasons. First, the "pervasively sectarian nature of the religious schools" might lead teachers there to participation in religious indoctrination. Second, a symbolic union of church and state was inherent in the use of parochial school classrooms to teach secular subjects at public expense, and so the

19. *Grand Rapids v. Ball*, 473 U.S. 373 (1985).

programs threatened to convey a message to students and the public that the government supported religion. Third, the programs effectively subsidized the religious functions of parochial schools by assuming the costs of education in secular subjects.

Brennan did not give any operational definition of the term *pervasively sectarian*. Nor did he cite any evidence beyond handbook statements about a "God-oriented environment" and "Christian atmosphere" to show that the parochial schools were such. The latter statements indicate that the parochial schools were religiously oriented, which is indisputable, but does it indicate anything about the way in which secular subjects are taught? Even assuming extensive sectarianism in the parochial schools, however, there was neither any evidence of religious indoctrination by teachers in the programs nor any strong likelihood of such indoctrination. Nor is it clear that even the classes in religion consisted of indoctrination as opposed to instruction about a religion.

The shared-time classes were restricted to secular subjects with no obvious religious content, the subjects were taught by full-time public school teachers, and the parochial schools were required to remove religious symbols from classrooms during the classes. Subjects like mathematics and physical education hardly lend themselves to religious indoctrination or instruction, and there is no reason to believe that public school teachers lack either the intelligence or the virtue to avoid religious indoctrination or instruction. Moreover, were public school teachers to attempt religious indoctrination or instruction, they would risk disciplinary action or even loss of their jobs.

The community education classes were likewise restricted to identifiably secular subjects with one exception (Christian arts and crafts) and were taught to nonpublic school children and adults of all faiths or none. Although the community education classes were taught by parochial school teachers, there is no more reason to suppose that those teachers would lack the intelligence or the virtue to avoid religious indoctrination when on the public payroll than there is that full-time public school teachers would. Nor is there reason to suppose that the presence of religious symbols in community education classrooms would induce teachers to participate in religious indoctrination.

The community education program involved classes in the humanities, subjects that cannot be taught without reference to religious meanings and influences. The Court might have had some justification for concern about the introduction of religious bias in those classes. But in spite of potential for religious or antireligious bias, certified teachers routinely teach humanities in the public schools and conscientiously strive for objectivity. There is no more potential for bias in teaching literature or history in parochial schools than in public schools, and there are no more grounds to question the objectivity of qualified parochial school teachers than that of public school teachers of those subjects.

Second, Brennan claimed that the use of parochial school classrooms to teach secular subjects inherently involved a symbolic union of church and state that threatened to convey a message to students and the general public that the government endorsed religion. Some, like Brennan and the justices who agreed with him, perceive a symbolic union of church and state in any use of church-related property for public purposes and so discern in the arrangement a message that government endorses religion. But the relevant question is not whether some might perceive a symbolic union of church and state in the arrangement. It is rather whether they should. In the shared-time program, only secular subjects were taught, only full-time public school teachers taught the subjects, and all religious symbols were removed from the classrooms when the subjects were taught. In the community education program, the classes (with one exception) were in secular subjects, open to the general public, and held after school hours. One might reasonably perceive a symbolic union of church and state in the community education classes in Christian arts and crafts. But the elaborate efforts of both programs to insulate other publicly funded classes from the religious functions of parochial schools should lead any citizen, even one of "tender age" (to use the Court's phrase), to conclude that the two programs were designed to promote only the things that belong to Caesar.

Last, Brennan claimed that the public funding of secular classes in parochial schools effectively subsidized the schools' religious functions. He conceded that all public welfare programs reduce individual citizen's out-of-pocket expenses and so increase the funds that they will have available for religious uses. What made the difference here, according to Brennan, was that the Grand Rapids programs provided direct and substantial aid to the church-related schools.

The second prong of the Schempp-Lemon test requires only that government assistance of individuals or groups have a primary effect that neither advances nor inhibits religion. The directness of aid to institutions, by itself, is irrelevant to the distinction between primary and secondary effects, and the substantiality of aid would be relevant only if the distinction is one of the relative importance or value of the effect. That was not the original meaning given to the distinction in the Schempp decision. In that decision Justice Clark understood the distinction to be one between the causal order of the secular and religious effects. If one applies the original Schempp meaning of the primary-effect test, the Grand Rapids programs had the primary effect of pupils learning secular subjects and the secondary effect of a religious school benefiting. The Brennan formulation of the primary-effect test rests on subjective value judgments, while the Clark formulation rests on an objective chain of causality.

The second case, *Aguilar v. Felton,*[20] involved a federal pro-

20. *Aguilar v. Felton,* 473 U.S. 402 (1985). *Agostini v. Felton,* 521 U.S. 203 (1997), implicitly overruled *Aguilar.*

gram of remedial instruction for poor children administered by New York City. Title I of the Elementary and Secondary Education Act of 1965 required that local school boards receiving federal funds provide the same remedial instruction for nonpublic school pupils as for public school pupils. The New York City program covered 300,000 pupils, including 183,000 in parochial schools. Under that program, public school teachers taught classes to parochial school students in parochial school classrooms, religious symbols were removed from the classrooms during the instruction, and supervisors, unannounced, visited the classes once a month.

The same majority as in the Grand Rapids case struck down the New York City program as an unconstitutional establishment of religion. Justice Brennan did not rest the decision on the primary-effect prong of the Schempp-Lemon test. Rather, he argued that the New York City program involved an excessive entanglement of government with religion. According to him, the presence of public school teachers in a pervasively sectarian parochial school necessitated monitoring to prevent religious indoctrination, and such monitoring excessively involved the government with religion. Again, we are not told what makes the parochial schools *pervasively* sectarian. The decision, however, left open the possibility of remedial classes for parochial school students in public schools or on neutral sites.

One can easily understand why Brennan chose not to rest his decision on the primary-effect test. The monitoring of the remedial classes reduced whatever risk of religious indoctrination or instruction there might otherwise be, and public funding of remedial instruction in parochial schools subsidized the religious functions of those schools no more than public funding off parochial school premises would. (Brennan, of course, would undoubtedly have found the same symbolic union of church and state in the program that he found in the Grand Rapids programs, had he chosen to express an opinion on the subject.) It is not easy, however, to understand why he should have found an excessive entanglement between government and religion in the monitoring, since the monitoring was minimal, and supervisors apparently carried out their duties objectively and professionally.

Dissenting Justice O'Connor directly questioned the utility of the excessive-entanglement test, and with good reason. Involvement of government and organized religion is inevitable. How does one determine when such involvement is excessive? In the very same term as *Aguilar,* for example, a unanimous Court upheld the application of minimum wage, overtime, and record-keeping requirements of the Fair Labor Standards Act to workers engaged in the commercial activities of religious organizations (*Alamo v. Secretary of Labor*).[21] The Court there, inter alia, rejected an excessive-entanglement argument on the ground that the government would need to make only routine factual inquiries. If it is routine and factual for the government to inquire whether workers are engaged in commercial or religious activities, then why is it excessive entanglement for the government to inquire whether public employees engage in religious indoctrination? There is no principled way to determine what degree of government involvement with religious educational organizations is constitutionally acceptable. Indeed, there is no need to do so if the involvement satisfies the secular purpose and primary secular effect prongs of the Schempp-Lemon test. In short, the excessive-entanglement prong of the Lemon test should be scrapped.

In *Bowen v. Kendrick,*[22] the Court in 1988, by the narrowest of margins, upheld the Adolescent Family Life Act on its face, but remanded the case to the lower court to decide whether the statute had been applied unconstitutionally in specific instances.

21. *Alamo v. Secretary of Labor,* 105 S. Ct. 1953 (1985).
22. *Bowen v. Kendrick,* 108 S. Ct. 2562 (1988).

The statute made grants available to public and private organizations for educating and counseling adolescents about problems connected with premarital sex, and some of the recipient private organizations had institutional religious ties. Chief Justice Rehnquist identified a valid secular purpose for the statute in the aim to eliminate social and economic problems connected with adolescent sexual activity. He held that the statute did not have the primary effect of advancing religion, despite the fact that teaching and counseling self-discipline in sexual matters coincided with religious doctrine, but only recognized that religious organizations could play a helpful role in communicating a secular message. On the statute's face, he saw no symbolic link between the secular message and religious doctrine. Social service organizations need be excluded from government grants only if they are pervasively sectarian, not if they are religious. Last, also on the statute's face, he found no excessive entanglement between government and religion. Monitoring would be necessary so that the secular message was communicated free of religious indoctrination, but there is no reason to assume that the organizations receiving the grants were pervasively sectarian, and so no reason to assume that such monitoring would involve excessive entanglement between government and religion.

Concurring Justice O'Connor noted that, if extensive violations of the prohibition of any use of public funds to promote religion were found, the lower court could fashion a broad remedy to correct the problem. Concurring Justice Kennedy would require the plaintiffs, on remand, to demonstrate that the organizations were pervasively sectarian and that the organizations used the grants for religious indoctrination.

Dissenting Justice Blackmun said that there were widespread violations of the establishment clause by recipients and argued that the recipient religious organizations were more akin to parochial schools than to church-affiliated colleges in pervasive sectarianism. He found the statute's primary effect to be one of promoting religion. He thought that there was a substantial risk that the secular message would not be separated from religious doctrine, and that the record showed that religious personnel had promoted the secular message in theological terms. Although government grants may constitutionally support social services by religious organizations, there is a difference between religious organizations running soup kitchens and religious organizations counseling pregnant teenagers. On the entanglement issue, Blackmun thought that the grants would involve frequent disputes about what was secular and what was religious. Last, he thought that there was a substantial risk of a symbolic link between religion and government where government funds religious personnel teaching and counseling impressionable teenagers. (The notion that teenagers today are impressionable seems almost Victorian.)

Rehnquist and the majority may be right that the statute is facially consistent with the primary-purpose and primary-effect tests of the establishment clause, but Blackmun is surely right that it will be difficult to distinguish what is secular in teaching and counseling on sexual matters from what is secular. For example, if a teacher says, "adultery is wrong," would this be contextually equivalent to saying, "adultery is a sin"? To this I would add that it is regrettable that Blackmun does not recognize that, by contrast, it is relatively easy to distinguish the secular and religious educational functions of parochial schools. To use Blackmun's own analogy with a twist, teaching secular subjects in parochial schools is more akin to running a soup kitchen than to teaching and counseling teenagers on sexual matters.

In *Zobrest v. School District*,[23] the Court in 1993, again by the

---

23. *Zobrest v. School District*, 113 S. Ct. 2462 (1993); see also *Arizona Christian School-Tuition Organization v. Winn*, 131 S. Ct. 1436 (2011).

narrowest of margins, upheld for the first time a program that placed a public employee in a role connected with instruction in a church-related school. A deaf student, Zobrest, asked the school district to provide a sign-language interpreter to accompany him to classes at a church-related high school, pursuant to the relevant federal and state statutes for aid to individuals with disabilities. Chief Justice Rehnquist maintained that the government was offering a religiously neutral service on the premises of a sectarian school as part of a general program that was in no way skewed toward religion. Indeed, according to Rehnquist, no funds traceable to the government ever find their way into sectarian school coffers. Second, Rehnquist argued that the task of a sign-language interpreter is quite different from that of a teacher or guidance counselor, and that nothing in the record suggests that a sign-language interpreter would do more than accurately interpret whatever material is presented to the class as a whole. The sign-language interpreter would, of course, be communicating religious as well as secular instruction to Zobrest, but that does not necessarily preclude the purpose and primary effect of the aid from being secular—namely, facilitating a handicapped student to obtain education in a school with the value-orientation of his choice.

In the late twentieth century dissatisfaction with public schools in some areas led to the charter-school movement. Proponents of charter schools advocated vouchers of specific amounts for parents of school-age children to pay tuition at an accredited school. A number of states adopted voucher systems, and some of them allowed parents to use the vouchers for their children to attend church-related schools. In 2002 the Supreme upheld one such plan (*Zelman v. Simmons-Harris*).[24]

Because the state perceived that the Cleveland public schools

24. *Zelman v. Simmons-Harris*, 536 U.S. 639 (2002).

were failing adequately to educate children, Ohio provided vouchers of up to $4,000 per pupil for low-income Cleveland parents to pay for their children's tuition at an accredited public or private school from kindergarten to the eighth grade. Eligible private schools included church-related schools, and most of the vouchers (82 percent) were used to pay tuition at the latter.

Chief Justice Rehnquist, speaking for a bare majority, thought that inclusion of church-related schools in the voucher plan satisfied the Schempp-Lemon test of religious establishment. He found a secular purpose (providing educational choice to parents), a primary secular effect (secular education), and minimal entanglement of government with religion. Four justices dissented, viewing financial support of religion as the primary effect of the vouchers used at church-related schools. This decision follows up on *Mueller,* since the vouchers went directly to parents and only indirectly to the schools. It is important to note, however, that vouchers went only to low-income parents, and so it is not clear that a future Court would approve a broader voucher system, although there is no obvious reason that, in principle, it shouldn't. Moreover, the narrowness of the vote in the case suggests that any new justice replacing one of the majority justices might lead to a different outcome.

Except for judges and lawyers, who are professionally committed to making razor-thin distinctions and to maintaining an integral system of case law, few would claim that the Court's decisions on government aid to religiously oriented schools or their students are consistent. On the one hand, as we shall see in the next section, the Court, by distinguishing the secular and religious functions of church-affiliated colleges and universities, has upheld direct aid to the colleges and universities for the construction of buildings exclusively devoted to secular uses. On the other hand, the Court, by failing to separate the secular and religious functions of church-related elementary and secondary schools, has disallowed direct aid to the schools for teaching secular subjects. On the one hand, the Court has upheld lending secular textbooks to students attending parochial students. On the other hand, until *Mitchell*, the Court disallowed lending other secular instructional material to such students. On one hand, the Court has upheld tax deductions to parents for the tuition and expenses of the secular education that their children receive at parochial schools. On the other hand, until *Zelman*, the Court had disallowed outright tuition grants and tax credits to such parents.

Although I and almost every other commentator find these Court decisions fundamentally inconsistent, the same cannot be said of the views of individual justices. At one extreme, some justices in the 1970s and 1980s (Blackmun, Brennan, Marshall, and Stevens) held a generally consistent position that almost all forms of government aid that ultimately benefited religiously oriented educational institutions of whatever level were constitutionally impermissible. These justices, by interpreting the establishment clause to prohibit governmental assistance to the secular functions of religiously oriented educational institutions, have taken a position hostile to any role of religion in the educational objectives of organized society as such. This radical privatization of religion in education seems to rest on an assumption that any religious association in pursuit of secular educational objectives poses a threat to civic virtue.

I do not want to be understood to say that there are no serious policy problems in connection with government aid to the secular components of religiously oriented schools or to their patrons. The principal policy objection to such aid, in my opinion, is that the aid would undermine the goal of schooling citizens of all classes, creeds, and colors in democratic values, since religiously oriented schools divide citizens along creedal lines and sometimes along lines of class and color. To cite an extreme example, many commentators think that state-supported sectarian schools in Northern Ireland have exacerbated the conflict there between Catholics and Protestants. That is not the root cause of the problem, but it is probably a factor. Many states are currently adopting or considering voucher plans to offer parents a choice between public and private schools. This is a matter for public debate and legislative decision. If the public supports and the legislature should adopt a voucher plan, I see no constitutional reason to exclude religiously oriented elementary and secondary schools on the basis of the establishment clause. Their inclusion would not only satisfy the secular purpose and primary secular effect prongs of the Schempp-Lemon test, but also support the free exercise of religion in parental choice of the value orientation of their children's education.

Nor do I maintain that there are no significant policy considerations regarding different forms of government aid (e.g., the merits of indirect aid over direct aid). I say only that a *constitutional* barrier to any substantial government aid to the secular functions of religiously oriented schools on the basis of the establishment clause is neither required by nor consistent with governmental neutrality toward religion. Dismantling many of the precedents establishing a constitutional barrier would open the way for reasoned discourse about the undoubtedly genuine policy choices and considerations.

GOVERNMENTAL AID TO CHURCH-AFFILIATED COLLEGES

In 1940, only half of the adult population had graduated from high school, and only an elite few attended or graduated from college. After the end of World War II, the numbers of those attending college radically expanded. The G.I. Bill provided federal funds for veterans to attend college, including accredited church-affiliated colleges that required theology courses, and many states provided tuition grants to many students to attend college, also including colleges that required theology courses. In addition, many states provided per pupil subsidies to the colleges. The G.I. Bill enjoyed broad public support, and no legal challenge to inclusion of church-affiliated colleges reached the Supreme Court. (There is a standing problem regarding such a challenge, since standing requires that the petitioner demonstrate concrete injury.)

But *Tilton v. Richardson*,[25] a case in which the petitioner, Tilton, challenged federal construction grants to religiously affiliated colleges and universities for buildings used exclusively for secular educational purposes (e.g., classroom buildings, libraries, dormitories), with monitoring by on-site inspections, did reach the Court in 1971. The Court upheld the grants at issue, finding that they had a secular purpose and a primary secular effect, despite the fact that the grants benefited the church-affiliated colleges and universities financially. The Court found that the record provided no basis for any assumption that religion so pervaded the secular functions of the church-related colleges and universities that those functions could not be separated from religious functions. In a subsequent case, *Roemer v. Board of Public Works*,[26] the Court in 1976 upheld annual state government subsidies to religiously affiliated colleges. The recipient institutions in the two cases required theology courses of all students, and the Court noted that the theology courses required by the recipient college in the Roemer case might involve elements of religious indoctrination.

In *Witters v. Dept. of Services*,[27] the Court in 1986 upheld state government payments to a blind student for pastoral training at a religious college. Speaking for the Court, Justice Marshall concluded that the payments, made directly to the student, did not have a religious purpose or a primary effect of advancing reli-

---

25. *Tilton v. Richardson*, 403 U.S. 672 (1971); see also *Hunt v. McNair*, 413 U.S. 1346 (1973).

26. *Roemer v. Board of Public Works*, 426 U.S. 736 (1976).

27. *Witters v. Dept. of Services*, 106 S. Ct. 748 (1986).

gion. But he remanded the case to the trial court to determine if the payments involved a symbolic union of church and state or an excessive entanglement of government with religion. Four concurring justices (Powell, Burger, Rehnquist, and O'Connor) stressed the fact that any advantages accruing to religion from the payments derived from a student's choice of the school and its program. Note that, although the payments were for Witters to obtain *pastoral* training—that is, training to be a pastor or a missionary—the Court found a *secular* purpose and primary *secular* effect—namely, assisting a handicapped person to receive the training. Query: Would not there be stronger constitutional case in favor of the validity of government aid to the parents of parochial school pupils for the *secular* education the pupils received?

5

RELIGIOUS ESTABLISHMENT
AND PUBLIC SCHOOLS AND
PUBLIC COLLEGES

ᛦᛦ

SECTARIAN RELIGIOUS INSTRUCTION
AND THE PUBLIC SCHOOLS

Elementary schooling in colonial America, even when supported by public funds, as in Massachusetts, was religiously oriented
and largely dominated by clerical authority. A transition, however,
developed in the years following the Revolution. Stimulated by
Enlightenment ideas and the authority of such prominent American thinkers as Benjamin Franklin and Thomas Jefferson, the goal
of a common school open to all eligible students, supported by
public funds, and free of sectarian instruction, received increas-
ing acceptance in American communities. Other, more practical
forces were also at work: the multiplication of Protestant sects, the
arrival of non-Protestant religious minorities, and the increased
number of religiously unaffiliated citizens. Since this diversity of
religion accompanied the rise of the public school, the measure of
the public school's contribution to religious formation became the
least common denominator of various creeds, usually a Protestant
common denominator. By the middle of the twentieth century,

the decline of traditional Protestant churches in the cities, the rise of utilitarian secular ideas about education, and the enthusiasm of some educationalists for a purely secular curriculum had radically reduced the contribution of the public schools to religious formation.

Some individuals and groups who wanted their children's education in public schools to include an element of religious instructions opposed the secular trend of public education in the twentieth century. Accordingly, many communities, beginning in Gary, Indiana, in 1914, responded with released-time programs. The Supreme Court reviewed two of these, with different outcomes: the released-time program of religious instruction conducted on public school premises disallowed in *McCollum*[1] and the released-time program of religious instruction conducted off public school premises allowed in *Zorach*.[2] Although there is at present no interest or impetus for new released-time programs of religious instruction for public-school pupils, the cases raise interesting theoretical questions, which I shall examine. Indeed, the views expressed by the Court in *McCollum* and by the dissenting justices in *Zorach* still resonate in current debates on and off the Court about the establishment clause and the role of religion in schools, both public and private.

In the McCollum case, the Court disallowed an Illinois released-time program of religious instruction. The Champaign Board of Education permitted a voluntary association of interested Protestant, Catholic, and Jewish organizations to offer classes of religious instruction to public school pupils whose parents signed printed cards signifying approval of their children attending one of the classes. The classes were held weekly in public school classrooms for a period of thirty to forty-five minutes. The school authorities did not pay the instructors, but the instructors were sub-

1. *McCollum v. Board of Education*, 333 U.S. 209 (1948).
2. *Zorach v. Clausen*, 343 U.S. 306 (1952).

ject to the approval and supervision of the superintendent of the schools. Students not participating in the program were required to pursue secular studies in a study period at the time appointed for the religious instruction classes. Likewise, students participating in the program were required to be present at the religious instruction classes.

The subjection of the religious instructors to the approval and supervision of public school authorities deserves scrutiny. The Board of Education's supervisory role might involve an inadmissible link between the public authority and the religious instruction. Of course, the Board might have intended the approval and supervision on the part of public school authorities as a procedural regulation rather than a substantive control over the religious instruction. The approval and supervision might have been designed simply to ascertain that the religious instructors would observe school rules and maintain discipline in the classroom. But the Board should have spelled this out and made clear what constituted approval and supervision. Otherwise, arbitrary action could easily transform a procedural regulation into a substantial control over the religious instruction, which would surely violate the religious establishment clause. But the Court never focused on this point, and it did not feature in the decision.

In the Zorach case, the Court approved a New York City released-time program of religious instruction. The New York City program permitted school pupils to leave the school buildings and grounds during part of the school day to attend classes or devotions at religious centers. The pupils were released on the written request of their parents, and those not released stayed in the public school classrooms for a study period. The religious instructors made weekly reports to school authorities of the released pupils who did not attend the instruction.

The Court and common opinion today understand the religious establishment clause to require that governmental actions be neutral regarding religion—that is, that they neither advance nor inhibit religion, and the Schempp decision articulated a two-fold test of that neutrality—namely, that governmental actions have a secular purpose and a secular primary effect. The Mc-Collum decision prohibited released-time religious instruction in public school classrooms, but the Zorach decision permitted released-time religious instruction outside public school buildings and premises.

I submit that to interpret the religious establishment clause to prohibit religious instruction on a voluntary basis inside or outside public school classrooms if an equally attractive alternative is available to nonparticipating students neither follows logically from the principle of neutrality nor is consistent with the Schempp test. Indeed, to do so would rather prefer unbelief over belief. Here we need to recall the central principle of the Pierce decision—namely, that the child is not "the mere creature of the state," and that parents enjoy the primary right, duty, and responsibility to educate the child.[3] Therefore, the state's role in public education is secondary and subordinate to that of the parents, and its task is to support rather than supplant parental choice. This is not to say that the state may not act where parents default or may not specify the minimum secular education required to achieve civic aims. But the state should not treat the pupil entrusted to it as its autonomous handiwork. To invert the roles of parent and state would establish an educational Leviathan.

Failure to understand clearly the respective educational roles of parent and state necessarily blurs the distinction between state *sponsorship* and state *permission* of religious instruction in public education, which, in my view, is constitutionally critical. As a result, every phase of public education will be considered as only a state activity and any kind of released time for religious instruc-

---

3. *Pierce v. Society of Sisters*, 268 U.S. 510 (1925).

tion on a voluntary basis a constitutionally prohibited religious activity by the state. Such reasoning may explain why *McCollum* failed to make a straightforward distinction between state-sponsored and state-accommodated religious instruction. If the public school offers pupils the opportunity for voluntary religious instruction at the request of their parents, then the public authority is only executing a supportive role in relation to the parents' choice. The public authority will not then be endorsing religious education. Rather, it is permitting pupils to obtain an educational objective that their parents choose for them insofar, and only insofar, as this is administratively feasible within the general civic secular aims of public education.

Thus understood, neither the purpose nor the primary effect of a released-time program is religious. Of course, there is an incidental benefit to religious activity by the instruction, but this is not contrary to the principle of neutrality. The purpose and primary effect are secular—namely, to accommodate the primacy of parental rights in the education of children. The public authority, which operates and controls the educational framework of the public schools as the surrogate of the parents, simply accommodates, when feasible, the reasonable desire of parents to include a measure of religious instruction for their children.

To deny that public schools may allow parents to choose what is effectively an elective of religious instruction, when feasible, would in fact establish secularism as the religion of the public schools. The public authority would then act to prevent parents from selecting a feasible amount of religious instruction as part of the formal education of their children. In other words, the public schools would be required to exclude religious instruction from that education. The product of such a constitutionally mandated policy would not be neutrality between government and religion. Rather, it would place the weight of its authority in public education on the side of the secular humanist creed.

Justice Black said in *McCollum* and repeated in his dissent in *Zorach* that released time for voluntary religious instruction invoked the state's compulsory education laws in order to assist religious sects. "Pupils compelled by law to go to school for secular education," he explained, were "released in part from their legal duty upon the condition that they attend religious classes."[4] In his view the state thus made religious sects the beneficiaries of its education laws. Justice Jackson in his dissent in *Zorach* voiced a similar complaint—namely, that the state first compelled each student "to yield a large part of his time for public secular education" and then released some of it to him "on condition that he devote it to sectarian religious purposes."[5] Thus the truant officer would dog the youngster who failed to attend the religious instruction classes.

But I submit that Black and Jackson misread the nature of the compulsory education laws, and that their misreading conflicts with the primacy of the parental rights recognized in *Pierce*. Those laws require only that a child secure formal schooling that includes the secular education designated as necessary to fulfill the duties of citizenship. The laws do not require that a child's formal education be exclusively secular. The state does not require that parents exclude religious instruction from their children's formal education. A child can fulfill the state's requirement of secular instruction by attendance at an accredited church-related school without any implication that the state thereby makes the churches beneficiaries. Surely the compulsory education laws would not operate any more to favor the churches if a child were to fulfill the state's requirement of secular instruction by attendance at a public school where religious instruction was available.

Indeed, the Pierce decision established the general right of parents to obtain for their child the religiously oriented education

4. *McCollum v. Board of Education*, 209–10; cf. *Zorach v. Clausen*, 316.
5. *Zorach v. Clausen*, 323–24.

of their choice on the view that those who nurture the child and direct the child's destiny "have the right, coupled with the high duty, to recognize and prepare him for additional obligations."[6] In the light of that decision and its philosophy of parental primacy, I do not see how the state's compulsory education laws could constitutionally insist on the exclusion of voluntary religious instruction as part of a child's formal education.

Religious instruction at home and at church, of course, remains freely and fully available to children attending public schools. This availability obviously limits the hostile effect of excluding on constitutional principle voluntary religious instruction from public schools. But it does not serve to refute the charge that such exclusion on principle would effectively establish the "religion" of secularism *within* the public schools. The believer is equal to the nonbeliever inside as well as outside the public school, and the believing parent retains the primary right to the formal as well as the informal schooling of the parent's child, as far as this is administratively feasible and compatible with the general civic aims of public education. Hence the Constitution cannot be interpreted consistently with the principle of neutrality to prohibit the child whose parents so wish from receiving religious instruction within the framework of the child's formal education in the public school, provided that an equally attractive alternative is available to pupils not participating in the religious instruction.

In *Schempp,* Justice Brennan wrote a long concurring opinion in which he comprehensively expressed his views on the religious establishment clause in relation to schools, both public and private. It is useful to consider some of them here. He maintained that "parents remain morally and constitutionally free to choose the academic environment in which they wish their children to

6. *Pierce v. Society of Sisters,* 535.

be educated."[7] But that choice, in his view, was simply between a public secular and a private sectarian education. The state could not "inhibit that freedom of choice by diminishing the attractiveness of either alternative, either by restricting the liberty of the private schools to inculcate whatever values they wish, or by jeopardizing the freedom of the public schools from private or sectarian pressures."[8] The parent who sends a child to the public school accepts "an atmosphere free of parochial, divisive, or separatist influences" and cannot fairly complain of the exclusion of religious instruction.[9] In this way Brennan sought to avoid the charge that the exclusion of religious influences from public education violated the parental rights of believers and preferred unbelief over religious belief.

Brennan, in my opinion, rightly insisted on the free exercise of parental choice in the education of their children. His own explanation would have been plausible if the parents of children attending church-related schools received recompense from the state for the schools' contribution to the secular educational requirements of citizenship. But, as the situation now stands, the secular functions of private, religiously oriented schools do not receive significant public funding, and parents may choose a religiously oriented education only if they or the sponsoring organizations can afford it. Even if the state did support parents' choice of a religiously oriented school to fulfill secular educational goals, why should not the children of believers in public schools have the opportunity to obtain religious instruction as an elective, with an equally attractive alternative available to those not participating in any? The believer is equal to the unbeliever inside as well as outside the public school, and religious parents have the primary right to choose religious instruction for their chil-

7. *Abington School District v. Schempp*, 374 U.S. 203, 242 (1963).
8. *Abington School District v. Schempp*, 242.
9. *Abington School District v. Schempp*, 242.

dren within as well as without the children's formal education in a public school if such instruction is feasible. By the same logic, of course, an equally attractive alternative should be available to those who do not participate.

What lies behind Brennan's sharp dichotomy between public and private schools is the philosophy "that the public schools serve a uniquely *public* function: the framing of American citizens in an atmosphere free of parochial, divisive, or separatist influences of any sort, an atmosphere in which children may assimilate a heritage common to all American groups and religions."[10] But the implication that religion is a "parochial, divisive, or separatist" influence against which it is the unique public function of the public school to protect its pupils is a thinly veiled profession of a secularist philosophy hardly consistent with the principle of neutrality. Perhaps unwittingly but no less certainly, Brennan assumed the secularist argument that religious instruction is somehow a threat to civic virtue. The demands of pluralism embodied in the principle of neutrality do indeed prohibit the state from sponsoring religious exercises or instruction as a common program for all students in the public schools, as we shall see in the next section. But the demands of pluralism and the principle of neutrality also prohibit the democratic state from excluding voluntary religious instruction in the training of citizens as a matter of constitutional principle. For the state to claim that the exclusion of voluntary religious instruction from the public schools is part of the school's proper and unique function would brand sectarian religion an enemy of the state and so violate the principle of neutrality.

The proposition that the public school is designed exclusively for secular education was not novel with Justice Brennan. Justice Jackson had declared as early as his dissent in *Everson* that the

10. *Abington School District v. Schempp*, 241–42.

public school was "organized on the premise that secular education can be isolated from all religious teaching."[11] Similarly, Brennan's concept of the public school's "uniquely *public* function" reflected the view of Justice Frankfurter in *McCollum* that "the public school is at once the symbol of our democracy and the most pervasive means for promoting our common destiny. In no activity of the state is it more vital to keep out divisive forces than in its school."[12] From this point of view, Frankfurter said that released time for voluntary religious instruction inculcated in those not participating "a feeling of separatism when the school should be the training ground for habits of community."[13]

Unfortunately, the philosophy of education that regards the public school as the unique vehicle of national unity is altogether too dominant. In the name of democracy, this philosophy would make the public school the community's agency of conformity rather than the parents' representative and so establish the public school as a secular temple to initiate the young in communal worship. It would supplant rather than support parental choice of religious instruction in the education of their children and prefer collective uniformity to individual freedom. In short, this philosophy of education would promote state absolutism rather than liberal democracy.

Political unity and community harmony are indeed values to be cherished, but they should not be purchased at the price of excluding parents' freedom to choose religious instruction for their children if this is feasible. Any realistic attempt to foster political unity and community harmony in a pluralist society like America should respect the primacy of parental rights. There are surely other ways in which our civic communion of mind, heart, and action can be fostered without sacrificing so fundamental a

11. *Everson v. Board of Education*, 330 U.S. 1, 23–24 (1947).
12. *McCollum v. Board of Education*, 231.
13. *McCollum v. Board of Education*, 227.

principle. For example, a required course in world religions might help to overcome religious separation through an understanding of religious differences. The presence of religious instruction in the public schools might likewise help to move students of various religions or none out of isolation into communication.

Similar to the claim that home, church, and private school remain available for the religious instruction of children whose parents so wish is the concession that objective courses about religion are constitutionally permissible in public schools. That is undoubtedly a useful idea, but why is voluntary religious instruction on constitutional principle not permissible? It should be fundamental to a liberal philosophy of education that parents should be free to specify an element of overtly religious instruction for their children insofar as this is administratively feasible within the general civic aims of public education.

Justice Brennan also argued in *Schempp* that religious instruction in the public school classroom would place the religious teacher "in precisely the position of authority held by regular teachers of secular subjects," lend "to the support of sectarian instruction all the authority of the governmentally operated public school system," and so unconstitutionally augment the "prestige and capacity" of the religious teacher for influence.[14] This argument assumes that *all* authority in the public schools, both that of the secular teacher and that of the religious teacher, derives primarily from the state and not from the parent. But such an assumption is completely at odds with the fundamental philosophy of a free society that the authority to educate the child rests primarily with the child's parents. Once the primacy of parental rights is recognized, then Brennan's argument fails, since the mantle of authority that the religious teacher, or indeed the secular teacher, assumes in the public school classroom is primarily

14. *Abington School District v. Schempp*, 374 U.S. 203, 262–63 (1963).

parental and only secondarily involves the state as the parents' surrogate. As a matter of fact, if no academic credit is given for the religious instruction, the authority of the religious teacher in the public schools would by no means be equal to that of the secular teacher.

Justice Black's opinion in McCollum pinned that decision in part on the use of the state's tax-supported public school buildings for the dissemination of religious doctrines. But not every use of public property or expenditure of public funds that is beneficial to religious organizations or activities necessarily violates the establishment clause. For example, the state not only may permit, but even must permit religious organizations to use public parks for religious purposes where the parks are open to other civic groups for similar use.[15] In the case of using public school classrooms for voluntary religious instruction, the use of public property and expenditure of public funds for lighting, heat, and application forms is for a secular civic purpose and primary effect—namely, accommodating parental choice in their children's education—and the benefit to religion incidental. Moreover, the *use* of the classrooms doesn't cost the public anything, and the other expenditures are small. Nor is the administrative involvement other than routine. The essential question is whether public authority may provide room for voluntary religious instruction within the framework of public education. If it may so do, then the use of public property, the incurring of incidental expenses, and the routine administrative involvement are constitutionally irrelevant.

Justice Frankfurter contended in *McCollum* that released time for voluntary religious instruction during school hours created an "obvious pressure on children to attend."[16] Now, this contention

15. *Niemotko v. Maryland,* 340 U.S. 268 (1951); *Fowler v. Rhode Island,* 345 U.S. 61 (1953).
16. *McCollum v. Board of Education,* 231.

may reflect the unarticulated premise that the state enjoys primary rights in the education of children, and so religious instruction
of public school students during school hours is state-sponsored
and state-endorsed. Or the contention may echo the argument
of Justice Black that released-time programs employ the state's
compulsory education laws to compel pupils to attend religious
instruction. The contention may also reflect a fear that a majority choosing religious instruction would psychologically pressure
those not participating to conform. According to Frankfurter,
"the children belonging to ... nonparticipating sects will thus
have inculcated in them a feeling of separatism.... As a result,
... [released time] sharpens the consciousness of religious differences, at least among some of the children committed to ... [the
public school's] care. These are consequences not amenable to sta-
tistics," that is, are unverifiable hypotheses.[17]

Whether psychological and social pressure constitute coercion, it is clear that the state cannot consistently with the principle of neutrality so weight a released-time program in favor of
participation as in any way to induce those not participating to do
so. The relevant question is whether a released-time program creates built-in pressures on students or their parents to participate.

If the state sponsors religious instruction or religious exercises
in the public schools, then the state is responsible for engendering
an inherent pressure on students to participate. But if the state
is not the sponsor, and an equal alternative is available to those
not participating, such psychological and social pressures as come
to bear on those not participating derive not from the state, but
from the fact that many parents choose religious instruction for
their children. The fact that children are young and impressionable does not affect the source of such pressures, which is the exercise of parental choice, and the pressures are not built into the

17. *McCollum v. Board of Education*, 227–28.

program itself. The public authorities are not obliged to insulate children any more than adults from an awareness of religious differences. Indeed, the state could not shelter them from the fact of religious diversity even if it wished to. The public schools may better serve their students by acquainting them with the normal incidences of religious differences that they will find in later life than by attempting to create an illusory impression of uniformity where none exists.

That a majority of parents might or does choose religious instruction with resulting psychological and social pressures on those not participating should be constitutionally irrelevant. If a majority of parents opted against religious instruction for their children, such pressures would then obviously operate *against* participation. Yet no one has suggested that believers would have a valid complaint that public authorities under those circumstances were illegally pressuring the believer's child against religious instruction. In fact, that was precisely the situation in the Champaign junior high school under the released-time program struck down in *McCollum*.[18] There 80 percent of the students did not participate in the program. Today, it is very unlikely that the proportion of participants anywhere would be higher. The proportion of parents choosing or rejecting religious instruction, in my opinion, should be accorded no constitutional weight. The nonparticipating parent exercises a fair choice as long as an alternative equal to religious instruction is offered to the nonparticipating parent's child. If a nonparticipating parent were to object to voluntary religious instruction on or off public-school premises, the parent would be objecting to the opportunity for the theist parent to choose a period of religious instruction for the parent's own child.

Justice Frankfurter's contention that released time during

18. *McCollum v. Board of Education*, Transcript of the Trial Record, 177.

school hours for voluntary instruction pressured children to participate may also reflect the conviction that the program involved did not offer an alternative that was equally attractive to those not participating. In my view, an equal alternative is the crux of the constitutional problem about released time. Unless that condition is fully satisfied, the built-in weight of the program would favor religious instruction over nonparticipation. The principle of neutrality prohibits such discriminatory treatment. But what constitutes an equal alternative?

Justices Frankfurter and Jackson, dissenting in *Zorach*, conceded what only the most doctrinaire secularist would deny: that the public school may close its doors to free students to repair to a place off the public school premises for religious instruction or religious exercises. Such a program of dismissed time would simply shorten a school day and allow each student to make whatever use the student wishes to make of the time. Of such a program, Frankfurter rightly concluded, no nonbeliever would have grounds for complaint. But parents of religious conviction may still ask why they, who enjoy primary rights regarding the education of their children, may not specify a period of religious instruction for their children within their formal schooling. In my opinion, dismissed time is a step in the right direction, but does not fully honor the rights of parents regarding the formal education of their children within the public schools themselves. In connection with dismissed time, we should note parenthetically that the Court in 1990 held that the Equal Access Act prohibits public high schools from barring religious group meetings on public school premises if the meetings are unrelated to curricular courses, and that this does not violate the establishment clause (*Westside Community Schools v. Mergens*).[19]

Practical difficulties with released-time programs may make

19. *Westside Community Schools v. Mergens*, 110 S. Ct. 2365 (1990).

religious instruction after school hours the most feasible solution. In that case the religious classes could be held on the school premises without violating the principle of neutrality as long as the facilities were equally available to all religious and cultural groups. Since the classes would not constitute part of the public school's course offerings, the school would not be obliged to provide an alternative to the religious instruction. However, devising a schedule for school busing in rural and suburban areas satisfactory to both those participating in extracurricular programs and those not participating might prove an insuperable problem.

In *McCollum,* Justice Frankfurter seemed to approve a recreation period as an acceptable alternative for those not participating in a released-time program of voluntary religious instruction conducted off public school premises. That arrangement, Frankfurter thought, would "not cut into public school instruction or truly affect the activities or feelings of the children who did not attend the church schools."[20] Most children, I am sure, would accept a recreation period as equal or superior to any instruction. But a student not participating, or at least the student's parents, not to mention a Court, might well feel that a choice restricted to a nonacademic period of recreation and a formal period of religious instruction would be weighted against the former. For the schooling of those not participating in released time for religious instruction would be altogether suspended while fellow students received formal instruction. If the chief purpose of a school is instruction, then those not participating in religious instruction might reasonably ask for secular instruction or extracurricular activity as an alternative. Of course, the recreation period might be coupled with academic alternatives to offer more than one alternative.

Far less attractive than recreation as an alternative, if at all

20. *McCollum v. Board of Education,* 224.

attractive, is a study period, which most students regard as unproductive and even involuntary detention. Indeed, it was a study period that was on offer in *McCollum* to those not participating in the Champaign released-time program. Terry McCollum was required to attend a study period during which he was often left to his own devices.[21] Similarly, under the New York released-time program off the public school premises, schooling was "more or less suspended" for those not released for religious instruction elsewhere.[22] This led Justice Jackson to charge that the public school served as a "temporary jail for a pupil who will not go to church."[23] In all probability, the majority in *McCollum* and the dissenters in *Zorach* would not have changed their opinion about the released-time programs for voluntary religious instruction at issue in those cases had those not participating been offered a more acceptable alternative than a study period. But they did object in part, and reasonably, to the adequacy of a study period as the only alternative to religious instruction. On the other hand, secular instruction or extracurricular activity scheduled at the same time as religious instruction would offer to those not participating an equal alternative. The additional alternative of a recreation period would increase the options for those not participating.

May or should students who attend religious instruction classes receive academic credit for their work? There is nothing in the nature of religious instruction as such to preclude academic credit. Many private and some public colleges and universities give credit for, and require courses in, theology, and students taking the courses receive academic credit. But the involvement of the state as supervisor of public elementary and secondary education should preclude it. Religious instruction in lower education would not

---

21. *McCollum v. Board of Education*, Transcript of the Trial Record, 255; cf. *McCollum v. Board of Education*, 227.

22. *Zorach v. Clausen*, 324.

23. *Zorach v. Clausen*, 324.

lend itself to the objective standards of higher education regarding the qualification of teachers or supervision over the curriculum. State control of the content of religious instruction and the qualification of religious instructors would be constitutionally impermissible, and so this should preclude academic credit. For the same reason, the state should not pay religious instructors.

Secular instruction at state expense with academic credit at the same time as religious instruction at sectarian expense without academic credit would surely offer an equal alternative to students who do not participate in a released-time program. Indeed, the state would thereby offer and pay for an academically more attractive alternative. But this paradox only serves to illustrate the deficiency of purely a priori analysis of problems arising under the establishment clause. The First Amendment does not prohibit apparent inequalities where the public authority acts for a secular civic interest that excludes a preferential design or weighting. In this case, the state has ample grounds to deny credit and financial support for sectarian religious instruction, although there is an apparent inequality in relation to credit and financial support of secular instruction.

Perhaps no released-time program would be administratively feasible if, improbably, all or most sects sought separate classes. Perhaps so few parents would want to participate, or so few religious organizations would be willing or able to provide instructors, that the administrative burden in establishing or maintaining the program would be disproportionate to its putative benefits. Perhaps religious instruction during school hours could not be linked to one or more acceptable alternatives. In the case of dismissed-time religious instruction on the school premises, perhaps the program would cause participating students to miss bus transportation to distant homes. But these are all policy considerations for the local school board, not the courts. In my opinion, the constitutional mandate of governmental neutrality toward religion would be fully satisfied if the released-time program remained open to all religious organizations and offered at least one acceptable alternative to those not participating.

From what I have said, it should be clear that I agree with the many commentators who regard *McCollum* and *Zorach* as fundamentally inconsistent. In my opinion, the two released-time programs at issue in those cases rise or fall together. The mere fact that the released-time religious instruction in the former case took place in the public schools and in the latter case off the public school premises is irrelevant. The real issue was the use of public school *time* for religious instruction. And resolution of that issue depends on the adequacy of the alternative to religious instruction. Both cases involved a study period as the alternative. If a study period is an inadequate alternative to voluntary religious instruction, then *McCollum* was rightly decided, and *Zorach* wrongly decided. On the other hand, if a study period is an adequate alternative, then *Zorach* was rightly decided, and *McCollum* wrongly decided.

I think that I have also made clear my view that there are two fundamental principles involved regarding the constitutionality of voluntary released-time programs in public schools. One is that the rights of parents in the education of their children are primary. The other is that those not participating should be offered an adequate alternative. If both principles are observed, then released time cannot be condemned on the basis of the establishment clause without violating the neutrality of governmental action toward religion.

STATE SPONSORSHIP OF PRAYER AND BIBLE-READING IN THE PUBLIC SCHOOLS

In 1951, the New York State Board of Regents recommended that the following prayer be recited in the public schools at the beginning of each school day after the pledge of allegiance to the flag: "Almighty God, we acknowledge our dependence upon thee, and we beg thy blessings upon us, our parents, our teachers, and our country." A local Board of Education adopted the Regents' prayer. The state courts upheld the prayer against a claim that it violated the religious establishment clause, and the plaintiffs carried the case to the Supreme Court.

In 1962, the Supreme Court held that recitation of the prayer in the public schools violated the Constitution (*Engel v. Vitale*).[24] The majority opinion by Justice Black argued that "the state laws requiring or permitting use of the Regents' prayer must be struck down because that prayer was composed by governmental officials as part of a government program to further religious beliefs."[25] In his view there was no doubt that the prayer officially established the religious beliefs expressed in the prayer. "Neither the fact that the prayer may be denominationally neutral, nor the fact that its observance on the part of students is voluntary, can serve to free it from the limitations of the establishment clause."[26] Moreover, laws officially prescribing a particular form of religious worship involve indirect coercion on individuals not participating.

A significant footnote dissociated the "unquestioned religious exercise" in recitation of the prayer from those "patriotic or ceremonial occasions" in which "school children and others are officially encouraged" to recite "historical documents, such as the Declaration of Independence, which contain references to the Deity" or to sing "officially espoused anthems which include the composer's professions of faith in a Supreme Being," or in which there are "manifestations in our public life of belief in God."[27]

Sponsors claimed that the prayer was nonsectarian, but it, implicitly if not explicitly, professed belief in the existence of God, his providence over human beings, and the effectiveness of prayer

24. *Engel v. Vitale*, 370 U.S. 421 (1962).
25. *Engel v. Vitale*, 425.   26. *Engel v. Vitale*, 430.
27. *Engel v. Vitale*, 435.

to him. That set of religious affirmations is surely sectarian, since religious persons may not believe in a provident God, and unreligious persons do not believe in any of them. It is also clear that the prayer was a religious exercise, that public authorities were sponsoring it as an integral part the common public school agenda, and that those who did not wish to participate had to petition to be excused from presence at its recitation. Students not wishing to participate had either to come after the prayer or to remain noticeably silent while other students prayed. In short, the Regents' prayer was an official prayer for the public schools.

Justice Douglas, concurring in a separate opinion, thought the issue was "whether the government can constitutionally finance a religious exercise."[28] That position needs to be nuanced, since government financing of religion may be incidental to a secular civic interest, as we shall see in the next chapter regarding military chaplains.

The sole dissent was by Justice Stewart, who thought that the local school board had only provided an opportunity for "those pupils who wish to do so" to "join in a brief prayer at the beginning of each school day."[29] There was, therefore, no establishment of an official religion. "On the contrary," he observed, "to deny the wish of these children to join in reciting this prayer is to deny them the opportunity of sharing in the spiritual heritage of our nation."[30] This position seems to ignore the fact that the state itself composed and sponsored the prayer.

One year after *Engel*, in 1963, the Court was confronted with a case of broader significance (*Abington School District v. Schempp*).[31] Two states, Pennsylvania and Maryland, had required at the opening of the public school day the reading by teachers of verses from the Bible (the Hebrew Bible) and the recitation of the Lord's Prayer

28. *Engel v. Vitale,* 437.   29. *Engel v. Vitale,* 444.
30. *Engel v. Vitale,* 445.
31. *Abington School District v. Schempp,* 203.

by students in unison. Individual students could be absent upon parental request.

The Court, in a majority opinion by Justice Clark, articulated a two-pronged test of governmental neutrality toward religion: a secular purpose and a primary secular effect. The states argued that the Bible-reading promoted moral values, countered materialism, supported democratic institutions, and taught literature. Applying the test of governmental neutrality, Clark held, without disputing the secular purpose of those objectives, that its primary effect benefited religion. (Recitation of the Lord's Prayer was evidently a religious exercise and fell under the umbrella of *Engel*.) Clark argued that the secular goals were "to be accomplished *through* readings ... from the Bible [italics added]."[32] The Bible-reading programs had "a pervading religious character," and so it manifested a secular purpose and had the primary effect of promoting religious inspiration, something "inconsistent with the contention that the Bible was being used as an instrument of nonreligious moral inspiration or as a reference for the teaching of secular subjects."[33] In other words, the effect prong of the original Schempp test was understood as primary in the sense of causally first, or direct, and secondary in the sense of causally second, or indirect.

Clark admitted, however, that one's education might not be complete without a course in comparative religion or the history of religion, when presented objectively, and that the Bible is "worthy of study for its literary and historical qualities."[34] Neither Clark nor the concurring opinions of justices Brennan and Goldberg, who said the same thing, explain how teaching about religion would differ from the teaching of religion. Undoubtedly, the composition of objective, academically accredited courses

32. *Abington School District v. Schempp*, 224.
33. *Abington School District v. Schempp*, 224.
34. *Abington School District v. Schempp*, 225.

about religion would prove a challenge. But this is a problem that has taxed the minds of educators in all subjects. The lower grades might begin with a descriptive study of the religious history of this country, and higher grades might undertake a comparative analysis of the major communities of belief. As Clark said, courses at various grade levels might study the Bible's literary and historical qualities.

Again, as in *Engel,* the sole dissenter was Justice Stewart. He thought that religious exercises at issue accommodated a common desire on the part of students and their parents to begin the school day with them. The issue, in his view, is whether those exercises coerce or psychologically pressure students to participate. Even under a law containing an excusal provision, if the exercises were held during the public school day and public authorities provided no equally desirable alternative for those who did not wish to participate, there is a likelihood that children might be under strong psychological pressure to participate. But there was no evidence in the record that there was such pressure in these cases, and so, according to him, the Court should not assume that there was. He would have remanded the cases to lower courts for further hearings on the issue. In short, Stewart equated the religious establishment issue in these cases to one of the free exercise of religion.

Twenty-two years later, in 1985, the Court struck down a 1981 Alabama statute that authorized a period of silence in public schools "for meditation or prayer" (*Wallace v. Jaffree*).[35] Justice Stevens, speaking for the Court, acknowledged that the framers of the establishment clause intended only to prohibit governmental preference of one Christian sect over another. Since later judicial decisions, however, recognized that the political interest in forestalling intolerance extends beyond intolerance among Chris-

35. *Wallace v. Jaffree,* 105 S. Ct. 2479 (1985).

tian sects or religious sects generally to intolerance toward unbelievers and the uncertain, Stevens argued that the establishment
clause today also prohibits governmental preference of religious
belief over unbelief. Applying the Schempp-Lemon test, he held
that the Alabama statute lacked a secular legislative purpose. He
claimed the legislative record not only demonstrated the purpose
of endorsing religion, but also the total absence of any secular
purpose not served by a 1978 statute that authorized a minute of
silence for meditation. Justice O'Connor, while declining to join
the Court opinion, concurred in the decision. Like the Court,
she interpreted the 1981 statute to endorse and sponsor voluntary
prayer in public schools.

Three justices dissented. Justice Rehnquist altogether rejected
the proposition that the establishment clause requires the government to be strictly neutral toward religion or prohibits the
government from endorsing prayer in general. Chief Justice
Burger objected to the Court's contention that the Alabama
statute endorsed prayer by specifying prayer as one permissible
mental activity during a moment of silence. In his view, striking
down the statutory mention of prayer manifested hostility rather
than neutrality toward religion. Justice White argued that the
Alabama statute did no more than answer the question, "May
students pray during the period of silence?" He also thought that
the Court should interpret the religious establishment clause less
stringently.

The first prong of the Schempp-Lemon test specifies that legislation regarding religion have a secular purpose. Stevens and
the majority understood purpose to mean the subjective motives
of legislators. But why should the subjective motives of legislators be deemed relevant except to help determine the objective
content of the legislation? Should the 1978 Alabama statute authorizing a minute of silence for meditation without mentioning
the possibility of prayer be deemed unconstitutional if it could

be demonstrated that the legislators voted for the statute in order to promote religion? Moreover, it will be difficult to prove specifically religious motives on the part of most legislators. In this case, for example, Stevens relied principally on a statement by the statute's chief sponsor *after* enactment, and the views of most legislators are unrecorded.

One could and should consider legislation without regard to the motives of individual legislators. Since the First Amendment guarantees freedom of religious exercise, thus constituting it a secular civic value, as well as prohibits religious establishment, the Alabama statute can be interpreted to have the secular purpose of facilitating that freedom and a secularly neutral primary effect with a secondary effect beneficial to religion.

Justice O'Connor alone considered this line of argument. She argued that the government may constitutionally facilitate citizens' freedom of religious exercise, but only where the government is responsible for conditions restricting that freedom. Because Alabama had done nothing to prevent public school students from praying silently, she argued, there was no restriction on religious freedom here. Is the matter so simple? As a practical matter, local governments control the activities of students in public schools six hours a day, five days a week. Unless specific time is allocated, the schedule of public-school events will necessarily limit the opportunity for students to pray silently during the day. It is, of course, true that the local government does not control the activities of public school students as comprehensively as the federal government controls the activities of military personnel. On the other hand, Alabama facilitated the religious freedom of public school students far less than the federal government facilitates the religious freedom of military personnel. Alabama did not make religious ministers or services available to public-school students. It only accommodated the schedule of public-school events to allow students a few moments to pray silently if they so wished. O'Connor might have reached a different conclusion had she asked whether that minimal accommodation was proportional to the limitations that Alabama imposed on students' religious freedom by its control of the public-school schedule.

The majority claimed that the Alabama statute, by specifying one potential use of the period of silence, endorsed prayer. Had the statute specified prayer as the only purpose of the period of silence or otherwise urged students to pray, the statute would rightly be said to endorse prayer. But the statute declared voluntary prayer to be only one of the uses to which students could put the period of silence. In this respect, the 1981 statute at issue in this case should be contrasted with the 1982 statute authorizing teachers to lead willing students in a prescribed prayer. The latter statute undoubtedly endorsed prayer and a specific prayer at that, and the Court had unanimously declared that statute unconstitutional at the time it agreed to review the 1981 statute.[36]

Even if the Court rightly decided that the 1981 statute lacked a secular purpose, the decision seems much ado about nothing. The plaintiff did not challenge the 1978 statute authorizing a minute of silence for meditation, and the Court conceded the secular purpose of that period of silence. Invalidating the 1981 statute, therefore, seems to have no practical effect. Moreover, as Justice White argued, a public school teacher could, consistently with the decision, answer "Yes" if a student asked whether the student could use the time for prayer. The statutory specification of silence "for meditation or prayer" hardly seems to endorse prayer, any more than a teacher's response to a student's question would.

In an unsigned opinion the Court in 1980 summarily invalidated a Kentucky law that required that copies of the Decalogue, paid for by private contributions, be posted in public school classrooms (*Stone v. Graham*).[37] At the bottom of the copies was a no-

36. *Wallace v. Jaffree*, 1704.
37. *Stone v. Graham*, 449 U.S. 39 (1980).

tice in small print that Western countries, including the United States, have adopted the Decalogue into their legal codes. The Court, however, found that no secular purpose was served by the posting, since the first part of the Decalogue is expressly religious, rather than secular. Justice Rehnquist dissented on the merits, and Chief Justice Burger and Justices Blackmun and Stewart would have heard oral arguments before deciding the case. The Court could have added, but didn't, that posting of the Decalogue along with other historical documents relating to the history of lawmaking (e.g., the Code of Hammurabi, the Magna Carta) might render the purpose of the posting secular.

In 1992 the Court invalidated an invocation and a benediction at public school graduation ceremonies because they were parts of the official program (*Lee v. Weisman*).[38] For the same reason, the Court in 2000 invalidated a district policy of student-led prayers before high school football games (*Santa Fe School District v. Doe*).[39] But if students initiated and led prayers at the games, the prayers would not have violated the establishment clause, since, according to Justice Kennedy, students on their own initiative may lead prayers before, during, and after the school day.

CREATIONISM IN THE PUBLIC SCHOOL CURRICULUM

Louisiana mandated that public schools teach creation science whenever evolution science was being taught; the statute explained the science as scientific evidence for creation and evolution and inferences from the evidence. The law also required guides for teaching creation science and protected teachers of creation science against discrimination. The Court in 1987 struck down the statute as an establishment of religion (*Edwards v. Aguillard*).[40]

38. *Lee v. Weisman,* 505 U.S. 577 (1992).
39. *Santa Fe School District v. Doe,* 530 U.S. 290 (2000).
40. *Edwards v. Aguillard,* 107 S. Ct. 2573 (1987).

Justice Brennan, joined by all members of the Court except Chief Justice Rehnquist and Justice Scalia, found no secular purpose for the statute. Its stated purpose was to protect academic freedom, but Brennan argued that outlawing the teaching of evolution, which the statute did unless creation was taught, or requiring the teaching of creation science, which the statute mandated if evolution-science was taught, did not further academic freedom. According to him, the legislative history demonstrated that the purpose of the statute was to narrow the curriculum, since teachers had authority to teach scientific theories other than evolution about the origins of the universe and life. The statute's one-sided provisions to assist and protect teachers of creation science indicated a purpose to discredit the theory of evolution. In short, the statute violated the religious establishment clause because it employed symbolic and financial support to achieve a religious purpose.

Justice Brennan found a religious purpose behind the statute—namely, to promote acceptance of the proposition that a supernatural being created humankind. He noted the historical linkage between the teachings of some religions and opposition to the theory of evolution and cited evidence that the legislators disdained supporters of evolution as secular humanists. He admitted, however, that the legislature could require scientific critiques and evaluations of the theory of evolution.

Brennan also agreed with the lower courts that summary judgment was appropriate. Subsequent to enactment of the statute, affidavits were submitted to challenge the finding that the statute had a religious purpose. He argued that the affidavits were immaterial, since experts were not participants in the legislative process, and to weigh subsequent affidavits would be to wage a Monday-morning battle of experts.

Justice Powell, with Justice O'Connor, also concurred separately. Powell began with an attempt to define creation and evolution. He had recourse to ordinary—that is, dictionary—use.

The word *creation* refers to the theory according to which a transcendent God made things out of nothing, and the word *evolution* refers to the theory that various forms of life had their origin in preexisting forms, with differences between the forms due to modifications over time. Given these definitions, Powell agreed that the statute had a religious purpose. Although the state argued that the statute had the secular purpose of promoting academic freedom, he denied that the cause of academic freedom gave the legislature a right to structure the public school curriculum so as to advance a particular religious belief. The legislative history, according to him, demonstrated such a religious purpose, and the lower courts had so found. Powell admitted, however, that the state could mandate the history of religious beliefs and comparative religion, since familiarity with religious beliefs and comparative religion may lend understanding to past and present events in such areas as Northern Ireland, the Middle East, and India.

Justice White wrote separately to indicate that he had doubts about the religious purpose of the statute, but deferred to the findings of the lower courts on the matter.

Justice Scalia, joined by Chief Justice Rehnquist, dissented. Since the Supreme Court of Louisiana never had an opportunity to resolve the question of what creation science is, Scalia was willing at this stage to accept at face value that creation science meant scientific evidence that the universe appeared suddenly. To justify constitutionally the inclusion of that subject in the public school curriculum, it is only necessary to find a secular purpose, and the coincidence of creation science with some religious beliefs should not lead to the conclusion that the statute mandating the former had a religious purpose. Moreover, sometimes the free exercise clause requires the government intentionally to favor religion, and sometimes the free exercise clause permits the government to do so. (Title VII of the 1964 Civil Rights Act, for example, requires private employers to accommodate religious practices.) In any case, federal courts should be reluctant to attribute unconstitutional practices to state legislators.

Scalia was thus not convinced that the statute had a religious purpose, or that finding such a purpose should always invalidate a statute. He then examined the legislative history to see if the statute had a secular purpose. Legislators asserted that the statute had a secular purpose, and, in his view, their statements should be accepted as sincere. The legislators' central concern was with the origins of life: that students have an opportunity to examine evidence that forms of life appeared suddenly, relatively recently, and changed little. The legislators' purpose was academic freedom, academic freedom here meaning the freedom of students not to be indoctrinated in the theory of evolution. According to Scalia, the people of Louisiana were entitled, as a secular matter, to have presented to their students in public schools whatever scientific evidence there may be against evolution. In conclusion, he argued that the purpose prong of the Schempp-Lemon test (discussed later) is unworkable, since it is difficult or impossible to ascertain the purpose of statutes from the subjective intentions of their framers.

The Court invalidated the Louisiana statute because it found the legislators intended thereby to advance particular religious views. The Court never explained why legislators' allegedly "bad" religious motives should ipso facto taint the legislation they pass. Indeed, the Court did not explain why the legislators' motives are relevant at all to the question of constitutionality. It is the language of criminal law to condemn action because of the agents' motives. To use such language to condemn legislators' actions calls for some explanation and justification.

The Court purported to apply the purpose prong of the Schempp-Lemon test. But, as previously indicated, the Schempp Court understood the purpose prong to refer to the objectives of laws as written. Court scrutiny of legislators' motives to determine whether statutes have a religious purpose began in *Ep-*

person v. Arkansas[41] and resurfaced in *Wallace.* The Court neither scrutinized nor relied on legislators' "bad" motives to invalidate released-time for religious instruction in public school classrooms, either in *McCollum* or in *Engel.* Similarly, the Court did not examine legislators' motives, much less argue that legislators' motives were "good," when it upheld subsidies for the bus transportation of parochial school pupils (*Everson*), released time for religious instruction off public school premises (*Zorach*), Sunday-closing laws (*McGowan v. Maryland*),[42] lending textbooks in secular subjects to parochial school pupils (*Allen*),[43] and aid to church-related colleges (*Tilton*).[44] Nor did any dissenter in the latter cases raise the issue of legislators' motives. Lawyers opposed to the governmental actions in at least some of those cases seem to have missed a sure-fire argument.

It might be argued that the motives of legislators who intend to achieve unconstitutional objectives are reprehensible, and so their legislation should be invalidated on that ground. This is arguably the theory behind those racial decisions that seem to invalidate legislation on the basis of legislators' discriminatory intent. Whatever the merits of that theory, it is not applicable to the facts of this case. The Louisiana legislators were only attempting to achieve objectives they considered constitutional, not to defy the Constitution or the Court.

It is beyond dispute that the legislators thought that they had found a constitutionally permissible way to accommodate citizens' religious beliefs, if that is what they were trying to do. The Court has always admitted that some accommodations of religious belief are constitutionally permissible. The Court may disagree with the legislators' understanding of what is constitutionally permis-

41. *Epperson v. Arkansas*, 393 U.S. 97 (1968).
42. *McGowan v. Maryland*, 366 U.S. 420 (1961).
43. *Board of Education v. Allen*, 392 U.S. 236 (1968).
44. *Tilton v. Richardson*, 403 U.S. 672 (1971).

sible under the establishment clause, but that hardly means that the Louisiana legislators intended to act unconstitutionally. The Court found their motives "bad" simply because they intended to "favor" certain religious views. Unless, however, *all* legislative attempts to accommodate religious beliefs are ipso facto unconstitutional, their intention to favor religion in constitutional ways deserves no legal or moral censure. The case of racial discrimination is altogether different, since an overwhelming public and professional consensus agrees that there is no constitutional way for legislators to favor racial discrimination.

Legislators' motives, or mind-sets, however, may be relevant to determining the *objective* purpose of the statute they write. What was the mind-set of the Louisiana legislators about the statute at issue? Justice Brennan argued that the legislators were motivated by a desire to discredit the theory of evolution because the theory runs counter to fundamentalist religious beliefs. Justice Scalia, on the other hand, argued that the weight of the evidence from the statute's legislative history indicated that the legislators were motivated by a desire to assure students the opportunity to hear both sides of the scientific question about the origins of matter and life.

Each justice scored some points. Both interpretations are plausible, but neither is conclusive. Undoubtedly, many will have a gut feeling that Justice Brennan is right. But gut feelings ought not to be determinative of judicial decisions. If evidence is conflicting, judges should interpret legislative intentions benignly, as they ordinarily do. Individual legislators made many statements claiming that they personally intended to promote what they called academic freedom, a secular objective. Only if one dismisses these statements as deliberately false can one say with any degree of probability that the legislature itself was motivated by a desire to promote religious beliefs.

Objective purposes are discovered from the effects that statutes necessarily produce or are likely to produce. In this light, the purpose of teaching creation science to public school students needs to be examined. Louisiana mandated the teaching of creation science whenever the theory of evolution was being taught, and that mandate was evidently thought necessary because creation science was not being taught to public school students. (Since the theory of evolution was already being taught in science courses, the statute's other mandate, that the theory of evolution be taught whenever creation science was taught, was essentially superfluous.) Thus the statute effectively promoted the teaching of creation science. But what is creation science? Is it a philosophical-theological or a secular-scientific theory?

The statute is not helpful in explaining the meaning of creation science. It simply equates creation science with scientific evidence for creation. The dictionary defines creation in the active sense as the act of God that brings the universe and finite things into existence. That, of course, is a philosophical-theological concept, and to mandate that it be taught, without presentation of other theories (e.g., the eternity of matter), would be to promote a philosophical-theological theory or religious belief about the relation of the universe and its inhabitants to a Supreme Being. Scientific evidence is incapable of confirming or denying creation in that sense. Louisiana legislators, however, probably meant something else by what they called creation, what the dictionary calls creation*ism* (italics added), the doctrine that the universe and all forms of matter and life result by their direct and immediate creation by God, not by evolution from preexisting matter. This interpretation is likely for several reasons. First, the title of the statute was the Creationism Act. Second, only a creationist interpretation would make intelligible the statutory dichotomy between origin by evolution and origin by creation. Third, creationism is the doctrine on the basis of which fundamentalist Protestants in the South have traditionally opposed the teaching of the theory of evolution in public schools.

Like the word *creation,* creationism in the active sense refers to the act of God that brings things into existence out of no pre-existing matter. For the legislature to promote creationism in the active sense would put the government on the side of a particular philosophical-theological theory or religious belief. In the passive sense, however, the word *creation* refers to what is created, and creationism to what is created directly and spontaneously. If creationism is taken in the passive sense, creation science would be concerned with the scientific evidence for the discrete appearance of different forms of matter and life, about how and when radically new forms of matter and life originated (e.g., plants, animals, human beings). So interpreted, creation science would be a purely scientific theory, although it would support a particular philosophical-theological position or religious belief.

Whether the Louisiana legislature meant creation science to be simply a theory about the discreteness, spontaneity, and relative recentness of the origins of different things cannot be determined from the statute alone. To determine that, one would have to know how administrators and courts in Louisiana define creation science. The proper procedure for the Court would have been to remand the case to the Louisiana Supreme Court to determine the meaning of creation science in the statute. Only then should the Court decide whether the state's mandate to teach creation science constitutes an unconstitutional promotion of a particular philosophical-theological position or religious belief.

In my view, the Court wrongly made legislators' subjective motives decisive in the case. Second, the Court's premise that all motives favorable to religion are "bad" was uncalled for. Third, the Court's conclusion that the state legislators had acted out of "bad" motives, as the Court defined them, lacked sufficient proof. Fourth, the legislators probably intended a meaning of creation science that is scientific and secular in content. For these reasons the Court was at best premature in striking down the Creationism Act as an establishment of religion. Despite these formidable objections, the Court, ironically, may have reached the right outcome for another reason, a reason that has nothing at all to do with the religious establishment question.

I have argued that creation science might be interpreted in a way compatible with purely scientific concerns, but even if it is, the statute would nonetheless have mandated the complementary teaching of a specific scientific theory. But government has no authority or competence to determine what is speculatively true, and it should not, therefore, presume to pick and choose among scientific theories, even if only to provide equal time for a specific theory. Government, of course, is necessarily concerned with practical matters in the course of promoting the common welfare. Government may and indeed must decide which subjects are to be taught, to whom, and when. Government, for example, may decide whether or which scientific subjects (e.g., biology, chemistry) are to be taught, whether the process of human reproduction should be included in a biology course, and the school grade in which the courses will be taught. Government may also insist that teachers observe the canons of science when presenting subject matter like evolution—that is, that they present problem areas within the general theory. (For example, Darwin never proposed that his theory dealt with the origin of living things from inanimate matter.) Louisiana intruded into the area of speculative truth when it mandated the complementary teaching of a specific allegedly scientific theory about the origins of matter and life.

The First Amendment's guarantee of free speech implicitly recognizes a distinction between thought and action. It protects expression of citizens' thoughts, at least thoughts unrelated to action. What was really at issue in the Edwards case, in my opinion, was the freedom of teachers to teach their subjects in the light of the best contemporary scientific understanding and in accord with the canons of science, not the freedom of students to be exposed to the teaching of creation science. The legislature can insist that individual science teachers adhere to the evidence for scientific theories and to the hypothetical nature of scientific theories, responsibilities that professional teachers fully recognize. To do more, as Louisiana did, would unconstitutionally restrict teachers' freedom to teach their subject.

The remedy for the potential cultural illiteracy that might result if students are not exposed to the theory of creation or creationism in the active sense does not lie in mandating equal time for the latter in science courses. Rather, it lies in finding a place for them in other courses. Concurring Justice Powell acknowledged, as justices in other cases have, that public schools are constitutionally free to teach the history of religious beliefs, since familiarity with religious beliefs is relevant to an understanding of past and present events. That is undoubtedly true, but intellectual curiosity is not fully satisfied by the history of ideas. Religious beliefs often represent answers to bona fide philosophical questions, and public schools should be free to provide an opportunity for higher-grade students to examine those questions rationally, albeit not scientifically. At least the religious establishment clause should not preclude them from having such an opportunity.

RELIGIOUS MEETINGS IN PUBLIC SCHOOLS AND PUBLIC COLLEGES

Some public universities (e.g., the University of Iowa) have departments of comparative religion, but the constitutionality of public universities maintaining those departments has never been challenged as a violation of the religious establishment clause. On the use of public university facilities for religious meetings, the leading case is *Widmar v. Vincent.*[45] Eleven members of a re-

---

45. *Widmar v. Vincent,* 102 S. Ct. 269 (1981); see also *Rosenberger v. University of Virginia,* 515 U.S. 819 (1995). But cf. *Christian Legal Society v. Martinez,* 130 S. Ct. 2971 (2010).

ligious group sought access to facilities of the University of Missouri at Kansas City. The university, citing a regulation against the use of facilities for "religious worship or teaching," denied the students group access. In 1981 the Court ruled in favor of the students.

Justice Powell, joined by six other justices, rested the decision on the First Amendment's guarantee of free speech. He labeled the university action a content-based exclusion of constitutionally protected religious speech and claimed that the university had failed to demonstrate any compelling state interest in the exclusion. He acknowledged that the state had a compelling constitutional duty not to establish religion at the university, but found a secular purpose and a primary secular effect in opening facilities to students for religious discussion where the facilities were available to students for other discussion purposes. Second, Powell argued, rather implausibly, that access of student groups would involve less entanglement of government with religion than denial of access for religious discussion would. Third, since freedom of religious speech and exercise were at stake in access to the facilities, he denied that the state had a compelling interest in further maximizing separation of church and state by means of the exclusion.

Justice Stevens concurred in the decision only because he concluded that the university had failed to show a rational justification for excluding the student group from access to the facilities. According to him a state university has the right to control the use of its facilities without demonstrating a compelling interest. Since user demands will almost inevitably exceed the available supply of facilities, a university cannot avoid making judgments about the academic value of different uses, and the university's academic freedom covers the right to determine who may teach, what may be taught, how it is taught, and to whom it is taught. But such limits need to be rationally justified, and he could not agree that the admixture of religious ceremonies provided a rational justification for suppressing religious discussion.

Justice White, dissenting, would permit but not require the university to grant student access to students for religious purposes. According to him, prayer and hymn singing dominated the student group meetings, and so religious worship, not religious discussion, was the issue here. He argued that exclusion of student groups from the use of university facilities for religious worship minimally burdened students' free exercise of religion, that the state need demonstrate only a permissible objective to justify exclusion of religious worship from university facilities, and that maximizing separation of church and state by such exclusion was a permissible objective.

Powell's characterization of the student group meetings as religious discussion seems rather disingenuous. The group's prayer and hymn singing would seem to mark its meetings as something more than religious discussion. Religious meetings consisting of religious discussion with an admixture of worship, however, may be one thing, and religious worship without significant discussion another, and it is probably better to restrict the Court's holding in the case to the former. For example, it is hardly likely that three of the justices who joined his opinion, Blackmun, Brennan, and Marshall, would hold that Catholic students have a constitutional right to use public-university facilities for the celebration of Mass, even with a dialogue homily and bidding prayers. Regarding religious worship without significant discussion, it is probably better to say that public universities may grant access to its facilities, but are not obliged to do so.

What degree of public interest should be necessary to justify the burden on students' free exercise of religious speech by a public university's exclusion of religious meetings from its facilities? Justice White thought that the university needed to demonstrate only a reasonable, not a compelling, public interest for imposing the burden. In his view the burden on the students in the case was only minimal, and they retained significant other options (e.g., joining local congregations or procuring off-campus facilities). He further argued that the university has a minimally rational public interest in maximizing the separation of church and state beyond constitutional requirements. But what is rational about maximizing separation of church and state *beyond* constitutional requirements? The principle of separation of church and state itself is presumptively the rational principle prescribing neutrality between government and religion. In the final analysis, therefore, the distinction between compelling and rational public interests seems to make no difference here.

One last word on the Widmar decision may be appropriate. The Court held that a state university may without violating the establishment clause, and indeed must, make its facilities available to student groups for religious discussion if it makes the facilities available to other student discussion groups. The majority justices here had no difficulty in distinguishing a primary secular effect in an open forum for all discussion groups from a secondary effect beneficial to religion. This invites the question of why many of the same justices cannot distinguish similar secondary effects from primary effects in the matter of government aid to the secular functions of religiously oriented grade and high schools. Of course, the aid to religion in *Widmar* benefits no institutional religious activity, but the First Amendment makes no distinction between institutional and autonomous religious activity. Simply as a matter of logic, therefore, justices have no reason to distinguish incidental religious beneficiaries of government support on the basis of their institutional or autonomous character. But perhaps more than logic lies behind Court decisions on government aid to parochial schools.

The Court in 2001 also upheld the use of public-school facilities for religious meetings after school hours (*Good News Club v. Mil-*

ford Central School).[46] The club proposed to use school classrooms after hours to sing religious songs, hear Bible lessons, memorize Scripture, and pray. Justice Thomas wrote the majority opinion, and three other justices joined his opinion. According to Thomas, public-school administrators could not deny students the use of facilities for religious meetings on the basis of content-based discrimination. He cited *Widmar* as an indistinguishable precedent. Justices Scalia and Breyer wrote separate concurring opinions. Justices Stevens and Souter, joined by Ginsberg, dissented. The decisions left open two further questions. Could administrators deny student use of public-school facilities for explicitly religious worship? Could administrators deny student use of public-school facilities for administrative reasons (e.g., distracting noise)? The decision also leaves open the question about religious ministers using the facilities for Sunday worship services at cost-based fees.

46. *Good News Club v. Milford Central School*, 533 U.S. 98 (2001); see also *Lamb's Chapel v. Center Mariches Union Free School District*, 508 U.S. 384 (1993), which Thomas cited along with *Widmar* as an indistinguishable precedent.

6

RELIGIOUS ESTABLISHMENT
AND OTHER QUESTIONS

MILITARY AND LEGISLATIVE CHAPLAINS

Since the Revolution, the United States government has re-
cruited military chaplains to provide for the spiritual needs of
military personnel, especially in combat operations. There is an
obvious secular civic interest in doing so. The government thereby redresses the lack of access to religious worship and counseling
available to civilians that the government creates when it enrolls
or conscripts citizens into military services. All but the most extreme secularists concede that this does not violate the religious
establishment clause, despite its incidental benefit to religion.
Moreover, the military services have an undeniable interest to
integrate the chaplains into their chain of command in combat
operations rather than rely on civilian chaplains. Whether that
structure is compatible with the religious mission of the chaplains' religion is one of conscience for the individual ministers
and the organizations they represent, not a constitutional question.

More debatable is the question of whether the religious establishment clause permits a state legislature to hire a chaplain to

open each day's sessions with a prayer. In *Marsh v. Chambers,*[1] the Court in 1983 held that it did. Chief Justice Burger, joined by five justices, argued that the long-standing history of the practice in state legislatures and Congress, including an imprimatur from the first Congress three days before passage of the final text of the First Amendment, clearly indicated an intention by the framers of the amendment not to prohibit legislative chaplaincies. Dissenting Justice Brennan, joined by Justice Marshall, argued that legislative chaplaincies run counter to the broad purposes of the establishment clause, and that historical practice should not override those purposes. Justice Stevens, dissenting separately, argued only that the state violated the establishment clause by employing a legislative chaplain of one denomination over the last sixteen years.

Chief Justice Burger argued plausibly that the framers of the establishment clause did not thereby intend to prohibit publicly funded legislative chaplaincies. On the other hand, Justice Brennan argued with equal plausibility that the phrase *establishment of religion* should be interpreted flexibly in the light of the general purposes rather than the specific intentions of the framers. These arguments, however, leave each justice with an unresolved problem of consistency. Burger does not explain how the historical approach he adopts in *Marsh* can be reconciled with the Schempp-Lemon test. Nor does Brennan explain how the developmental approach he adopts in *Marsh* can be reconciled with his rigid position on the Schempp-Lemon test regarding government aid to support the secular functions of church-related schools that only incidentally benefits religion. Perhaps the Court could have reached the same outcome if it had called the issue a political question—that is, one reserved to the decision of the legislature and not to the Court.

1. *Marsh v. Chambers,* 103 S. Ct. 3340 (1982).

TAX EXEMPTION OF CHURCH PROPERTY
USED FOR RELIGIOUS WORSHIP

The Court in 1970 upheld tax exemptions of the property of religious and charitable organizations, even property used for religious worship (*Walz v. Tax Commission*).[2] Chief Justice Burger, writing for the Court, did not apply the Schempp-Lemon test, but appealed to the fact that such tax exemption avoided what he regarded as excessive entanglement between government and religion. In this way the government manifested "benevolent neutrality" toward religion when tax exemption of church property was coupled with tax exemption for charitable organizations. Justice Brennan, separately concurring, stressed the fact that tax exemption of churches and other fraternal organizations fostered freedom of association. Justice Douglas, the sole dissenter, raised his usual objection to any financial support of religion.

Peter Finley Dunne's famous cartoon maintained that the Supreme Court follows the election returns. In this case the Court anticipated adverse popular reaction had it ruled against tax exemption for churches. It is very probable that adverse popular reaction would have led to a constitutional amendment to overturn the decision. Burger did not claim that the tax exemption of churches had any secular purpose other than avoiding excessive entanglement of government with religion. In my view Brennan filled that lacuna by claiming that tax exemption of churches for religious worship facilitated freedom of association and freedom of religious exercise.

CHURCHES AND ZONING

Denial of a liquor license provided the unlikely background for a 1982 Court decision on the establishment clause (*Larkin v.*

2. *Walz v. Tax Commission*, 397 U.S. 664 (1970).

Grendel's Den).[3] Grendel's Den was a restaurant in Cambridge, Massachusetts, and had applied for a license to sell alcoholic beverages. The Holy Cross Armenian Church, whose back wall was ten feet from that of Grendel's Den, opposed the application. Since a Massachusetts statute required rejection of liquor license applications when the governing authorities of a church or school within a radius of 500 feet objected, the local commission denied a license to Grendel's Den. The Den sued to obtain a license, and the Court on appeal agreed with the Den's contention that the Massachusetts statute violated the establishment clause.

Chief Justice Burger, joined by all members of the Court except Justice Rehnquist, admitted that the statute's aim to protect the neighborhood environment of churches was secular, but Burger contended that the statute had the direct and immediate effect of advancing religion. By delegating veto power to churches over roughly one million square feet of commercially valuable property, the statute handed over discretionary governmental power to the churches. Moreover, the statute did not require the churches to exercise their veto power in a religiously neutral way, with the potential result that churches might favor liquor license applications by their own members over those by others. Burger argued in a similar vein that this fusion of ecclesiastical and secular authority involved impermissible church-state entanglement and promoted political divisiveness along religious lines.

Justice Rehnquist thought the whole case silly and the holding bad. He accused the majority of latching onto the "veto" feature to convert a sensible liquor zoning law into a sinister attack by religious organizations on secular government. In his view, the Massachusetts statute, which had originally banned liquor licenses within the specified radius of churches, adopted the simple expedient of asking churches to voice objections before man-

3. *Larkin v. Grendel's Den*, 103 S. Ct. 505 (1982).

dating denial of licenses to sell liquor at neighboring premises. The purpose of the statute was to protect citizens in their exercise of religion from the incompatible activities of liquor outlets, and the way to determine whether the activities of liquor outlets are incompatible with religious activities is to ask those responsible for the religious activities. As to the majority's concern about churches using their required approval to favor liquor licenses for their own members, he thought that issue absent from the present case and would leave it to be considered on another day.

The decision in *Larkin* elevates form over substance. The majority conceded that a total ban on liquor sales within a reasonable radius of churches would not constitute an establishment of religion. What the Massachusetts statute at issue did was to permit liquor licenses in areas near churches unless the churches objected. The Court suggests that churches might effectively approve nearby liquor franchises when applicants for the franchises were members of their congregations. Not only is there no evidence to support that hypothesis, but the suggestion seems to this writer to lack plausibility on its face. One might argue, irrespective of the establishment clause, that the statute privatizes public power and so violates due process. Students of government and public administration have long inveighed against delegating public power to special interest groups. Had the Court relied on the due process clause rather than the religious establishment clause, the decision would have made more theoretical and practical sense.

PUBLICLY SPONSORED CHRISTMAS DISPLAYS
ON PRIVATE AND PUBLIC PROPERTY

In 1984, by the narrowest of margins, the Court upheld the constitutionality of a municipally owned Christmas display, including a Nativity crèche, in a private park (*Lynch v. Donnelly*).[4]

4. *Lynch v. Donnelly,* 104 S. Ct. 2376 (1984).

Each year the city of Pawtucket, Rhode Island, in cooperation with its downtown retail merchant association, erected a display during the Christmas season in a park owned by a nonprofit group and located in the heart of the shopping district. The display comprised both purely secular figures like Santa Claus and the figures of Mary, Joseph, and the infant Jesus. Individual residents of Pawtucket and the Rhode Island affiliate of the American Civil Liberties Union sued to enjoin the practice. The District Court granted the injunction, and the Court of Appeals affirmed. The Supreme Court reversed.

Chief Justice Burger, speaking for the Court, noted at the outset that the Constitution does not require complete separation of government and religion, but mandates governmental accommodation of religion. According to him, there is an unbroken history of official acknowledgment of the role of religion in American life, and the Court has consistently declined to take an absolutist view of the establishment clause. Applying the Schempp-Lemon test, he concluded that the crèche display had the secular purpose of celebrating a traditional public holiday, conferred no substantial or impermissible benefit on religion, and created no deep political division along religious lines.

Justice Brennan, joined by three justices, reached diametrically opposite conclusions about the crèche display when he applied the Schempp-Lemon test. According to him, the sectarian exclusivity of the Nativity scene indicates a religious purpose beyond the secular purpose of celebrating a holiday season, the scene's inclusion in the municipal display places a governmental imprimatur on Christian religious beliefs, and non-Christians will be offended by that imprimatur.

Perhaps the most interesting feature of this decision is its revival of the Zorach reasoning. The chief justice does not expressly endorse accommodating public events to sectarian needs, as *Zorach* did, but he basically relies on a similar norm of civic culture to interpret the establishment clause here. The difficulty with this approach is that decisions after *Zorach* have substituted the criteria of secular purpose and primary secular effect for the norm of civic culture. Accordingly, Burger adds to his Zorach reasoning an application of the Schempp-Lemon test and the Lemon factor of political divisiveness.

Sometimes the purpose prong of the Schempp-Lemon test is interpreted to require assessment of the subjective intentions of government actors, and these may be ambiguous. From that perspective Burger gave municipal authorities the benefit of the doubt about their motives for including the crèche in the Christmas display. But his arguments on the effect of the inclusion seem to this writer rather weak. He argued that the crèche display satisfied the effect prong for two reasons. First, display of the crèche benefits religion no more than textbook and transportation aid to students attending church-related elementary and secondary schools or tax exemption of church property does. Second, display of the crèche advances religion no more than the recognition of the holiday or exhibition of religious paintings in government-supported museums does. Both of these reasons misconstrue the fundamental question that the Schempp-Lemon test posed about the effects of governmental action regarding religion.

The question to be asked about effects under the Schempp-Lemon test is whether an effect beneficial to religion is primary or secondary, not whether an effect is large or small. If textbook and transportation aid to students attending church-related schools can be said to pass the effect prong of the test, that will be because the benefits to religion are incidental to the secular learning and student safety, not the other way around. Likewise, if tax exemption of church property passes the effect prong of the test, that will be because the benefits to religion are incidental to the aid to the freedoms of association and religious exercise. The question under the effect prong of the test is whether the benefit accruing to the Christian religion here is simply an incidental by-product of celebrating a public holiday. On this point Burger is silent and Brennan persuasive. The crèche display enhances the celebration of a public holiday only as a consequence of fostering a religious atmosphere.

The second reason alleged by Burger would equate the crèche display with recognition of Christmas as a holiday and with the exhibition of religious paintings in publicly supported museums. That equation ignores very significant differences between the two cited examples and the crèche display. To recognize Christmas as a holiday does no more than close government offices and give government employees a day of rest, while the crèche display visibly thrusts majority religious beliefs in the faces of unbelievers. Similarly, exhibition of paintings on religious subjects make works of art available to citizens of all religious beliefs or none, while the crèche display is not presented to the public for its artistic merit.

Justice O'Connor, in a concurring opinion, attempted to circumvent these difficulties with applying the effect prong of the test by reinterpreting the test itself. According to her, the establishment clause aims to interdict governmental endorsement or disapproval of religion. Accordingly, she would interpret the purpose and effect prongs to invalidate governmental actions only if the latter are designed to endorse or disapprove religion or, irrespective of purpose, if they convey a message of endorsement or disapproval. This interpretation would not require invalidation of a governmental practice merely because it causes, *even as its primary effect,* advancement or inhibition of religion.

The majority and minority also disagreed whether the crèche display passed the Lemon test of political divisiveness. The crèche display involved no administrative entanglement of government and religious institutions, but the dissenting justices found a reason to invalidate the municipal display of the crèche on the grounds that the display caused division of the body politic along religious lines. The disagreement of the justices about the political divisiveness of the display is hardly surprising. Justices who view the crèche as symbolic of a shared culture quite naturally do not view its display as divisive, while justices who view the crèche as symbolic of Christian beliefs quite naturally view its display as divisive. This reinforces what critics have long suggested—namely, that the political divisiveness criterion has little or no independent merit. All laws or governmental administrative actions are likely to be controversial; some will be divisive along religious lines, and judicial decisions cannot avert politico-religious divisions in any case.

The most disturbing feature in this and so many other establishment decisions is their ad hoc quality. A majority here, purporting to apply the Schempp-Lemon test, upholds a government-sponsored display of an unmistakably religious event, while majorities in other cases, including the dissenters in this case, invoke the test to invalidate government aid to the unmistakably secular functions of church-related primary and secondary schools. The public, with or without legal education, can be forgiven a certain cynicism about the rational consistency of many of the Court's religious establishment decisions.

Five years later, in 1989, the Court, by the narrowest margin, invalidated the Christmas display of a privately owned crèche in the Allegheny county courthouse in Pittsburgh, Pennsylvania, a crèche adorned by a banner proclaiming, "Gloria in excelsis Deo" (*Allegheny v. American Civil Liberties Union*).[5] That decision effectively overruled *Lynch*. In the same case, six justices in three separate opinions upheld the Christmas display of a menorah, a tree

5. *Allegheny v. ACLU*, 472 U.S. 573 (1989). On display of the Ten Commandments in public buildings, see the conflicting results in *Van Orden v. Perry*, 545 U.S. 677 (2005) and *McCreary County v. American Civil Liberties Union of Kentucky*, 545 U.S. 844 (2005). On religious symbols on public land, see *Pleasant Grove City v. Summum*, 555 U.S. 460 (2009) and *Salazar v. Buono*, 130 S. Ct. 1803 (2010).

with holiday ornaments, and signs saluting liberty on the steps of the nearby City-County building. Two justices, Blackmun and O'Connor, supported both decisions and found a secular message in the second display, despite the fact that the menorah, like the crèche, is unmistakably a religious symbol.

CHURCH PROPERTY DISPUTES

Recurring and often bitter disputes between different groups of church members have cast courts in the position of referee in adjudicating rights to church property. In a nineteenth-century case the Court held that it must decide the ownership of church property claimed by two groups of members of a local congregation according to where the highest authority in the church rests (*Watson v. Jones*).[6] In 1979 Justice Brennan, speaking for himself and four other justices, held, contrariwise: that the courts must decide the ownership of church property on neutral principles of property law (*Jones v. Wolf*).[7] Just how there can be neutral principles of law when such a dispute involves different religious claims is not clear. Dissenting Justice Powell, speaking for three other justices, observed that the new rule failed to account for the fact that religious organizations are governed as much by religious as legal principles. If local church property is registered in the name of the church's highest governing authority, however, the new rule should not adversely affect a hierarchical church, and there has been no evidence that the new rule has resulted in decisions different from the results under the old rule.

SUNDAY LAWS

Sunday laws of the colonial period reflected an exclusive concern with fostering Christian observance of the Lord's Day. The Massachusetts law prohibited employment and business on Sun-

6. *Watson v. Jones*, 80 U.S. 697 (1872).
7. *Jones v. Wolf*, 443 U.S. 595 (1979).

day, except for works of necessity or charity. First adopted in 1653 for the observance of the Lord's Day, the law represented an effort by the Bay Colony's theocracy to enforce the religious observance of second-generation Puritans. Today almost every state has laws making illegal on Sunday some form of labor or sales that would be legal if performed on weekdays. These laws are similar in origin and wording.

Expanding commerce at highway shopping centers in the 1950s presented a challenge to enforcement of the Sunday rest. Despite condemnation by Christian groups and economic loss to local merchants, the easy convenience of the shopping centers and the free time available on Sunday sent Sunday sales soaring. In many instances the shopping centers were outside the jurisdiction of local ordinances, and ancient statutes did not provide for an effective statewide regulation of Sunday sales. Many states reacted by enacting new, more specific legislation and by enforcing old Sunday laws more energetically. In turn, opponents of Sunday laws looked to the courts for relief. Opponents claimed that Sunday laws violated the religious establishment and free exercise of religion clauses. (We shall consider here only the Supreme Court treatment of the religious establishment objection and consider the free-exercise objection in the next chapter.)

In *McGowan v. Maryland*,[8] the Supreme Court in 1961 upheld the Sunday laws of three states (Maryland, Massachusetts, and Pennsylvania). Chief Justice Warren, speaking for the entire Court except dissenting Justice Douglas, rejected the contention that the Sunday laws in dispute were religious legislation. These laws, he conceded, "are undeniably religious in origin" and "still contain references to the Lord's Day."[9] Now, were fostering Christian observance of the Lord's Day the exclusive or primary purpose of Sunday laws today, they could not be sustained in face

8. *McGowan v. Maryland*, 366 U.S. 420 (1961).
9. *McGowan v. Maryland*, 446.

of the First Amendment's injunction against a religious establishment.

Warren, however, found that the basis for the Sunday laws before the Court was no longer exclusively or primarily religious.
Under review were not the Sunday laws of the colonial era, but
Sunday laws with a modern gloss. By 1961 the legislative basis for restricting work and sales on Sunday was economic and
recreational—namely, to preserve healthy conditions of employment and competition and to safeguard a common day of rest and
recreation. The highest courts of the three states had passed on
the constitutionality of the laws and authoritatively interpreted
them on a secular basis. Warren did not go so far as to say there
was no constitutionally objectionable language in the Sunday
legislation or its judicial interpretation. What he did conclude
was that the statutory purpose "was no longer solely religious,"
and that, "for the most part, they [the Sunday laws] have been
divorced from the religious orientation of their predecessors."[10] In
short the Court found that the religious purpose of the Sunday
laws was at the present time neither exclusive nor primary, and
that the secular purpose of the present laws was sufficient to provide a legitimate legislative basis.

What is the secular basis commonly asserted in favor of the
Sunday laws? It is that the laws provide a respite from work for
almost all citizens and simultaneously ensure fair conditions of
retail competition. (Some citizens would perform necessary work
on Sundays (e.g., telephone workers, doctors). Of course, the day-
of-rest purpose could be fulfilled adequately by a regulation that
prescribed one day a week of rest without specifying Sunday. But,
Warren observed, "it seems plain that the problems involved in
enforcing such a provision would be exceedingly more difficult

---

10. *Gallagher v. Crown Kosher Supermarket*, 366 U.S. 617, 626 (1961); this was a
companion case on the Massachusetts Sunday law.

than those enforcing a common day-of-rest provision."[11] Moreover, he argued, "the state seeks to set aside one day apart from all others as a day of rest, repose, and tranquility, a day that all members of the family and community have the opportunity to spend and enjoy together."[12] (The idea of Sunday as a day of family and community togetherness seems almost quaint in the present cultural context.)

No doubt many advocates are subjectively motivated by religious conviction. Others are subjectively motivated by economic considerations. But that is irrelevant. The basis of the legislation should rest on the power of the state to protect the health, safety, and welfare of citizens. The legislature may recognize as harmful the economic conditions that tend to foster work and competition seven days a week and institute a common day of rest and recreation. If the legislature may do this, may it not accommodate its legislation to the day of rest desired by the majority of its citizens? One effect of the legislation, of course, is to prefer the orthodox Christian day of rest, but this does not make the legislation religious legislation. On this point, Warren remarked, "It would seem unrealistic for enforcement purposes and detrimental to the general welfare to require a state to choose a common day of rest other than that which most persons would select of their own accord."[13]

Opponents of Sunday laws also objected that the legislative classification of permissible and prohibited work and business on Sunday was arbitrary and so violated the Fourteenth Amendment's equal protection clause. Classifications of and exemptions from prohibited work and business on Sunday have been the product of pressure from almost every lobby, and the result is almost a crazy quilt. Yet the general rationale of Sunday laws is fairly clear. The legislatures of the three states wished to establish

11. *McGowan v. Maryland,* 451.   12. *McGowan v. Maryland,* 450.
13. *McGowan v. Maryland,* 452.

a day of rest by more or less comprehensively forbidding unnecessary work and business on Sunday. If we take into account the recreational activities proper to a day of rest, many of the apparent anomalies of classification dissolve.

But even if substantial anomalies remain, legislatures may recognize degrees of harm and act accordingly. To exercise discretion in the choice of means to combat the perceived evils of harm in certain business activities is part and parcel of the legislative function of classification. For these reasons the Court is and should be reluctant to interfere with even nearly whimsical classifications when these are part of a scheme of economic legislation. Justice Holmes once said insightfully that objection to the reasonable basis of legislative classification is the "usual last refuge of constitutional arguments."[14] And Warren on this issue concluded that "on the record before us, we cannot say that these statutes do not provide equal protections of the laws."[15]

STATUTES FORBIDDING EMPLOYERS FROM REQUIRING WORK ON EMPLOYEES' RELIGIOUS DAY

In 1985, the Court struck down on the basis of the establishment clause a Connecticut statute that forbade employers from requiring employees to work on the latter's religious day of rest (*Thornton v. Caldor*).[16] Thornton managed a department of Caldor's Waterbury, Connecticut, store. After Connecticut revised its Sunday laws, Caldor opened stores in the state and required managerial employees to work every third or fourth Sunday. Thornton worked thirty-one Sundays in 1977 and 1978. In October 1978 he was transferred to a store in Torrington and continued to work Sundays during the first part of 1979. Later that year,

---

14. *Buck v. Bell,* 274 U.S. 200, 208 (1927).
15. *McGowan v. Maryland,* 428.
16. *Thornton v. Caldor,* 105 S. Ct. 2914 (1985).

advised by a lawyer of the existence of the statute, he invoked its protection. Caldor offered to transfer him to a position in Massachusetts, a state that required businesses like Caldor's to close on Sundays, or to a lower position in Torrington. Thornton rejected Caldor's offer, resigned, and filed a grievance against Caldor.

Caldor claimed that Thornton had not been discharged within the meaning of the statute, and that the statute, in any case, violated the religious establishment clause. The Connecticut Supreme Court, ruling only on Caldor's religious establishment claim, held that the statute lacked a secular purpose and had the primary effect of advancing religion.

Chief Justice Burger, joined by all members of the Court except Justice Rehnquist, affirmed. Burger focused his attention on the primary effect of the statute. According to him, the statute armed workers whose religion mandated a day of rest other than Sunday with an absolute and unqualified right not to work on whatever day they designated as a religious day of rest, and so religious concerns automatically prevailed over the secular interests of employers and fellow employees. Concurring Justice O'Connor argued that the statute conveyed a message of endorsing religion and so advanced religion in that way. But she expressly approved the requirement of Title VII of the 1964 Civil Rights Act that employers make reasonable accommodation of the religious practices of their employees. Justice Rehnquist dissented without opinion.

The reference in the statute to the Sabbath of an employee's choice makes clear that the statute was designed to benefit those with religious objections to work on a particular day of the week. Burger made no claim that the Connecticut legislators were motivated by a desire to benefit religion. Rather, he argued the primary effect of the statute, whatever the motives of the legislators, was to advance the position of those who observe the religious practice of a day of rest other than Sunday over those who do not.

Burger's argument is superficial. Closer analysis would yield a different result. If the statute is interpreted as an attempt to remove economic pressures on citizens to act against their conscience, its purpose would be to advance the moral integrity of citizens, not their specific religious practices. This is not an unusual legislative objective. Since 1940, for example, Congress has granted exemption from military service to individuals conscientiously opposed to all wars on the basis of religious belief. The Court has not only approved that exemption, but even broadened it to include humanist conscientious objectors (*U.S. v. Seeger*).[17] Many states exempt Sabbatarian businessmen from Sunday laws, which the Court has never considered an establishment of religion.

Burger argued, in effect, that the statute, by exempting religious objectors from private work rules, preferred the objectors to the secular interests of other employees and employers. That argument is premature. There is no evidence in the record that employees without religious objections to work on Saturdays or Sundays would be unwilling to work more shifts on those days. Moreover, there is no evidence that Caldor could not induce Thornton's fellow employees to work additional Sundays by offering them extra pay. But let us assume that the statute did work hardship on unwilling employees without religious objections to working on Sundays, or that the statute would increase costs to consumers substantially. Let us even assume that these public interests are compelling or substantial. It would still not follow that the public interest in accommodating religious conscience lacks the secular purpose and the primary secular effect of fostering the moral integrity of citizens.

Connecticut required that private employers arrange their work schedule to accommodate those with religious objections to working on particular days of the week. In essence, its statute

17. *U.S. v. Seeger*, 380 U.S. 163 (1965).

regulated the private economic marketplace regarding employer-employee and employee-employee relations and did so for the secular purpose and primary secular effect of facilitating the *moral* integrity of the state's citizens, not their religious practices. There are reasons, perhaps substantial reasons, that Connecticut might have chosen not to compel private employers to accommodate employees with religious objections to working on a particular day of the week. But there is a rational and secular public interest to support such governmentally compelled accommodations. It is precisely the function of a legislature to choose between conflicting public interests. If, as I believe, fostering the moral integrity of citizens is both a secular and a rational objective of government, then the Court has no business imposing its own judgment about the relative weight of the conflicting public interests. By doing so, the Court constituted itself a superlegislature over what was essentially regulation of the marketplace.

The Connecticut might have been wiser to mandate only reasonable accommodation of religious objectors to working on particular days of the week. Perhaps the Connecticut Supreme Court should have avoided the religious establishment issue by holding that Caldor's offer of another position without work on Sundays sufficiently satisfied the statute. Or perhaps Thornton's previous work on Sundays made his present claim suspect. But the case came to the Court on only one issue: whether the statute constituted a religious establishment. On that single issue, the Court should have found none.

EXEMPTION OF RELIGIOUS EMPLOYERS
FROM TITLE VII

Another religious establishment case, *Corporation v. Amos*,[18] involved the exemption of religious organizations from the 1964

18. *Corporation v. Amos*, 107 S. Ct. 2862 (1987).

Civil Rights Act's Title VII prohibition of religious discrimination by employers. An engineer working at a nonprofit gymnasium operated by the Mormon Church was dismissed when he failed to certify that he was a Mormon. He and others brought suit challenging the application of the exemption to the nonreligious activities of religious organizations. The Court in 1986 unanimously upheld the exemption as compatible with the religious establishment clause.

Justice White, joined by the Chief Justice and Justices Powell, Scalia, and Stevens, agreed with the District Court that the legislative history demonstrated a secular purpose for the exemption—namely, avoidance of governmental interference in religious affairs. As to the exemption's effects, White interpreted the exemption to permit rather than promote discrimination by religious organizations and said that the exemption lifted a burden from religious organizations rather than conferred a benefit on them. Four justices concurred in the judgment as applied to the nonprofit activities of religious organizations because exemption of those activities avoided the necessity of deciding on a case-by-case basis which activities of religious organizations are religious and which are not.

White was satisfied that the exemption had no religious purpose, although more cynical critics might plausibly contend that a desire to favor particular religions motivated many legislators, and that fear of the political clout of particular religious organizations motivated even more of the others. Considering the effects prong of the Schempp-Lemon test, White was satisfied that the exemption had the effect of insulating religious organizations from governmental interference. That may be so, but exemption also had the effect of permitting religious organizations to practice religious discrimination in activities unrelated to religious exercise. Questions remain about which effect is primary, and about how one determines primacy. In any case, White's argument that the exemption merely allowed religious organizations to discriminate in employment seems somewhat disingenuous.

Justice O'Connor, in her concurring opinion, reiterated her view that the Lemon test is incapable of resolving conflicts between requirements of the religious establishment and religious exercise clauses. She again suggested a new test. The first prong of the new test would ask whether legislators had a religious purpose—that is, a religious motive. If they did not, the first prong was satisfied. A second prong would ask whether a reasonable person would regard the net effect of governmental activity as an endorsement of religion. I have already criticized substituting legislators' subjective motives for the objective purpose of statutes as revealed in their text and so see no necessity for O'Connor's first prong. But her second prong is much more to the point because it focuses on effects from an objective perspective, however elusive that objective.

As of the late 1980s, three justices (O'Connor, Rehnquist, and Scalia) were on record as favoring a reexamination of all or part of the Lemon test. Justice O'Connor's endorsement test is one possible reformulation, but return to the original Schempp test is better. The first prong of the Schempp test asked whether a bona fide, objective secular purpose can be claimed for the statute as revealed in its text. The second asked whether the secular or the religious effect (assuming there are both) is primary, understanding primary to mean first in the order of causality. The Lemon case added the nebulous prong of excessive entanglement. The Schempp-Lemon test, as interpreted by many justices in the 1980s, equated purpose with legislators' motives, primary with what justices think more important, and excessive entanglement with what judges think too much. If the Schempp-Lemon test is so interpreted, it will remain what it has indeed become—namely, a Rorschach test.

THE MINISTERIAL EXCEPTION

The Supreme Court in 2012 unanimously recognized and broadly interpreted a ministerial exception from employment discrimination laws (*Hosanna-Tabor Evangelical Lutheran Church v. Equal Employment Opportunity Commission*).[19] Cheryl Perich was a teacher in an Evangelical Lutheran school in Redford, Michigan. She took a leave of absence because of a medical disability (narcolepsy) and sought to return to her position in the middle of the school year. The school refused to reinstate her, and she, instead of pursuing the church's internal reconciliation process, threatened to sue the church and school unless they reinstated her. Church officials withdrew her "call" to the ministry and fired her. She then brought suit against the church and school with the Equal Employment Opportunity Commission under the federal American Disabilities Act. She had mostly taught secular subjects such as math and music, but also taught religion classes and attended prayer services with the students in the chapel.

Chief Justice Roberts, speaking for the whole Court, held that the establishment clause prohibited the government from appointing ministers, and that the free-exercise clause prohibited it from interfering with religious groups' freedom to select them. Although Perich's religious duties at the school consumed only forty-five minutes of each school day, Roberts did not think that that fact was decisive. She had received and completed religious training for her position, and the church considered her a minister. When she declined to follow the church's required procedure for resolving the dispute and proposed to pursue litigation, church officials withdrew her ministry and terminated her employment. Roberts contended that one of the prime purposes of the religious guarantees of the First Amendment was to prohibit

19. *Hosanna-Tabor Evangelical Lutheran Church v. Equal Employment Opportunity Commission*, 132 S. Ct. 694 (2012).

general interference in the internal affairs of religious groups and the selection of their leaders in particular. He left the possibility of criminal prosecution of ministers and other protections of employees for future resolution.

Justice Thomas wrote separately to say that courts should stay out of the business of trying to determine which church employees are ministers and which are not. In his view the very question is a religious matter, and attempts to form a civil definition of ministry would risk disadvantaging religious groups whose beliefs and practices are unconventional.

In another concurring opinion Justice Alito, joined by Justice Kagan, thought that it was a mistake to focus on the word *minister*, which Protestants normally use, but which Catholics, Jews, Muslims, Hindus, and Buddhists do not. Rather, he would grant exemption to any church employee who leads a religious organization, conducts religious services, or serves as a teacher of its faith.

Although federal statutes prohibiting employment discrimination on the basis of race, sex, age, and disability have no explicit exception for church employees, lower courts had for forty years applied a ministerial exception and decided only whether a particular job was sufficiently religious to qualify as ministerial. The lower courts had generally construed the exception broadly. Given that precedent and the unanimity of the Supreme Court's decision in the Perich case, why did the Justice Department, in support of the Commission, seek to limit the ministerial exception to church employees performing exclusively religious functions? The probable answer is that the department did so for political reasons—namely, to score points with the electorate by espousing the cause of a worker with a disability.

RELIGIOUS TESTS AND STATE OFFICEHOLDERS

The Constitution (Art. 6, cl. 3) prohibits religious tests for federal officeholders, but says nothing about state officeholders. The omission was quite deliberate, since several states at the time of the Convention had religious establishments and could hardly be expected to ratify the Constitution if it contained a provision undermining their church-state system. In 1961, the Court filled that archaic lacuna, holding unanimously that religious tests for state officeholders was, through the due process clause of the Fourteenth Amendment, unconstitutional (*Torcaso v. Watkins*).[20]

The governor of Maryland had appointed Torcaso to the office of notary public, but Torcaso refused to declare his belief in the existence of God, as Maryland required of all officeholders. Torcaso brought suit to obtain his commission, and the Supreme Court upheld his right to the commission without declaring his belief in the existence of God. According to Justice Black, who spoke for the Court, neither a state nor the federal government can force a person "to profess a belief or disbelief in any religion," nor can a state or federal government impose legal requirements that "aid all religions against nonbelievers."[21]

20. *Torcaso v. Watkins*, 367 U.S. 488 (1961).
21. *Torcaso v. Watkins*, 495.

7

THE FREE EXERCISE
OF RELIGION

THE VALUE OF RELIGIOUS FREEDOM

Most liberals today endorse religious freedom for the same reason that they endorse freedom from governmental restriction of individual choice generally—namely, that the autonomous will of each individual constitutes what is good for that individual, and that governments should not restrict that choice unless it conflicts with the freedom of others. From this point of view, it does not matter what individuals choose or about what they choose. Thus most liberals today endorse religious freedom because it involves freedom, not because it involves religion, and because it insures civic peace in a pluralist society. But liberalism can be incorporated into a public philosophy that links freedom to development of the human person, a public philosophy that John Hallowell called integral liberalism.[1] Then the principle of religious freedom will be seen as valid, not only because it involves freedom in a generic, objectively purposeless sense, but

---

1. John B. Hallowell, *Main Currents in Modern Political Thought* (New York: Henry Holt, 1950), 330–35.

also and especially because it involves a freedom fundamental to the being and fulfillment of the human person.

The human person is endowed with an intellect capable of seeking truth and a will capable of freely deciding to act in accord with it. Human persons are inclined by nature to seek truth, especially the ultimate truth about their destiny, and they assent to religious truth by their will freely and rationally adhering to it. Human persons are likewise by nature inclined to order their lives in accord with the ultimate truths about their destiny as perceived by their intellects, and they have the freedom to choose to do so. The search for religious truth and the freedom to act accordingly are thus fundamental to the being and well-being of the human person. From the integrally liberal point of view, religious freedom is of a qualitatively higher order than the freedom to select items from the shelves of a grocery store.

Religious freedom, of course, necessarily involves the freedom to believe or disbelieve anything in religious matters. No one can force another to believe or disbelieve anything, and so governments cannot coerce individuals to assent *internally* to religious beliefs. Moreover, although governments might try, and have tried, to compel external profession of religious beliefs, Western liberal democracies today absolutely guarantee the freedom to profess any or no religious belief.

Liberal democracies guarantee freedom of religious worship as well as freedom to profess religious beliefs. Only rarely would acts of worship threaten substantial public interests, but some acts of worship might. Human sacrifice in religious rites, for example, would surely run counter to the very substantial public interest in human life. Religious rites in which participants handle deadly snakes to demonstrate their faith would threaten the same public interest regarding both participants and audience, and religious rites involving self-mutilation would conflict with a substantial public interest in the physical integrity of citizens. We shall consider later a Supreme Court case in which an untraditional Indian religious rite ran counter to a rational, but not compelling, public interest.

RELIGIOUS PROSELYTISM

Most of the Supreme Court cases on religious proselytism and the free exercise clause arose in the 1940s and concerned the activities of Jehovah's Witnesses. The first of these cases was *Cantwell v. Connecticut.*[2] Jesse Cantwell, a Jehovah's Witness, was arrested and convicted of breaching the peace. In the course of sidewalk proselytizing in New Haven, Cantwell stopped two men and with their permission played a record that attacked the Catholic Church and all organized religion. The two men, Catholics, were incensed by the content of the record and told Cantwell to go away. He was not offensive to the listeners, entered into no argument with them, and upon their objection picked up his materials and walked away.

Speaking for a unanimous Court, Justice Roberts overturned the convictions. Although he admitted that the common-law offense of breach of peace included acts or words likely to produce violence, he argued that such provocative language, to be considered an invitation to a breach of the peace, must consist of profane, indecent, or abusive remarks directed to the person of the hearer. In the instant case he found no assault or bodily harm, no truculent bearing, no intentional discourtesy, and no personal abuse. Indeed, the defendant, when challenged, simply picked up his materials and walked away. Nor was the sound of the phonograph shown to have disturbed residents of the street, to have attracted a crowd, or to have impeded traffic. The Court ruled that, in the absence of a statute narrowly drawn to define and punish specific conduct constituting a clear and present danger to a sub-

---

2. *Cantwell v. Connecticut,* 310 U.S. 296 (1940).

stantial public interest, the defendant's communication raised no menace to public peace and order that would render him liable to a conviction for breaching the peace. Accordingly, the First Amendment by way of the Fourteenth protected his speech and activities, and for the state to determine beforehand whether his solicitation of funds was religious infringed his religious liberty.

Two years later, the Court unanimously upheld the conviction of a Jehovah's Witness for breaching the peace (*Chaplinski v. New Hampshire*).[3] The traffic officer on duty at the intersection where Chaplinski was distributing literature escorted him to the police station. On the way to the station, they met the city marshal, and Chaplinski called the marshal a "damned racketeer" and a "damned Fascist."[4] Thereupon, Chaplinski was arrested and convicted of breaching the peace. Justice Murphy, upholding the conviction, held that "fighting words," those that "by their very utterance inflict injury or tend to incite an immediate breach of the peace,"[5] were not protected by the First Amendment.

In 1942, the Court decided a case in which Jehovah's Witnesses contested local license taxes on persons selling printed matter or canvassing for their sale (*Jones v. Opelika*).[6] The taxes varied from fifteen dollars per year to two and a half dollars per day in Opelika, Alabama, and were two and a half dollars per day in Fort Smith, Arkansas. The Witnesses, convicted of violating the ordinances that required the licenses, complained that application of the fees to their missionary activities abridged their freedom of religious exercise under the First Amendment.

By the narrowest margin, the Court upheld the convictions. Justice Reed, speaking for the majority, held that the only constitutional question was "whether a nondiscriminatory license fee, presumably appropriate in amount," may be imposed on sell-

3. *Chaplinski v. New Hampshire*, 315 U.S. 568 (1942).
4. *Chaplinski v. New Hampshire*, 569.   5. *Chaplinski v. New Hampshire*, 572.
6. *Jones v. Opelika*, 316 U.S. 584 (1942).

ers of religious literature,[7] and that "the First Amendment does not require a subsidy in the form of fiscal exemption" for such sellers.[8] Chief justice Stone, speaking for the dissenters, saw the question as "whether a flat tax, more than a nominal fee to defray the expenses of a regulatory license, can be constitutionally laid on a noncommercial, nonprofit activity devoted exclusively to the dissemination of ideas, educational and religious in character, to those persons who consent to receive them."[9] In his judgment a flat tax unrelated to the defendants' activities or the receipts derived from them restrained in advance the freedom taxed and tended to suppress its exercise. Stone also stressed the cumulative effect of such local taxes on the missionary activities of itinerant evangelists.

One year later, in 1943, by the same narrowest majority (Justice Rutledge having succeeded Justice Byrnes), the Court overturned the convictions of Jehovah's Witnesses for violating a similar Pennsylvania law (*Murdock v. Pennsylvania*).[10] Justice Douglas, speaking for the new majority, repeated the arguments of Stone in the Jones case and commented that "the mere fact that the religious literature is 'sold' by itinerant preachers rather than 'donated' does not transform evangelism into a commercial enterprise."[11] (Justice Douglas' father was an itinerant preacher.) Accordingly, Douglas held that "the constitutional rights of those spreading their religious beliefs through the spoken and printed word are not be gauged by standards governing retailers or wholesalers of books."[12] The Court thus recognized an exemption from general revenue license taxes for itinerant evangelists incidentally selling religious literature.

In the following year the Court extended the Murdock prin-

---

7. *Jones v. Opelika*, 593.   8. *Jones v. Opelika*, 595.
9. *Jones v. Opelika*, 604.
10. *Murdock v. Pennsylvania*, 319 U.S. 105 (1943).
11. *Murdock v. Pennsylvania*, 111.   12. *Murdock v. Pennsylvania*, 111.

ciple to exempt from payment of a similar license fee a Jehovah's Witness who both maintained his home in the taxing municipality and earned his entire living from the sale of religious literature (*Follett v. McCormick*).[13]

On the same day as *Murdock*, the Court affirmed the right of Jehovah's Witness preachers to distribute from door to door handbills advertising a meeting, contrary to a city ordinance (*Martin v. Struthers*).[14] The ordinance of Struthers, Ohio, forbade knocking on the door or ringing the bell of a private residence in order to deliver a handbill. In defense of the ordinance, the city argued that it was designed to prevent crime and to assure privacy in an industrial community where many citizens worked on night shifts and slept during the day, but the Court held these reasons insufficient to justify the ordinance.

Justice Black, speaking for the majority, found that the ordinance controlled the distribution of literature and substituted community judgment for that of the individual householder. Although Black accepted the validity of "reasonable police and health regulations of the time and manner" of distributing literature to protect the leisure of citizens against intrusion and their property against burglary, he thought that the ordinance curtailed the freedoms of speech and press too broadly.[15] He pointed out that the law of trespass protected the householder who posted a notice against uninvited distributors, and that the registration and licensing of distributors for purposes of identification could control abuse by criminals. Justice Murphy, joined by Justices Douglas and Rutledge, agreed with Black, but argued further that "freedom of religion has a higher dignity under the Constitution than municipal or personal convenience."[16] Thus these three justices added freedom of religious exercise to the freedoms

---

13. *Follett v. McCormick*, 321 U.S. 573 (1944).

14. *Martin v. Struthers*, 319 U.S. 141 (1943).

15. *Martin v. Struthers*, 147. 16. *Martin v. Struthers*, 151–52.

of speech and press. Justice Frankfurter concurred in the decision insofar as it struck down an invidious discrimination favoring ordinary vendors over distributors of literature. Three justices dissented. Justice Reed, speaking for the dissenters, argued that the ordinance prohibited only the distribution of handbills, circulars, and other printed advertisements, not the distribution of literature. He did not deem the classification discriminatory, since the adverse reactions arising from the distribution of the former materials might be judged more serious than those from the distribution of other materials or the activities of ordinary vendors.

The nature of the Witnesses' claim to the free exercise of religion is clear—namely, that they had the right to implement their general religious duty to preach their beliefs and proselytize unbelievers by door-to-door solicitation. The ordinance did not compel them to act against their religious consciences or impede them from the performance of any specifically religious duty. Rather, they were denied one useful means of fulfilling their religious duty to proselytize.

The public interests that the ordinance sought to secure were of relatively low weight. The prohibition of door-to-door distribution of handbills bore only a tenuous relation to the prevention of crime, since the municipality could require distributors of handbills to register and obtain a license for a nominal fee. More substantial was the public interest in securing the privacy of residents against the nuisance of door-to-door distributors of handbills. But the majority argued that an individual desiring privacy could assure it by posting a notice prohibiting uninvited visitation, and that the rights to freedom of expression overrode whatever such public interest was at stake. On the other hand, the dissenters argued that the ordinance was the most efficient way to protect the privacy of residents, and that the legitimacy of such a public interest sufficiently justified the limitation on the freedom of expression.

Unlike the decision in *Murdock,* the Court in *Martin* created no exemption for religiously motivated distributors of handbills from door to door. Rather, the Court established a principle applicable to all noncommercial distributors. The justices in both cases, however, disagreed about the standard to be applied in determining whether public interests justify limitations on the exercise of First Amendment rights. In both cases, the majority required local governments, in effect, to demonstrate substantial or compelling public interests, and the minority was willing to sustain any arguably reasonable legislative determination of even a low public interest.

Although American law recognizes that parents or guardians have the primary responsibility in raising children, the state may intervene to restrict parents' or guardians' control to safeguard the well-being of children. The Supreme Court case on this point regarding children and religious proselytism is *Prince v. Massachusetts.*[17]

Mrs. Sarah Prince, a Jehovah's Witness, had legal custody of her nine-year old niece, Betty Simmons. Although a school official had on a previous occasion warned Mrs. Prince not to do so, she took Betty with her on the evening of December 18, 1941, to preach and distribute religious pamphlets on the sidewalk of a street intersection in Brockton. Betty held up copies of the pamphlets for passersby to see, and a canvas bag hung from her shoulder, on which the names of the periodicals and the price (5 cents) were printed. No one received a copy from Betty or gave her money. Mrs. Prince was convicted of violating Massachusetts' child labor laws, which forbade boys under twelve and girls under eighteen to "sell, expose, or offer for sale any ... periodicals in any street or public place" and made parents or guardians criminally liable if they compelled or permitted minors under their control

17. *Prince v. Massachusetts,* 321 U.S. 158 (1944).

to work in violation of the prohibition.[18] Mrs. Prince was convicted, and the Supreme Judicial Court upheld the conviction. She appealed to the U.S. Supreme Court.

Mrs. Prince's appeal rested both on the freedom of religious exercise guaranteed by the First Amendment, made applicable to the states by the Fourteenth, and on her primary parental right under the due process clause of the Fourteenth Amendment. She thus claimed two liberties. One was Betty's—namely, to observe the tenets and practices of her faith by preaching and by distributing religious pamphlets, as Is. 11:6 says, "a little child shall lead them." The other one was for herself as guardian to teach those tenets and practices to Betty.

By the narrowest majority, the Court upheld Mrs. Prince's conviction. Speaking for the majority, Justice Rutledge acknowledged the right of children to exercise their religion and the right of parents or guardians to encourage children's exercise of their religious beliefs. But neither the right of religious exercise nor the right of parental control were without limitation. According to him, the state's authority over children's activities is broader than its authority over similar activities of adults. To ensure "the healthy, well-rounded growth of young people," the state may seek to avert "the crippling effects of child employment, more especially in public places, and the possible harms arising from other activities subject to all the diverse influences of the street."[19] Specifically, the "exercise of the right to engage in propagandizing the community, whether in religious, political, or other matters, may and at times does create situations difficult enough for adults to cope with and wholly inappropriate for children."[20] Such employment of children, he argued, might cause "emotional excitement and psychological or physical injury."[21]

Justice Murphy, speaking for the dissenters, admitted that the

18. *Prince v. Massachusetts*, 160–61.   19. *Prince v. Massachusetts*, 168.
20. *Prince v. Massachusetts*, 169–70.   21. *Prince v. Massachusetts*, 170.

power of the state to control religious and other activities of children is greater than its power over similar activities of adults, but he argued that, in dealing with direct or indirect restrictions of religious freedom, the state has the burden of proving the compelling public interests at stake. "If the right of a child to practice its religion ... is to be forbidden by constitutional means, there must be convincing proof that such a practice constitutes a grave and immediate danger to the state or to the health, morals, or welfare of the child."[22] In his opinion, the state had failed completely to sustain its burden of proof, and the mere possibility of harm from the distribution of religious literature was insufficient justification for restricting Betty's freedom of religious exercise. Moreover, he thought that such religiously motivated activity under the auspices of a guardian was likely to be immune from the usual harmful influences of the street corner.

Mrs. Prince's claim of religious conscience was to a right to allow and encourage her niece to distribute religious literature on street corners as part of a general duty to preach the word of God. Since there were available to Mrs. Prince's ward other methods of implementing this duty, such as visiting private homes and publicly distributing handbills unconnected with soliciting funds, Mrs. Prince's claim of religious conscience was not pressing from the viewpoint of the threatened impact of the child-labor laws on her own religious or moral integrity, or on that of her ward. This is not to say that Mrs. Prince's claim was trivial, but merely that she and her ward had other options by which they could fulfill their obligations, both to their religious consciences and to the law.

The public interest at stake in the Prince case involved the child's welfare, and this interest was asserted to be not only generic with respect to the effect of child labor, but specific with respect to the proselytizing activities of Betty. Since Mrs. Prince

---

22. *Prince v. Massachusetts*, 174.

claimed an exemption for the religiously motivated activities of her ward from regulations that her lawyers conceded were valid for identical, secularly motivated activities, the public interest to be weighed against her claim had to rest specifically on the harmful results of Betty's participation in her aunt's proselytizing activities. Although the majority expressed concern for Betty's physical well-being, the main emphasis seems to have been concern for her psychological and moral development. For its part, the minority attempted to show that there was no proof of any danger to Betty's physical safety, mental health, or moral virtue.

In summary, Mrs. Prince's claim of religious conscience was of a relatively low order. In the view of the minority, the public interest against Mrs. Prince's claim to exemption for her niece's proselytizing activities was unproved and rated low. But in the view of the majority, the public interest in denying her exemption from the child-labor laws of Massachusetts was of moderate rank and superior to her claim.

RELIGIOUS BELIEFS AND
PUBLIC SCHOOLING

Many states require patriotic exercises in public schools—namely, saluting the flag and reciting the pledge of allegiance—and these exercises led to one of the sharpest controversies on the rights of religious conscience in the history of American law. The Board of Education of Minersville, Pennsylvania, had mandated that all teachers and students participate in a program of saluting the flag and pledging allegiance. Two public-school children, Lillian and William Gobitis, refused for religious reasons to salute the flag, and they were expelled from the school. (The Gobitis children were Jehovah's Witnesses, and they believed that to salute the flag would be to worship a graven image, contrary to the injunction of Ex. 20:4–5.) Since the children were of the age for which the state required attendance at an accredited school, their parents had to send them to a private school. This entailed a substantial financial burden, and so the father of the children brought suit in a federal district court to enjoin the local authorities from exacting the children's participation in the flag-salute ceremony as a condition of their attendance at the Minersville public school. The District Court granted the injunction, and the Court of Appeals affirmed it. Minersville then appealed to the U.S. Supreme Court.

Justice Frankfurter, speaking for eight members of the Court, overturned the lower courts and upheld the requirement of participation in the program of saluting the flag (*Minersville v. Gobitis*).[23] For him, the only question concerned the legitimacy or rationality of the programs. He then argued that a free society is founded on "the binding tie of cohesive sentiment ... fostered by those agencies of the mind and spirit which may serve to gather up the traditions of a people, transmit them from generation to generation, and thereby create the community of a treasured common life which constitutes a civilization."[24] And so he said that a free society may use the educational process to inculcate that sentiment. Against the claim of Gobitis that Witnesses should have an exemption from participating in the flag-salute ceremony because of conscientious objection to it, Frankfurter argued that such an exemption "might introduce elements of difficulty into school discipline" and "might cast doubts in the minds of other children which would weaken the effect of the exercise."[25]

The sole dissenter in the Gobitis case was Justice Stone. In his view, the law sustained by the Court as applied to the Gobitis children did more than suppress freedom of speech and prohibit the free exercise of religion. "By this law, the state seeks to coerce these children to express a sentiment which ... violates their

23. *Minersville v. Gobitis,* 310 U.S. 586 (1940).
24. *Minersville v. Gobitis,* 596.
25. *Minersville v. Gobitis,* 600.

deepest religious convictions."[26] If the guarantees of civil liberty are to have any meaning, he argued, they must be deemed "to withhold from the state any authority to compel belief or the expression of it where that expression violates religious convictions, whatever may be the legislative view of the desirability of such compulsion."[27] On the role of the Court to review the legislative determination of the issue, Stone defended "a searching judicial inquiry into the legislative judgment where prejudice against discrete and insular minorities may tend to curtail the operation of ... political processes ordinarily to be relied on to protect minorities."[28]

A year and a half after the Gobitis decision of 1940, the West Virginia Board of Education ordered that a salute to the flag become a regular program in the public schools of the state, and that all teachers and pupils participate in the salute. Failure by the pupils to conform was considered insubordination to be dealt with by expulsion, and some children of the Jehovah's Witness faith were expelled from school and others threatened with expulsion for failure to participate in the ceremony. Officials also threatened to send such children to reformatories for juvenile delinquents, and their parents were prosecuted or threatened with prosecution for causing delinquency. A number of these parents brought suit to enjoin enforcement of the regulation against themselves, their children, and other Witnesses. The federal district court issued the injunction, and the Board of Education appealed directly to the Supreme Court.

This time the Witnesses won their case in the high court (*West Virginia v. Barnette*).[29] Justice Jackson, speaking for six members of the Court, noted that compelling flag salutes required an "affirmation of a belief and an attitude of mind" and held that

---

26. *Minersville v. Gobitis*, 601.   27. *Minersville v. Gobitis*, 604.
28. *Minersville v. Gobitis*, 606.
29. *West Virginia v. Barnette*, 319 U.S. 624 (1943).

legislatures had no constitutional power to require such an affirmation.[30] He thought that "the action of the local authorities in compelling the flag salute and pledge ... invades the sphere of intellect and spirit which it is the purpose of the First Amendment to reserve from all official control."[31] Since there was no power to make the flag salute a legal duty in the first place, Jackson accordingly did not find it necessary to inquire whether nonconformist beliefs would exempt the Witnesses from a duty to salute. Against the judicial restraint urged by Frankfurter, Jackson argued that "the very purpose of the Bill of Rights was to withdraw certain subjects from the vicissitudes of political controversy, to place them beyond the reach of majorities and officials, and to establish them as legal principles to be applied by the courts."[32]

Jackson thus reformulated the issue in the flag-salute cases as one of freedom from compulsion of any expression rather than one of freedom from words or actions prohibited by an individual's religious conscience. But concurring Justices Black and Douglas emphasized that claim of conscience:[33] "Neither our domestic tranquility in peace nor our martial effort in war depend on compelling little children to participate in a ceremony which ends in nothing for them but a fear of spiritual condemnation." And Justice Murphy, also concurring, insisted that "official compulsion to affirm what is contrary to one's religious beliefs is the antithesis of freedom of worship."[34] For his part, dissenting Justice Frankfurter repeated his view that the only issue was whether legislators could reasonably prescribe the flag salute at all. Since the requirement was admittedly not designed to be discriminatory, he would not strike it down because it hurt or offended dissidents.

The claim of religious conscience represented by Gobitis and

---

30. *West Virginia v. Barnette*, 633.
32. *West Virginia v. Barnette*, 648.
34. *West Virginia v. Barnette*, 646.

31. *West Virginia v. Barnette*, 642.
33. *West Virginia v. Barnette*, 644.

Barnette was the same—namely, a claim that a specific, negative, and absolute religious belief prohibited the act of saluting the flag required by the state. As such, the claim was of the highest order because there was no way for the individual to obey the law and at the same time preserve the individual's religious and moral integrity. The penalties for nonconformity in the two cases were different, at least in the short run. Gobitis was penalized by the financial costs of private schooling, while Barnette was threatened with imprisonment. But Gobitis might have been forced into Barnette's position in the long run, and, in any case, the penalties coercing both were severe.

The countervailing public interest asserted in these cases concerned the development of patriotic attitudes in the young, and even Frankfurter thought the flag-salute exercises to be of marginal utility for this purpose. The Gobitis majority rested its decision on a judicial philosophy of deference to legislative judgments and on an unwillingness to make exceptions for dissenters from facially nondiscriminatory laws, not on a high public interest regarding compulsory flag salutes. The Barnette majority assumed a broader role for the Court in reviewing legislation affecting civil liberties and avoided a grant of exemptions for conscientious objectors to flag salutes by invalidating any compulsion of expression from pupils unwilling to participate for any reason or motive. In effect, Jackson held that compulsion of flag salutes represented no constitutionally valid public interest.

Members of the Amish religion directly challenged the public interest in the education of children beyond the eighth grade, viewing such education as a corrupting involvement in what they consider irreligious worldliness. The Amish people, who live in tightly knit farming communities, had been prosecuted in several states for refusing to obey laws that require children to attend school until the age of sixteen. The Wisconsin Supreme Court had ruled that the compulsory education law, as applied to the

Amish children, violated the First Amendment's guarantee of the free exercise of religion. Wisconsin then brought the case to the U.S. Supreme Court.

Chief Justice Burger, speaking for the Court, upheld the Wisconsin decision in favor of the Amish parents (*Wisconsin v. Yoder*).[35] According to him, there was ample evidence that ordinary secondary education contravened the basic religious tenets and practice of the Amish faith, regarding both the parents and their children, and that the state's claim of a supervisory role over the children did not override this claim to the free exercise of religion. The Amish parents had indicated their willingness to provide vocational training with a few hours of formal study each week as an alternative to conventional high-school education, but the state refused to accept the alternative. Under these circumstances the state had the burden of demonstrating that the loss of one or two years of secondary education would impair the physical or mental health of the children or render them unable to support themselves as adults or detract from their ability to discharge the duties and responsibilities of citizenship. This burden the state failed to sustain to the Court's satisfaction. The Court avowed that its holding did not resolve questions of potential conflict between the wishes of parents and the wishes of their offspring, although it noted the strong legal tradition in favor of parental rights in the upbringing of their children. And the Court took pains to distinguish the Amish claims from those based on philosophical and personal choice, thus intimating that the states may regulate home schooling.

Justice Stewart, joined by Justice Brennan, concurred in the judgment and opinion of the Court, but emphasized that the decision involved no question involving the rights of Amish children to attend public or private schools against the will of their

35. *Wisconsin v. Yoder,* 406 U.S. 205 (1972).

parents if they wished to do so. Justice White, joined by Justices Brennan and Stewart, also concurred in the judgment and opinion of the Court, but only after concluding that the state had not demonstrated that Amish children who leave school after the eighth grade are unable to acquire academic skills for adult life if they later abandon their parents' faith. Justice Douglas concurred in the case of one Amish parent whose child testified that her religious views were opposed to high-school education, but he dissented in two other cases in which the children had not testified. He would have remanded the latter cases for new hearings on the religious views of the children, which views he would have made determinative of the cases. Douglas also disagreed with the Court's attempt to reserve exemption from compulsory secondary education to those motivated by religious views in the traditional sense.

The claims of religious conscience by the Amish parents in these cases, which all the justices except Douglas assumed to be identical with that of the children, were of the highest order—namely, that they not be coerced into sending their children to participate in schooling that they deemed contrary to their religion. Against these claims of the Amish parents, the Court held the public interest in compelling one or two years of formal secondary education beyond grade school to be of relatively low priority. But Justice Douglas would ascertain the wishes of the children in every case, and Justices Brennan and Stewart would reexamine the public interest of the welfare of children in properly presented cases of conflict between them and their parents. The Court's attempt to distinguish opposition to compulsory secondary education based on philosophical or personal views seems to be inconsistent with the Seeger[36] and Welsh[37] decisions. Perhaps, however, Burger wished only to distinguish opposition

36. *U.S. v. Seeger,* 380 U.S. 163 (1965).
37. *Welsh v. U.S.,* 398 U.S. 333 (1970).

to compulsory secondary education based on a concept of *moral duty*, whether conventionally religious or not, from one based on views about what is educationally desirable. In any case, the Court here recognized a claim of religious or moral conscience, and only such a claim, to exemption from the prescriptions of facially nondiscriminatory laws.

EXEMPTIONS FROM SUNDAY LAWS FOR SABBATARIAN BUSINESSMEN

Sabbatarian entrepreneurs in two of the Sunday law cases before the Court in 1961 (*Braunfeld v. Brown* and *Gallagher v. Crown Kosher Supermarket*)[38] contended that the free exercise clause requires states with Sunday laws to exempt entrepreneurs who observe another day of the week as a religious day of rest. Such an exemption, they argued, would achieve the state's interest in a day of rest for all citizens and simultaneously relieve Sabbatarian businessmen of the economic burdens imposed on them by the Sunday laws. Sunday laws do not command Sabbatarian businessmen to do anything contrary to their religious beliefs, but the laws do create a situation where the businessmen are pressured financially to do so. If the businessman obeys his conscience, he will close his store on Saturdays, and if he obeys the Sunday laws, he will close his store on Sundays. If he does both, he will suffer serious financial loss and perhaps risk bankruptcy. The financial impact of Sunday laws thus both provides a strong incentive for Sabbatarian businessmen to do business on Saturdays—and thereby act against their religious beliefs—and penalizes them if they follow their religious beliefs. Since a state can achieve the secular purpose of Sunday laws without imposing an indirect burden on their religious observance, they argued, the application of the laws to them was discriminatory and a violation of the free exercise clause.

38. *Braunfeld v. Brown*, 366 U.S. 599 (1961); *Gallagher v. Crown Kosher Supermarket*, 366 U.S. 617 (1961).

A central question was whether the states could in fact achieve the secular goal of their Sunday laws if they extended exemptions to conscientious Sabbatarian businessmen. Chief Justice Warren pointed out several ways in which he thought that exemptions might adversely affect the secular aims of Sunday laws. First, enforcement problems would be more difficult, since there would be two or more days to enforce rather than one. Second, to allow only people who rest on a day other than Sunday to keep their businesses open on that day might well provide these people with an economic advantage over their competitors who remain closed on that day. Third, because of the potential competitive advantage, unscrupulous entrepreneurs might assert that religious convictions compelled them to close on a less profitable day, and a state might object to conducting an inquiry into the sincerity of merchants' asserted religious beliefs. Fourth, exempted employers might hire only employees whose religious beliefs qualified them for the exemption, and a state might reasonably oppose the injection of a religious factor into the employment picture. Finally, if exemptions for conscientious Sabbatarians did assure a day of rest for all citizens without upsetting the balance of competition or creating other problems, the exemptions would still undermine the common day of rest and recreation that the Sunday laws were designed to provide.

Justice Douglas objected to Sunday laws in principle, but added that the laws imposed an economic penalty on those who observe Saturday rather than Sunday as the Sabbath, and so constituted state interference with the free exercise of religion. Justices Brennan and Stewart dissented only in the two cases in which Sabbatarians claimed that the Sunday laws infringed the free exercise of their religious beliefs. Brennan admitted that the laws do not compel affirmation of a repugnant belief, that the laws affected Sabbatarian religious observance only indirectly, that granting exemptions to Sabbatarians would make Sundays a little noisier and the task of the police a little more difficult, and that the exempted non-Sunday observers might get an unfair competitive advantage. But the mere convenience of having everyone rest on the same day could not justify making one or more religions economically disadvantaged. The free exercise of religion, in Brennan's view, is a preferred freedom and may be infringed, even indirectly, only to prevent the grave and imminent dangers of criminal actions or other substantive evils. Stewart felicitously described a legally mandated common day of rest as "enforced Sunday togetherness."[39]

The nature of the Sabbatarian businessmen's claim of religious conscience to exemption from the Sunday laws was clear. The laws did not demand that Sabbatarian businessmen operate on Saturdays, nor did they prohibit any religious practice or implementation of religious or moral duties. Rather, the laws put financial pressure on Sabbatarian businessmen to operate on Saturdays, which was specifically and absolutely contrary to their religious beliefs, or penalized them if they closed their stores in Saturday as well as Sunday. The Sabbatarian businessmen's claim of conscience was of a moderately high order, but not the highest, since Sunday laws did not require work on Saturdays or forbid any religious practice or duty.

The Court held that the public interest against granting exemptions to Sabbatarian entrepreneurs was based on the likelihood of administrative difficulties and competitive imbalance. Justices Brennan and Stewart assigned much less value to a common day of rest and recreation, administrative convenience, and competitive balance than the Court did. They thought the public interests in denying exemptions to be of relatively low value, while the majority thought them to be of at least moderate value. (One should note that, at the time of the decision, ten

39. *Braunfeld v. Brown*, 616.

states granted exemptions, apparently without any serious problem.) More importantly, Brennan and Stewart argued that only a
compelling public interest could constitutionally justify denying
exemption to Sabbatarian businessmen from commercial regulations that financially penalized their religious beliefs. The question of what standard the Court should apply to cases of religious
objectors to otherwise nondiscriminatory laws or regulations of
general applicability will recur in subsequent cases, especially the
Smith case.[40]

SABBATARIANS, PACIFISTS, AND UNEMPLOYMENT COMPENSATION ELIGIBILITY

Mrs. Sherbert, a Seventh Day Adventist, would not accept
work on Saturday, a day on which the tenets of her religion prohibited labor, and she failed to find employment involving no
work on Saturdays. She thereupon applied for unemployment
compensation, but the state agency denied the application because
she failed to accept suitable work—that is, work including Saturdays, when it was offered to her. The South Carolina Supreme
Court upheld the decision of the state agency, and Mrs. Sherbert
appealed to the U.S. Supreme Court.

Although South Carolina did not command Mrs. Sherbert to
work on Saturdays under threat of criminal penalties, its denial of
unemployment benefits threatened her with severe financial penalties unless she accepted work on Saturday and so induced her to
act against her religious beliefs and penalized her if she observed
them. Her claim is thus a moderate one and similar to the claim
of the Sabbatarian businessmen for exemption from Sunday laws.

The state's main argument for disqualifying Mrs. Sherbert
from unemployment compensation was that to grant her claim
would open the workers' fund to unscrupulous applicants who

40. *Employment Division v. Smith*, 494 U.S. 872 (1990).

might feign religious objections to work on Saturday. The public interest thus asserted against allowing her claim was principally to administrative convenience in preventing fraudulent access to the fund, although the state did argue incidentally that recognition of her claim might make it more difficult for employers to schedule Saturday work.

Justice Brennan, speaking for six members of the Court, found no compelling interest on the part of South Carolina to disqualify Mrs. Sherbert from eligibility to receive unemployment compensation (*Sherbert v. Verner*).[41] Justice Stewart concurred separately, but he insisted (rightly) that the Sherbert decision was inconsistent with *Braunfeld*, the case on Sabbatarian businessmen and Sunday laws. The majority held that the state's claim of a public interest against fraudulent access to its unemployment compensation fund was too low to justify the financial penalty that denial of Mrs. Sherbert's application would impose on her if she fulfilled her religious duty or pressure on her to act contrary to her perceived duty. Justices Harlan and White, dissenting, pointed out (rightly) that the effect of the Court's decision was to give applicants for unemployment compensation unwilling to work on Saturdays for religious reasons a standing superior to that of those unwilling to work on Saturdays for other reasons. The case is thus a clear example of exemption from a facially nondiscriminatory law of general applicability in favor of religious objectors.

Nearly twenty years later, in 1981, a nearly unanimous Court, Rehnquist alone dissenting, upheld the unemployment eligibility of a Jehovah's Witness who quit his job for what he claimed were religious reasons (*Thomas v. Review Board*).[42] Thomas was a Jehovah's Witness and worked in a foundry that produced sheet steel for industrial uses. When the foundry closed, he was transferred

---

41. *Sherbert v. Verner,* 374 U.S. 398 (1961).
42. *Thomas v. Review Board,* 450 U.S. 707 (1981).

to a department producing tank turrets. All other departments to which he could have been transferred also produced armaments, and so he asked to be laid off. After the company denied his request, he quit and applied for unemployment compensation. The Indiana unemployment compensation board denied the application on the ground that Thomas had not terminated his employment for work-related good cause, and the Indiana Supreme Court sustained the board.

The Indiana Supreme Court rejected Thomas' contention that he had terminated his employment for religious reasons. Thomas admitted that he had no religious objections to producing raw materials destined for use in armaments, but he was unable to articulate to the satisfaction of the court precisely why his religious beliefs permitted him to do so and would not permit him to produce the armaments themselves. Moreover, another Jehovah's Witness in the same position as Thomas had no religious scruples about accepting work producing armaments. From this the Indiana Supreme Court concluded that there was nothing intrinsically incompatible between the pacifist religious beliefs of Jehovah's Witnesses and work producing armaments.

Chief Justice Burger, speaking for the Court, rejected the conclusion of the Indiana Supreme Court about the religious nature of Thomas' convictions. The religious beliefs of Jehovah's Witnesses forbid participation in war, and Thomas held the honest conviction that those beliefs extended to armament production. In Burger's view, the line that Thomas drew between armament production and the production of raw materials for armaments was not unreasonable, and his conduct in quitting his job should be considered an exercise of religious belief.

Indiana, by conditioning receipt of unemployment compensation upon conduct proscribed by Thomas' faith, imposed a severe, though indirect, financial burden on the exercise of religion protected by the First Amendment. That burden, according to

Burger, could be justified only if it was the least restrictive means to achieve a compelling public interest. Indiana alleged two justifications of the burden placed on workers with beliefs like those of Thomas: the financial integrity of the unemployment compensation fund and the social undesirability of probing the religious beliefs of employees. Burger summarily dismissed both of these asserted public interests as insufficiently demonstrated to be compelling.

Last, Burger found no violation of the establishment clause for Thomas to receive the benefit of unemployment compensation precisely on account of his religious beliefs. Burger admitted that a tension exists between the requirements of the free exercise clause and the religious establishment clause in cases like Thomas', but argued that the obligation of government neutrality in the face of religious differences resolved this tension.

Justice Rehnquist, dissenting, would not require Indiana to make an exception for religious believers like Thomas. Rehnquist admitted a current tension between the two religious clauses of the First Amendment, and he identified social welfare legislation since the Great Depression, judicial incorporation of the First Amendment into the Fourteenth, and especially interpretations of both clauses as causes of the tension. He would not read the free exercise clause to ban indirect financial burdens on religious exercise in order to achieve minimally rational public interests. Applying that standard, he concluded that the free exercise clause did not require Indiana to recognize Thomas' eligibility for unemployment compensation. On the other hand, Rehnquist would not read the religious establishment clause to ban aid to religion involving no support of proselytizing activities. Applying that standard, he concluded that the religious establishment clause would not prohibit Indiana from recognizing Thomas' eligibility if it chose to do so.

The position of the Indiana Supreme Court denying the religious nature of Thomas' beliefs about armament production seems arbitrary, and the U.S. Supreme Court rightly rejected it. The only threshold legal question about claims to freedom of religious exercise concerns the honesty of the asserted religious conviction, not the quality of the reasoning process to that conviction. However a believer arrives at a conclusion about whether one's religious beliefs prohibit an activity, the individual perceives the conclusion no less than the premises as a religious duty. Of course, the more remote the conclusion from the premises, the more doubt may be cast on the sincerity of the believer's asserted conviction about the conclusion.

For the rest, the Thomas case is a carbon copy of the Sherbert decision eighteen years before. The Court in the latter case applied the compelling public interest test to determine whether indirect financial burdens on religious exercise were justified. The Court applied the same test in *Thomas,* but Rehnquist, echoing dissenting Justice Harlan in *Sherbert,* would have applied the minimally rational public interest test. The question of which test to apply is critical, since the standard chosen will effectively determine the outcome of most such cases. If the compelling public interest test is applied, claimants like Sherbert and Thomas are almost certain to win, and if the minimally rational public interest is applied, they are almost certain to lose.

Sherbert and Thomas were confronted with a stark, if indirect, conflict between their perceptions of religious and moral obligation and the requirements of public law. Conscience threatened them with loss of religious and moral integrity if they performed specific acts (work on Saturdays, working on armament production), and public law threatened them with severe financial deprivation if they did not (ineligibility for unemployment compensation). Other conflicts are not so stark. Conscience may prescribe a general religious or moral duty (e.g., to preach the gospel), and public law may prohibit specific means (street proselytism by or with minors). In the latter situation, conscience does not threaten individuals with loss of religious or moral integrity if they obey the law, since alternate means are available to fulfill the perceived duty to preach the gospel. The justices, however, have made little or no attempt to adapt the constitutional standard to fit different types of conflict between conscience and law.

In *Thomas*, Burger would require governments to show not only that there are compelling public interests to justify the burdens their laws impose on religious exercise, but also that the means chosen to achieve such interests are the least restrictive. In this respect Burger formulated the compelling public interest test more stringently than *Sherbert* did. The inclusion of a least-restrictive-means component in the compelling public interest test would not seem to have much import for the decision in *Thomas*, but it might in other cases (e.g., the alternative of civilian service for selective conscientious objectors to war might be a less restrictive means than military conscription).

If Rehnquist is less sensitive than the majority to the claims of religious conscience to exemption from public laws, he is also more sensitive than the majority to the implications of such exemptions for interpreting the establishment clause. Burger and the majority accepted the preference accorded to religious believers like Thomas on the ground that the preference fulfills a government obligation to be neutral in the face of religious differences. But Rehnquist indicated pointedly that the preference, if legislatively mandated, could not survive the "complete separation" language of *Everson* and asked why Burger did not apply to the Thomas case the Schempp prongs of a secular purpose and a primary secular effect that neither advances nor inhibits religion. Rehnquist is at least correct that the issue deserves more analysis than it received from Burger in *Thomas* or from Brennan in *Sherbert*. Moreover, if preference for Thomas does not offend the establishment clause because the government has an obligation to be neutral in distributing the benefits of unemployment compensation in the face of religious differences, then why should not the same reasoning justify, even oblige, government support of the secular component of religiously oriented education?

Six years later, in 1987, the Court, over the dissent of now Chief Justice Rehnquist, again ruled in favor of the right of a Sabbatarian unwilling to work on Saturdays, in this case a convert to the Seventh Day Adventist religion, to receive unemployment benefits (*Hobbie v. Unemployment Appeals Commission*).[43] The later holding in *Smith*[44] declined to apply the compelling public interest standard used in the Sherbert, Thomas, and Hobbie cases to a claim for exemption from a criminal law of general applicability, but left those unemployment cases in place on their own facts.

RELIGIOUS BELIEFS AND ADMINISTRATION OF THE GOVERNMENT'S OWN AFFAIRS

In a number of cases in the 1980s, the Court has held the free exercise clause does not require the government to demonstrate a compelling public interest if, in administering its own affairs, the government restricts an individual's religious exercise. One of these involved the U.S. Air Force dress code, which prohibits the wearing of any headgear indoors and unauthorized headgear outdoors. Goldman was an Orthodox Jewish rabbi, a clinical psychologist, and an Air Force officer. He sought to enjoin application of the regulation to himself on the ground that wearing a yarmulke was a religious exercise protected by the First Amendment, and the Court, by the narrowest margin, ruled in 1986 against him (*Goldman v. Weinberger*).[45]

Justice Rehnquist, speaking for the Court, declined to follow the compelling public interest standard that the Court had

43. *Hobbie v. Unemployment Appeals Commission*, 107 S. Ct. 1046 (1987).
44. See n. 40, supra.
45. *Goldman v. Weinberger*, 475 U.S. 503 (1986).

adopted in *Sherbert* regarding the religious exercise of civilians. Because the military has a special need for discipline, he argued, courts should be far more deferential to decisions by military authorities than to those by civilian authorities, and he found the dress regulation a reasonable exercise of professional judgment about what was necessary for military discipline. Whether exceptions for Goldman and other Orthodox Jews to wear yarmulkes while on duty would be compatible with discipline was a matter for military authorities to decide.

Concurring Justice Stevens was concerned about what an exception for Orthodox Jews would imply for other religious claims of military personnel to exceptions (e.g., Sikhs to wear turbans, Rastafarians not to cut their hair) and about the damage that exceptions might inflict on uniformity in the military services. Still more important, in his view, was the necessity for the government to treat all religions uniformly, and he thought that the Air Force regulation did so.

Dissenting Justice Brennan noted that Orthodox Jewish males regard wearing a yarmulke not merely as a religious exercise, but also as a religious duty. He criticized deference to military authorities in matters of constitutional right, foresaw no serious discipline problem if Orthodox military personnel were permitted to wear yarmulkes, and challenged the asserted interest in uniformity when military authorities permitted personnel to wear rings. In his view the compatibility of other dress exceptions for religious reasons could be decided in appropriate cases. Against Justice Stevens, Brennan argued that the existing Air Force dress regulation does distinguish between religions, favoring mainstream (Christian) religious over those prescribing special garb.

Dissenting Justice Blackmun thought that the Air Force could justifiably weigh the cumulative costs of dress code exceptions for religious reasons to military discipline as well as the cost of permitting an exception for Goldman. But he also thought that the government had failed to show any significant cost to discipline if Goldman and other Orthodox Jews were permitted to wear yarmulkes. Neutral principles, such as that of safety, could distinguish the case of yarmulkes for Jews from the turbans of Sikhs, and, in any case, the government had not demonstrated how many individuals would seek exceptions from dress code rules for religious reasons.

Dissenting Justice O'Connor would, contrary to the view of Rehnquist, test the validity of government regulations affecting the religious exercise of military personnel by the same standard as the one applied to government regulations affecting the religious exercise of civilians. Accordingly, O'Connor would require military authorities to demonstrate that regulations serve important government interests, and that exceptions for religious reasons would substantially harm those interests. O'Connor agreed that discipline is a military necessity, but could see no substantial harm if Goldman and other Orthodox Jews were permitted to wear yarmulkes on duty. In fact, the Air Force had raised no objection to Goldman wearing a yarmulke on hospital duty during the first four years of his service.

At first glance the conflict between the government and Goldman seems to be categorically clear-cut: the government seems to be commanding Goldman not to wear a yarmulke, and his religion is commanding him to do so. In fact, the case is not so categorically clear-cut. Goldman voluntarily participated in an R.O.T.C. program and thereby contracted to serve in the Air Force. At the time of this case, Goldman had nearly completed his tour of military duty and sought to renew his contract. The actual conflict, therefore, is between a hypothetical command of the government that Goldman not wear his yarmulke on duty *if* he wishes to continue to serve in the Air Force and the claim by Goldman to a right to employment by the military without being required to doff his yarmulke while on duty.

Only Brennan inquired about the nature of Goldman's religious claim, emphasizing that Orthodox Jewish males regard the wearing of a yarmulke as a religious duty. As previously noted, however, Goldman is claiming a right to wear a yarmulke in the Air Force when on duty. He remains free to fulfill his religious duty, but not in the Air Force when on duty. Only were he a conscript would his choice be categorically between obedience to the government and obedience to his conscience.

All the justices found that the public interest against granting Goldman and other Orthodox Jews an exemption from the headgear—namely, military discipline—was unsubstantial. Indeed, Justice Blackmun found none at all against an exception for Orthodox Jews to wear yarmulkes when on duty. (Some, however, might wish to argue that *any* exception from military regulations would seriously undermine military discipline, at least by inviting more.) Most of the justices reached different conclusions because they used different tests. Rehnquist and Stevens, for example, used the minimum rationality test and accordingly sustained the government regulation, and O'Connor used the compelling public interest test and accordingly ruled for Goldman. The relevant test seems irrelevant in the case of Blackmun, who presumably uses a minimum rationality test, but finds no minimally rational public interest in denying Goldman and Orthodox Jews an exception from the government regulation.

The decisive issue for most justices, therefore, seems to concern which test to apply to cases involving religious exercise claims of rights by military personnel against military regulations. It seems to this writer that the minimum rationality test is appropriate regarding *volunteer* military personnel. In this connection, Justice Steven's point that exemptions for other religious groups might be incompatible with military discipline indicates why a minimum rationality test is more practical. On the other hand, the compelling public interest test might be more appropriate to use regarding claims of rights to religious exercise by *conscripted* military personnel, and this might then require the government to offer alternative civilian service to such claimants.

In the same year, the Court ruled against an American Indian who objected on religious grounds to a requirement that his daughter have a Social Security number in order for him to be eligible for welfare aid (*Bowen v. Roy*).[46] Roy claimed that assignment of the number would rob her spirit and use of it cause evil to befall her. His original objection was to obtaining the number, but when it was indicated that the Social Security Administration had already assigned a number to his daughter, Roy objected to governmental use of the number. The District Court enjoined use of the number and denial of benefits if Roy did not provide the number on an application form. The Supreme Court overturned both injunctions.

Chief Justice Burger and other members of the Court except Justice White agreed that governmental use of the number did not affect Roy's beliefs or his actions, and that Roy could not claim that he was denied the free exercise of his religion because the government did not act according to his beliefs. Burger argued further that the case of the government conditioning benefits on recipients obtaining a Social Security number was distinctly different from one where the government compels them to do so. A rule admitting no exceptions is religiously neutral and serves an important government interest in preventing fraud.

Justice Blackmun concurred with Burger on the reversal of the injunction against government use of a number for Roy's daughter, but he would have remanded the case to the district court to determine whether the government would force Roy to supply the number on his application for welfare benefits. If so, Blackmun thought that the Sherbert test of a compelling public inter-

46. *Bowen v. Roy*, 476 U.S. 693 (1986).

est should apply; if not, the issue would be moot. Justice Stevens judged the issue of forcing Roy to supply the number on his application form either moot or not ripe.

Justice O'Connor dissented from the reversal of the district court order enjoining denial of benefits. The issue, in her view, was not moot, since the government had not yet categorically indicated what it would require of Roy. On the merits, she saw no difference between compelling acts contrary to religious beliefs and conditioning benefits on the performance of such acts. Applying the Sherbert test, she found no important government interest served by requiring Roy to supply a number on his application form for welfare benefits, since only a few applicants would raise religious objections to supplying a number. Dissenting Justice White would have affirmed the district court order, both respecting governmental use of the number and respecting denial of benefits to Roy if he failed to supply the number.

From the religious exercise perspective, Burger properly distinguished governmental use of Social Security numbers from governmental compulsion of action by Roy contrary to his religious beliefs. Roy may believe that his daughter will suffer evil if the government uses a number for her, but Roy himself is not thereby forced to do anything. Were the government to require that Roy supply the number on his welfare application, however, there seems little point to distinguishing between governmental compulsion of cooperation and government conditioning benefits on cooperation. Surely, to deny benefits to the needy unless they perform an act pressures them to act as much as, or almost as much as, the threat of imprisonment. Nor does the problem of fraud if Roy fails to supply his daughter's number on an application form seem at all substantial. The Social Security Administration already has the number and can enter it on the application form.

In another case involving religious claimants against government administrators (*O'Lone v. Shabazz*),[47] the Court by the narrowest margin deferred to prison officials as to the reasonableness of freeing Muslim prisoners from work duty in order to attend Muslim religious services on Friday.

An Indian group sought to prevent the Forest Service from constructing a paved road through land used by Indians for religious purposes, which construction, it claimed, would violate its exercise of religion. The Court denied that the Indians were being deprived of any right of religious exercise (*Lyng v. Northwest Indian Protective Association*).[48]

Justice O'Connor, joined by four other justices, held that the free exercise clause did not require the government to conduct its own affairs in ways that comport with particular religious views. She thought that the Roy decision was directly apposite. Like Roy, O'Connor claimed, the Northwest Indians claimed that construction of the road would hinder their spiritual development, and any attempt to distinguish the two cases on the basis of the relative effects of governmental action on religious exercise would impermissibly require the Court to determine the truth of religious beliefs. When, as here, it is a question of the indirect effects of governmental action that makes the practice of religion difficult, but neither coerces action contrary to religious belief nor penalizes the exercise of religion, the religious exercise clause does not apply, and so the government does not need to show a compelling public interest for its action. Whatever the limits protecting a religious objector from the indirect effects of governmental action, they do not depend on the consequences of the action on the objector's spiritual development. In short, the government had a right to use its own land without regard to the religious effects on the Indians.

O'Connor did, however, endorse the government's efforts to

47. *O'Lone v. Shabazz*, 482 U.S. 342 (1987).
48. *Lyng v. Northwest Indian Protective Association*, 485 U.S. 439 (1988).

accommodate the Indians' religious beliefs and practices. The Regional Forester selected a route that avoided archeological sites and was as far as possible removed from present sites of Indian spiritual activities. Alternate routes had been rejected for several reasons. They would have required the purchase of private land, soil along the routes would be too unstable for a road, and the routes would traverse other areas of ritualistic value to the Indians.

O'Connor rejected the dissenters' proposal that the free exercise clause should cover land-use effects on values central to the Indians' religious beliefs. In her view the Court could not distinguish between values central to religious beliefs and those peripheral without making determinations about religious beliefs. Moreover, a further claim might be made that exclusion of non-Indians was central to the Indians' religious practices and spiritual development.

Justice Brennan, joined by Justices Blackmun and Marshall, dissented. He did not accept the Court's distinction between restraints that coerce actions contrary to religious beliefs or penalize religious exercise, on the one hand, and restraints with indirect adverse effects on religious exercise, on the other. The free exercise clause is directed against any form of governmental action that frustrates or inhibits religious practice. Brennan interpreted prior decisions to support his position.

Brennan, citing the trial court, claimed that the environmental and physical attributes of the "high country" were an indispensable part of the Indians' religious practices and essential to their ceremonials. The proposed road would virtually destroy the Indians' ability to practice their religion and completely prevent them from doing so. Against the destructive effects on the Indians' religious practices, the road would serve public interests that are neither compelling nor commensurate. In fact, Brennan did not see any need for the road at all.

As to the Roy precedent, Brennan argued that the assignment

and use of a Social Security number affected only the internal affairs of the government, whereas the land-use issue at stake in the present case had external effects. Government use of a Social Security number did not affect Roy's daughter's religious exercise, but the roads would affect the Indians' religious exercise.

Brennan recognized that a decision in favor of the Indians might lead to objections to any human use of government lands by others. A conflict of cultures was at the heart of the case, and the free exercise clause should protect Indian use of land central and indispensable to their religious practices. Such land included more than the land necessary for the survival of Indian religion or the land deemed sacred by them. Indians themselves could make clear what land was central to their religious practices, although any claim that exclusion of others from government land was central to the Indians' religious practices would pose a formidable religious establishment problem.

The central issue in this case was whether the free exercise clause should extend to protect religious objectors from administrative governmental actions. The Court held that the religious exercise clause does not apply to the indirect effects of governmental actions that make the practice of religion more difficult, but neither coerce action contrary to religious belief nor penalize the exercise of religion, and so the government does not need to demonstrate compelling public interests for its actions. This makes practical sense, since to apply the compelling public interest standard of protection to the indirect effects of every administrative governmental action would cripple routine decision-making in many areas.

But should the free exercise clause offer no protection at all when governmental actions indirectly hinder religious practices, albeit without coercion to act contrary to one's religious beliefs? I think not. The free exercise clause should require that the government demonstrate the *reasonableness* of its actions specifically with respect to their indirect effects on religious practices. In other words, the government should be required to show that there are no satisfactory alternatives that would have no or less adverse effects on religious practices and would adequately achieve legitimate, albeit not compelling, governmental objectives, This protection would be of no help to the Indians here, assuming some necessity for the road and the unavailability of alternate routes. It might, however, help religious objectors in other situations. It is surely no serious burden on the government to require that it accommodate religious practices when that can be done at little or no cost to secular public interests.

Brennan had an alternative to resolve the problem He would have the free exercise clause protect only practices central to religious beliefs from the indirect effects of administrative governmental activities and apply the compelling public interest standard. But could a court deny any claim that a practice was central to religious belief without judging the theological accuracy of the claim or the truthfulness of the claimant?

On the relevance of *Roy* to the present case, Brennan makes the better argument. In the former case, governmental use of a Social Security number would, according to Indian religious belief, have adverse effects on the spiritual development of Roy's daughter, but it would in no way have interfered with her or his religious exercise. In the present case, on the other hand, construction of the road was alleged to interfere with the Indians' religious practices.

The majority and dissenting justices also disagreed on two factual issues: the effect of the road on Indian religious practices and the need for the road. O'Connor thought that the road would only make Indian religious practices more difficult; Brennan argued that the road would make the practices impossible. O'Connor accepted the necessity of the road; Brennan denied its necessity.

Free Exercise of Religion

THE SMITH DECISION AND
ITS AFTERMATH

Oregon prohibited the use of peyote. Two Indians were fired from their jobs with a private drug rehabilitation clinic because they, while on work duty, ingested peyote, a hallucinogen, in a ceremonial rite of the Native American Church. They then applied for unemployment compensation, but the state agency denied them eligibility because they had been dismissed for work-related misconduct. The state courts ruled that the denial of benefits to them violated the free exercise clause. After remand from the U.S. Supreme Court, the Oregon Supreme Court ruled that Oregon law provided no exception from the criminal drug law for the religious use of peyote and continued to hold that the denial of unemployment compensation benefits violated the free exercise clause.

In 1990, the U.S. Supreme Court ruled in favor of the state (*Employment Division v. Smith*).[49] Justice Scalia, joined by four other justices, defined the issue presented by the case as whether the free exercise clause permitted Oregon to include religious use of peyote within the general criminal prohibition of use of the drug and consequently to deny unemployment benefits to persons dismissed from their jobs because of such religious use. He distinguished the present case from the flag-salute cases, in which the free exercise clause was held to entitle the religious objectors to exemption from neutral laws of general applicability, on the ground that the cases were hybrid cases—that is, cases that involved communicative activity protected by the free speech clause. He also distinguished the present case from the Sherbert line of cases on the ground that those cases involved unemployment compensation, the eligibility criteria for which invite con-

49. See n. 40, supra.

sideration of particular circumstances, and not criminal laws of general applicability. He pointed out that the Court had not invoked the Sherbert test in cases of the 1980s involving religious claimants for exemptions from the government's regulation of its own activities.

In short, he would not apply the compelling public interest test to require exemptions from generally applicable criminal laws. Nor did he think it possible to limit the impact of exemptions by requiring a compelling public interest only when the prohibited conduct is "central" to the individual's religion. If the compelling public interest test is to be applied at all, then it should be applied across the board to all actions thought to be religiously mandatory. Moreover, if the test is adopted for religious exceptions, many laws will not meet the test. Any society adopting such a system would be courting anarchy, and the danger would increase in direct proportion to the society's religious diversity. A state may elect to grant religious exceptions, but if it doesn't, that consequence should be preferred to a system in which each conscience is a law unto itself, or one in which judges decide the relative importance of all laws.

Justice O'Connor concurred in the judgment, but rejected the majority reasoning. She would have relied on the compelling public interest test and held that Oregon passed that test, largely because she rated high the risk that cumulative exceptions for diverse religious objectors would undermine the general prohibitions of criminal laws.

Justice Blackmun, joined by Justices Brennan and Marshall, dissented. He would adhere to the compelling public interest test of claims of exemption for religious reasons, and he found no such interest in the present case, for the following reasons. First, Oregon had not deemed it necessary to enforce its drug laws against religious users of peyote. Second, there is no evidence that religious use of peyote is harmful. Third, the risk of a flood of exceptions is purely speculative, and twenty-three states and the federal government have mandated an exemption for the religious use of peyote. Blackmun concluded by stressing that the use of peyote by the Indians was an essential ritual of their religion.

In the facts of this case, it is difficult to see how or why the Indian plaintiffs could advance any claim to exemption to perform a religious rite during work hours, especially the use of a prohibited drug in a drug-rehabilitation clinic, and if they were fired for good cause, then the denial of unemployment compensation seems appropriate. But the Court treated the case without regard to the time and place of the Indians' presumptively religious use of peyote. Assuming that abstract state of the question, Scalia concluded that the Oregon drug laws imposed only an indirect burden on the Indians' free exercise of religion, and that the free exercise clause provided no basis for exemption from a criminal law of general applicability. Scalia was right that the burden was indirect, but why should the compelling public interest be jettisoned? Scalia has a point about the risk that exemptions for religious objectors from criminal prohibitory laws might invite a flood of exceptions and so undermine the law, but O'Connor using that test reached the same judgment as Scalia. Evidently, the majority was determined to put this type of religious claim permanently off the Court's docket. As a footnote to the case, Oregon one year later passed a law permitting the sacramental use of peyote by Native American Indians.

The Smith decision aroused opposition from many religious groups, and Congress in 1993 passed the Religious Freedom Restoration Act (RFRA) to restore the compelling public interest test of claims to exceptions for religious reasons from laws of general applicability. According to RFRA, a law that substantially burdens a religious practice needs to demonstrate a compelling public interest to justify it, and the means to achieve that interest needs to be the least restrictive.

Archbishop Flores of San Antonio applied for a permit to enlarge the Catholic Church in Boerne, Texas. The permit was denied on the ground that the existing church building was a historical monument protected by a local ordinance. Flores then sued in reliance on the RFRA. He won in the lower court, and the city of Boerne appealed to the Supreme Court.

Justice Kennedy, joined by five other justices, ruled for the city, holding the RFRA unconstitutional because Congress has no power under sec. 5 of the Fourteenth Amendment to define or enlarge the substance of civil rights (*Boerne v. Flores*).[50] According to him, the power granted to Congress by the Fourteenth Amendment to enforce sec. 1 extends only to preventive or remedial measures. Although he cites some points favorable to his position, he ignores the forest for the trees. Bingham, the author of sec. 1, in which sec. 5 was originally part, stated repeatedly that the purpose of the amendment (sec. 1) was to guarantee rights guaranteed in the Bill of Rights, the rights of citizens as such— indeed, innate rights. Congress intended to write a blank check for its own use, not the Court's. (The Radical Republicans were so called for good reason.) Moreover, Kennedy seems oblivious of the first Justice Harlan's powerful dissent in *The Civil Rights Cases*.[51] Harlan there argued persuasively that the first sentence of the amendment defined citizenship, and that Congress could enforce the rights of citizens as such. Kennedy's opinion reads like a conclusion in search of premises. The majority may be right that the RFRA goes too far as a matter of policy, and they undoubtedly were not happy with receiving a slap on the wrist from Congress, but matters of policy should be left to legislatures, as conservative justices often remind us.

The Court's current interpretation of the free exercise clause can be summarized as follows. First, the government may not

50. *Boerne v. Flores,* 521 U.S. 507 (1997).
51. The Civil Rights Cases, 109 U.S. 3 (1883).

overtly or covertly ban a religious practice without demonstrating a compelling public interest.[52] Second, the government may not coerce individuals to act contrary to their religious beliefs without demonstrating a compelling public interest. Third, the government may not, without demonstrating a compelling public interest, deny unemployment compensation to those who have declined to accept suitable work for religious reasons when no criminal law is involved. Fourth, the government may manage its own affairs in ways that have only incidental effects on some or even all religions. Fifth, the government may deny exemption from criminal laws generally prohibiting activities to those objecting on religious grounds.

52. Cf. *Church of Lukumi Babalu Aye v. Hialeah,* 113 S. Ct. 2217 (1993).

8

CONSCIENTIOUS OBJECTORS
TO WAR

※

CONSCRIPTION AND PACIFISM

The first conscientious objectors to military service in America were members of religious sects opposed to war as a matter of principle. Chief among these were the Quakers, the Mennonites, and the Brethren. There were also smaller pacifist sects like the Shakers. They won recognition from colonial legislatures and exemption from militia duty. They were legally required but rarely forced to pay special taxes or hire substitutes in the course of Indian conflicts, the French and Indian War, and the American Revolution.[1] During the Civil War, the states exempted religious conscientious objectors to war, but they were obliged to pay set fees or hire substitutes. Some pacifists objected to the fees both as taxes on conduct dictated by conscience and as equivalent to personal participation in waging war. Some also objected on the latter ground to the hiring of substitutes and even to the payment of general taxes earmarked to cover military expenses.

The Civil War brought the first federal conscription of men

1. For the history of conscientious objection to war in America, see Lillian Schlissel, ed., *Conscience in America* (New York: Dutton, 1968).

into the United States Army. The Federal Conscription Act of 1863 made all men between the ages of twenty and forty-five liable to military service if called upon by the president, but it allowed the payment of $300 in lieu of service and the hiring of a substitute. As a result of petitions by pacifist churches, Congress in 1864 granted exemption from combatant military service to "members of religious denominations who ... are conscientiously opposed to the bearing of arms, and who are prohibited from doing so by the rules and articles of faith, and the practice of said religious denominations."[2] Those qualifying for the exemptions, however, were to be drafted into military service as noncombatants and assigned to duty in hospitals or care for freedmen. As an alternative, they could avoid military service entirely by paying $300 for the benefit of sick and wounded soldiers. Even the accommodations of the Draft Act of 1864 were unacceptable to those conscientious objectors who considered any cooperation with the armed forces a betrayal of their principles, and they accordingly refused to serve in military hospitals. When Northern officials found that neither alternate service nor payment for a substitute was acceptable to such pacifists, they arranged to parole them for the duration of the war.

Conscription was not needed again until World War I. The Selective Service Act of 1917 granted exemptions from combatant military service to conscientious objectors affiliated with a "well-recognized religious sect or organization [then] organized and existing ... whose ... creed or principles forbid its members to participate in war in any form."[3] The act required all such persons to be inducted into the armed services, but allowed them to serve in noncombatant capacities declared by the president. In the Selective Services Cases,[4] the provision for conscientious objectors

2. 13 U.S.C. 9; Schlissel, ed., *Conscience in America*, 98.
3. 40 U.S.C. 76, 78; Schlissel, ed., *Conscience in America*, 133.
4. The Selective Service Cases, 245 U.S. 366, 389–90 (1918).

was upheld against constitutional attack as an establishment of religion, and conscription in general was upheld against constitutional attack as a form of involuntary servitude prohibited by the Thirteenth Amendment.

Those claiming exemption as conscientious objectors during World War I included members not only of traditional pacifist religious sects, but also of newer sects like Seventh Day Adventists and Jehovah's Witnesses. Some pacifist churches advised their eligible members to register and accept noncombatant military service, but some pacifists took exception to this policy because it placed them under military jurisdiction. On March 16, 1918, Congress authorized the secretary of war to grant furloughs without pay to enlisted conscientious objectors who would then work on farms or in Red Cross units under civilian control. Military directives to this effect were not issued until June and July 1918. There were also groups whose objection to war was not religiously motivated: socialists, radicals, and humanists, who were opposed to war on purely philosophical grounds. The Adjutant General of the Army, in a directive of December 10, 1917, declared that "'personal scruples against war' should be considered to constitute 'conscientious objection,' and such persons should be treated in the same manner as other 'conscientious objectors.'"[5]

In the Selective Training Act of 1940, Congress broadened the exemption afforded conscientious objectors in 1917. The act exempted from combatant military service anyone who, "by reason of religious training and belief, is conscientiously opposed to participation in war in any form."[6] Thus Congress determined that religious training and belief rather than formal membership in a recognized pacifist church was required for qualification as conscientious objectors.

The act also provided that any person qualifying for an exemp-

5. Schlissel, ed., *Conscience in America*, 130.
6. 54 U.S.C. 889; Schlissel, ed., *Conscience in America*, 214.

tion from combatant military service because of conscientious objection was liable to induction into the armed forces for assignment to noncombatant military service as defined by the president. But if an individual was also found to be conscientiously opposed to such noncombatant military service, he was liable to assignment to "work of national importance under civilian direction."[7] Conscientious objectors to noncombatant service under military authorities were accordingly assigned to perform work in Civilian Public Service camps, and members of such churches as the Quakers would supervise them. In any event, these camps furthered the work of the Civilian Conservation Corps. Some conscientious objectors to noncombatant as well as combatant military service freely sought work in mental hospitals or social agencies, and others were volunteers for medical experimentation. Conscientious objectors participating in the Civilian Public Service program were not paid, and they received none of the fringe benefits granted soldiers on active service. They either supported themselves or their families or churches did.

Jehovah's Witnesses were a class apart as conscientious objectors during World War II. They were generally refused classification as conscientious objectors to participation in war in any form because they believed in the use of force in defense of "Kingdom interests" and in the waging of "theocratic" wars commanded by Jehovah. They also claimed exemption as ministers, because the church considered every member a minister of the gospel, but these claims were likewise generally denied. After the outbreak of hostilities in Korea in 1950, the question about exempting Jehovah's Witnesses arose again, and the Supreme Court in 1955 upheld the claim of one of their members to such exemption (*Sicurella v. U.S.*).[8]

Sicurella, who was a Jehovah's Witness, registered with his lo-

7. 54 U.S.C. 889; Schlissel, ed., *Conscience in America*, 214.
8. *Sicurella v. U.S.*, 348 U.S. 385 (1955).

cal draft board in 1948. He worked forty-four hours a week at a Railway Express office, but he was at first classified as qualified for exemption as an ordained minister. After the outbreak of the Korean War, he was reclassified as eligible for general service. He then filed a claim as a conscientious objector. When his claim was disallowed and he failed to report for induction into the armed services, he was convicted of violating the Universal Military Training and Service Act of 1948, and a federal court of appeals affirmed the conviction. The Supreme Court overturned the conviction and accepted Sicuralla's claim to exemption as a conscientious objector.

The issue was whether, in view of his acceptance of the use of force to defend "Kingdom interests" and his willingness to fight in "theocratic" wars commanded by Jehovah, Sicurella could qualify for exemption as a conscientious objector to participation in war in any form. Justice Clark, speaking for the Court, thought that Sicurella could and did. Acknowledging that there were certain inconsistencies and obscurities in the petitioner's claim, Clark pointed out that Sicurella was admittedly sincere, that the force accepted by him to defend "Kingdom interests" involved no arms or "carnal" weapons, that "theocratic wars" were unlikely, and that, in any case, such wars were not the shooting wars Congress had in mind. Justices Reed and Minton dissented on the ground that the petitioner admitted that he would use force to defend "Kingdom interests" and participate in "theocratic wars" in some carnal form.

In 1948 Congress amended the language of the 1940 statute to declare in section 6 that "religious training and belief" was defined as "an individual's belief in a relation to a Supreme Being involving duties superior to those arising from any human relation but ... not [including] essentially political, sociological, or philosophical views, or a merely personal moral code."[9] Thus the

9. 50 U.S.C.A., App. § 456; Schlissel, ed., *Conscience in America*, 255, 263.

act of 1948 apparently excluded exemption for humanist conscientious objection to war.

In 1965 the Supreme Court unanimously held that the test of belief in relation to a Supreme Being is not whether a given belief in God is orthodox, but whether it "occupies a place in the life of its possessor parallel to that filled by orthodox belief in God" (*U.S. v. Seeger*).[10] One claimant admitted his skepticism about the existence of God, but acknowledged a "belief in, and devotion to, goodness and virtue for their own sakes and a religious faith in a purely ethical creed."[11] A second claimant acknowledged belief in a Supreme Reality to which human beings were partially akin, and he called his opposition to war religious in the sense that religion is the "sum and essence of one's basic attitudes to the fundamental problems of human existence."[12] The third claimant, in order to describe the grounds of his opposition to war, defined religion as "consciousness of some power manifest in nature which helps man in the ordering of his life in harmony with its demands."[13]

The Supreme Court found that all three claims to exemption as conscientious objectors were not based on a merely personal code, but on "the broader concept of a power or being, or faith, to which all else is subordinate or upon which all else is ultimately dependent."[14] The construction of the statutory language about religious training or belief in relation to a Supreme Being was undoubtedly broad and historically tenuous, but the alternative, as Justice Douglas pointed out,[15] would have raised a constitutional question about whether the statutory exemption preferred some religious beliefs over others and invidiously discriminated between different forms of religious expression. At any rate, the Court did insist that a claim to exemption as a conscientious ob-

10. *U.S. v. Seeger*, 380 U.S. 163, 166 (1965).
11. *U.S. v. Seeger*, 166.   12. *U.S. v. Seeger*, 168.
13. *U.S. v. Seeger*, 169.   14. *U.S. v. Seeger*, 174.
15. *U.S. v. Seeger*, 188.

jector had to be based on ethical grounds that transcend the individual's own desires for himself.

Five years after *Seeger*, in 1970, the Supreme Court applied the rationale of that decision to cover a conscientious objector who denied even more explicitly that his views on war were religious in the traditional sense (*Welsh v. U.S.*).[16] Welsh was convicted in a federal district court of refusing to submit to induction into the armed forces and sentenced to three years' imprisonment. A federal court of appeals affirmed the conviction, but the Supreme Court, in a five-to-three vote, reversed it "because of its fundamental inconsistency with *United States v. Seeger.*"[17]

Justice Black, speaking for four justices, interpreted *Seeger* to apply to any individual who "deeply and sincerely holds beliefs which are purely ethical or moral in source and content but which nonetheless impose on him a duty of conscience to refrain from participating in any war at any time."[18] Although Welsh struck out the word *religious* on his conscientious objector application and later characterized his beliefs as formed by reading in the fields of sociology and history, Black argued that the claimant's description of his beliefs as nonreligious was inconclusive and even unreliable, since few registrants are aware of the broad scope of the word *religious* as used in section 6(j) of the Universal Military Training and Service Act of 1948.

Nor did Black think that section 6(j)'s "exclusion of those persons with essentially political, sociological, or philosophical views, or a merely personal moral code, should be read to exclude those who hold strong beliefs about our domestic and foreign affairs or even those whose conscientious objection to participation in all wars is founded to a substantial extent upon considerations of public policy."[19] According to him, only two groups were excluded from the statutory exemption for conscientious objectors

16. *Welsh v. U.S.*, 398 U.S. 333 (1970).   17. *Welsh v. U.S.*, 335.
18. *Welsh v. U.S.*, 340.   19. *Welsh v. U.S.*, 342.

to war: namely, those whose beliefs are not deeply held and those whose beliefs rest solely on considerations of policy or expediency and not at all on moral or religious principles.

Justice Harlan concurred in the result, but not in Black's statutory construction.[20] He accepted the result in order to salvage congressional policy from what he conceived to be the constitutional infirmity of a religious establishment. Congress could not grant exemptions to theistic conscientious objectors and at the same time deny exemptions to nontheist conscientious objectors. And so Harlan chose to save the congressional policy of exemptions by extending them to nontheists by judicial fiat.

Justice White, joined by two other justices, dissented.[21] First, White argued that Welsh had no standing to object to granting exemption only to theists. Second, he found no violation of the establishment clause in the selective grant of exemptions, since Congress may have had in mind the purely practical consideration that religious conscientious objectors are unsuitable for military service. Third, Congress may have granted the exemptions to safeguard the freedom of religious exercise, just as some states grant exemptions from Sunday laws to Sabbatarian businessmen, and he saw no reason to strike down the statutory exemption for religious conscientious objectors "because it does not reach those to whom the free exercise clause offers no protection whatsoever."[22]

As a result of the Seeger and Welsh decisions, a question arises about the continuing validity of the statutory distinction between a belief involving recognition of duties superior to those arising from any human relations and one involving recognition of duties on the basis of essentially political, sociological, or philosophical views, or a merely personal code. How can moral judgments about war be divorced from human relations, political analysis, philosophical views, or personal moral codes? Apparently, the

---

20. *Welsh v. U.S.*, 344.   21. *Welsh v. U.S.*, 367.
22. *Welsh v. U.S.*, 374.

essence of the distinction after the two decisions is whether a claimant to classification as a conscientious objector recognizes a moral force or order that transcends him as an individual. Thus a conscientious objector to war will qualify for an exemption under the statute if his objection is grounded on considerations irreducible to personal whim or expediency.

Although there was no question of the sincerity of Seeger (and the other claimants) and Welsh, the decisions in their cases would admittedly complicate the administrative difficulties of determining the sincerity of later applicants for classification as conscientious objectors. Between 1966 and 1970, the number of men in the conscientious-objector classifications (1-O and 1-A-O) increased over 100 percent. A partial response to some of the difficulties may lie in the options for substitute service that are already authorized for those exempted from the obligation of military duty.

The relatively generous provisions of Selective Service regulations for pacifists, as interpreted and enlarged by the Court, had limitations. Pacifists were required to register with local draft boards, and those exempted from military duty were required to perform alternate civilian service. Several pacifists objected to the latter requirement on moral grounds and failed to report for assigned alternate civilian service. They were convicted for failing to do so, but the Supreme Court refused to review the convictions.[23]

Pacifists may object to combatant military service, to all service in the military, and even to various forms of cooperation or support of war (e.g., registration for the draft, alternate civilian service). The further an individual presses his conscientious objection to war beyond combat service, the more doubts may arise about the sincerity of the individual's representations. Assuming

---

23. *Holmes v. U.S.*, 391 U.S. 936 (1968); *Hart v. U.S.*, 391 U.S. 956 (1968); *Boardman v. U.S.*, 397 U.S. 991 (1970).

the individual's sincerity, however, only the individual can judge
how extensively the individual's moral principles apply. But, of
course, the further an individual presses the individual's conscientious objection to war in the matter of associated activities, the
more substantial may be the public interest opposed to the claim.

CONSCRIPTION AND SELECTIVE CONSCIENTIOUS OBJECTION TO WAR

The issue of exemptions for selective conscientious objectors to
war arose to a high level of popular discussion and legal adjudica-
tion during the controversial Vietnamese War. After a number
of futile efforts to secure Supreme Court review of the status of
conscientious objectors to the war,[24] the Court decided one case
(*Gillette v. U.S.*).[25] Guy Gillette, who based his objection to the
war on humanist rather than traditionally religious grounds, was
convicted of failing to report for induction at the end of 1967, and
a federal court of appeals affirmed the conviction.

On March 8, 1971, over the sole dissent of Justice Douglas,
the Court gave its long-awaited decision, ruling against Gillette.
The sweep of the Court opinion and the margin of the vote left
little room for doubt about the current constitutional status of
selective conscientious objectors to war. Justice Marshall, speaking for the majority, admitted by silence the petitioner's standing to challenge his induction on the basis of his conscientious
objection to service in Vietnam, but agreed with the circuit court
that the petitioner did not qualify for the statutory exemption as
a conscientious objector to participation in war in any form. Thus
the Court was confronted with the petitioner's constitutional
claim to exemption based on the religious guarantees of the First
Amendment.

24. *Mitchell v. U.S.*, 386 U.S. 972 (1967); *Spiro v. U.S.*, 390 U.S. 956 (1968); *U.S. v. Sisson*, 398 U.S. 267 (1970).
25. *Gillette v. U.S.*, 401 U.S. 437 (1971).

On the establishment issue, Marshall held that there were valid secular purposes for exempting pacifists, and so the exemptions did not favor pacifist religions. Such exemptions might reflect the congressional view that pacifists would make poor soldiers or a congressional concern for "the hard choice that conscription would impose on conscientious objectors to war as well as respect for the value of conscientious action and for the principle of supremacy of conscience."[26]

Marshall also found valid, religiously neutral reasons for limiting the exemptions to conscientious objectors to all wars. He cited the difficulty of distinguishing morally motivated from purely political objection to a particular war. (The government had argued that objection to a particular war is necessarily political—that is, that the judgment against a particular war must be based on the same factors that the government had considered and authoritatively evaluated when it decided to wage the war.) He claimed that the large number of variables involved (the purposes of the war, the legality of the war, the means employed in the war, the character of the foe, the character of the allies, the place of the war, and the destruction necessary to achieve the goals of the war) made moral judgment about a particular war uncertain. He cited the difficulty of determining sincerity, the advantages that might accrue to the more articulate, the better educated, the better counseled, and Catholics and others holding the just-war theory, as well as the danger of governmental involvement in determining a person's character, beliefs, and religious affiliation. Marshall also recognized the further risk to which the government's argument pointed—namely, that exemption for selective conscientious objectors might open the doors to a general principle of selective disobedience to law.

For these reasons, Marshall concluded that selective conscien-

26. *Gillette v. U.S.*, 453.

tious objectors to war are not unconstitutionally denied freedom of religious exercise by denial of exemption from military service. "The incidental burdens felt by persons in the petitioner's position are strictly justified by substantial governmental interests that relate directly to the very impacts questioned."[27] "More broadly," he added, almost in passing, "there is the government's interest in procuring the manpower for military purposes pursuant to the constitutional grant of power to Congress to raise and support armies."[28]

Justice Black concurred in the judgment of the Court, but only in the reasoning of the majority opinion restricting the statutory exemption to pacifists.[29] Justice Douglas was the only dissenter.[30] Stressing the moral plight of all conscientious objectors to war, he found the denial of exemption to selective conscientious objectors an invidious discrimination that violated the Fifth Amendment's guarantee of due process of law.

Marshall's analysis of the establishment clause issue and the exemption of pacifists was straightforward and conformed to previous Court decisions, especially *Schempp*. He argued well that the reasons Congress offered for denying exemption to selective conscientious objectors were substantial and did not show religious discrimination. Indeed, even Douglas did not base his dissent specifically on this issue.

But Marshall's analysis of the religious exercise issue was inadequate, since he did not consider whether the substantial governmental interests against a grant of exemptions were equivalent to the compelling public interests required by *Sherbert*. Nor did Justice Brennan, who was the author of the Sherbert decision, nor did Black, who had always insisted on evidence of the highest public interests to justify governmental restrictions on dissenters, nor did Douglas, who dissented. If the government is required

27. *Gillette v. U.S.*, 462.
29. *Gillette v. U.S.*, 463.
28. *Gillette v. U.S.*, 462.
30. *Gillette v. U.S.*, 463.

to show substantial or compelling public interests specifically against granting exemptions to selective conscientious objectors to war, then the government should likewise be required to demonstrate the inadequacy of civilian service as an alternative. Alternate civilian service, perhaps for a longer period of time than conscripted military service, might obviate administrative difficulties and discourage selective disobedience to law. Neither the government nor the Court considered this alternative.

Gillette lost decisively, the Court rating as substantial the public interests at stake against his claim to exemption. Selective conscientious objectors to war represent the highest claim of conscience—namely, an absolute duty not to do what the law commands, which involves participating in the killing of human beings. Despite the strength of these moral claims, the Court ruled against them because it rated high the opposing public interests. This illustrates the obvious principle that no claim of conscience, however high, is likely to be recognized as a constitutional right when judges rate high the public interests opposed to them.

Selective conscientious objectors to participation in the Vietnamese War failed to persuade the public and Congress that vindication of their claims to exemption was compatible with equitable administration of the draft system. Their exemption while others fought was politically unpalatable to the American public. Selective conscientious objectors may be more likely to have their claims to exemption from a future draft vindicated if an acceptable alternate service to the public, possibly for a longer period than military service under the draft, can be devised. The present system of a purely voluntary army has, at least for now, eliminated the question of exempting conscientious objectors from military service.

MILITARY PERSONNEL AND CONSCIENTIOUS OBJECTION

The armed services have permitted and currently do permit personnel to apply for discharge or noncombatant duty on the basis of their pacifist conscientious objection to war. But service personnel who would challenge decisions of military authorities, whether regarding the legality of the decisions or on the basis of conscientious objection to them, have no direct legal recourse in civilian courts. Military authorities derive their jurisdiction from Congress' broad power under Article 1, sec. 8, of the Constitution to make all laws "necessary and proper" for the "government and regulation of the land and naval forces" of the United States, and civilian courts have generally adhered to a policy of abstention in matters of military regulations. Nor have service personnel ever successfully gained a hearing for challenges to their disposition by the president as commander-in-chief. Nor have civilian courts directly reviewed the proceedings and decisions of military courts.

Civilian courts, however, have reviewed such proceedings and decisions collaterally by means of the writ of habeas corpus, in which cases the scope of inquiry is limited to questions of the jurisdiction of the military tribunal over the subject matter and person on trial and of the legal authority for the sentence imposed. Many servicemen attempted in civilian courts to challenge their assignment to Vietnam,[31] but only one obtained a full review on the merits.

The one conscientious objector to participation in the Vietnamese War in military service who gained a full review on the merits was Louis Negre. Negre would accept service elsewhere,

---

31. The Supreme Court denied certiorari in the following cases: *Levy v. Corcoran*, 387 U.S. 915 (1967); *Luftig v. McNamara*, 387 U.S. 945 (1967); *Noyd v. McNamara*, 395 U.S. 683 (1969).

but objected to any duty in Vietnam. He was inducted into the Army in 1967 and ordered to Vietnam in 1968. He then sought discharge from the Army as a conscientious objector, but was judged not to qualify, principally because his objection did not extend to all war. After exhausting his administrative military remedies, he petitioned for a writ of habeas corpus in a federal district court. The district court denied his petition, and the court of appeals for the ninth circuit affirmed. The Supreme Court granted certiorari along with the Gillette case.

The Gillette and Negre cases were decided in the same opinion, and the decision in the latter case was the same as in the former case. A majority of eight justices voted against Negre over the sole dissent of Justice Douglas (*Negre v. Larsen*).[32]

Negre's military status played no prominent part in the Court opinion, since, if Gillette, a civilian, had no constitutional right as a conscientious objector to exemption from the draft, then a fortiori a military subject like Negre had no constitutional right to refuse assignments as a conscientious objector. In fact, Negre was no longer on active duty at the time of the decision, as he had been discharged under honorable conditions.[33]

Many military personnel who were conscientious objectors to participation in the Vietnamese War never received a hearing before the Court on the merits of their legal and moral objections to service in Vietnam. Negre did receive a hearing but, like Gillette, lost decisively. The moral claims of military personnel against service in conflicts they deem immoral are as high as those of selective conscientious objectors who refuse induction into the armed forces during the conflict they deem immoral. But the public interests opposed to recognition of the former claims, because of the demands of military discipline, are even higher than the public interests opposed to recognition of the latter claims.

32. *Negre v. Larsen*, 401 U.S. 437 (1971).
33. *Negre v. Larsen*, 440, n. 2.

9

REGULATION OF
RELIGIOUS ORGANIZATIONS
AND PERSONNEL

꙰

The First Amendment guarantees the free exercise of religion. There is no doubt that the free exercise clause absolutely protects freedom of religious belief and the freedom to adhere to any religious organization an individual may choose, but the freedom to act in accord with one's religious beliefs is not absolutely guaranteed. Important secular public interests may run counter to religiously motivated activities. Organizations' religious practices in soliciting funds, liability for taxes, conditions of employment, and methods of recruiting and retaining members are the main areas where religious practice may trigger government regulation.

SOLICITATION OF FUNDS

In soliciting funds, individuals and groups may falsely represent themselves to the public. Governments not only prosecute fraud when it occurs, but also try to prevent it from happening in the first place. In *Cantwell v. Connecticut*,[1] three Jehovah's Wit-

1. *Cantwell v. Connecticut*, 310 U.S. 296 (1940).

nesses were convicted of violating a Connecticut statute that required solicitors of money for religious causes be certified by a local welfare official. The Supreme Court in 1940 unanimously overturned the convictions, holding the statute an unconstitutional abridgment of the defendants' rights to religious exercise. Specifically, the Court held that the statute was a prior and prohibited restraint upon the exercise of religion because the statute empowered a public official to decide whether a solicitor's cause was religious. The Court noted, however, that the state might subsequently punish any fraudulent solicitation of funds under religious pretenses.

Four years later, in 1944, the Court reviewed another case involving a conflict between individuals claiming a right to freedom of religious exercise and the public's interest in preventing fraud (*U.S. v. Ballard*).[2] Donald and Edna Ballard were convicted of using the mails to solicit funds by false and fraudulent representations of their religious beliefs. The defendants were accused of falsely representing that they had been selected as divine messengers, that they had the power to heal and cure diseases the medical profession considered incurable, and that they had in fact cured hundreds of afflicted persons. The indictment charged that the defendants knew these claims to be false, and that the defendants made these claims with the intention of cheating and defrauding the public.

The defendants sought at the trial to establish the truth of their religious beliefs as a defense, but the trial judge restricted the Ballards' defense to their good faith in the matter of the beliefs. When the case went to the jury, the judges instructed the jury not to consider the truth or falsity of the defendant's claims of supernatural powers, but only whether the defendants believed their claims to be true. The jury found the defendants guilty of

2. *U.S. v. Ballard*, 322 U.S. 78 (1944).

fraud. The Ballards appealed, and the Court of Appeals reversed the convictions and ordered a new trial, holding that they were entitled to submit to the consideration of the jury a defense based on the asserted truth of their religious beliefs.

The Supreme Court divided three ways. Justice Douglas, speaking for five justices, held that the trial court correctly excluded the question of the truth or falsity of the defendants' religious beliefs, but remanded the case to the court of appeals to review other issues. According to Douglas, "heresy trials are foreign to our Constitution," and human beings "may not be put to the proof of their religious doctrines or beliefs."[3] Thus religious beliefs may not be submitted to a jury charged with determining their truth or falsity.

Chief Justice Stone, joined by two justices, dissented. Stone argued that some counts in the indictment had charged the Ballards with fraudulent procurement of money by knowingly making false statements about their religious experiences, and that these counts were susceptible of negative proof. If one asserted that one had had a religious experience in San Francisco on a certain day, Stone thought that it should be open to the government to submit to the jury proof that such a one had never been there. Or if one asserted that one had in fact cured hundreds of persons by the use of spiritual powers, the government should be able to submit evidence that no such cures had ever taken place. But Stone's main argument was that the case went to the jury on the single issue of whether the Ballards believed that the religious experiences they claimed had in fact occurred, and the jury had found against them. Since "the state of one's mind is a fact as capable of fraudulent misrepresentation as is one's physical condition or the state of one's bodily health," Stone argued that none of the defendants' constitutional rights had been violated.[4]

3. *U.S. v. Ballard*, 86.
4. *U.S. v. Ballard*, 90.

They were prosecuted for the fraudulent procurement of money "by false representation as to their beliefs, religious or otherwise," and so the jury's judgment of guilty should be simply reinstated.[5]

Justice Jackson, the other dissenting member of the Court, would have dismissed the indictment altogether and "have done with this business of judicially examining other people's faith."[6] Thus Jackson would not have allowed the jury to consider even the issue of the defendants' good faith. But he would not bar the government from prosecuting religious leaders for fraud if they made false representations about matters other than their religious beliefs or experience—for example, if they represented that funds were solicited to construct a church when they were in fact converted to personal use.

Jackson made four points to support his position. First, religious insincerity cannot be dissociated from religious truth, since what a person believes depends on what the person considers believable. Second, any inquiry into the intellectual honesty of religious beliefs by unbelievers would be biased. Third, religious belief implies the possibility of doubt, and government is not competent to determine what degree of skepticism or disbelief in religious representations amounts to actionable fraud. Fourth, members of a religious sect get what they pay for, and any wrong they suffer relates not to the money they part with so much as the mental poison they may get, "precisely the thing the Constitution put beyond the reach of the prosecutor."[7]

Another case in California involved an allegation of fraud similar to that in *Ballard*. David Supple left a substantial portion of his estate to various Catholic charities, which bequests a grandnephew contested on the ground that the will had been obtained by fraud and undue influence. The allegation was that the Catholic Church promised to shorten the period of purga-

---

5. *U.S. v. Ballard*, 90. 6. *U.S. v. Ballard*, 95.
7. *U.S. v. Ballard*, 95.

tion that the testator and deceased relatives would otherwise be obliged to undergo after death to expiate their sins in exchange for the performance of certain good works, which included gifts to the church and affiliated agencies. The grandnephew further alleged that this representation was false.

The California court of appeals affirmed the decision of a lower court admitting the will to probate (*In re Supple's Estate*).[8] Following the majority in the Ballard case, the appellate court held that California would not allow inquiry into the truth or falsity of religious beliefs and pointed out that no allegation had been made that the Catholic clergymen did not actually believe the teaching attributed to them—that is, there was no allegation of bad faith. The latter point raises the interesting prospect that, had such an allegation been made, the Catholic beneficiaries would have had to argue the sincerity of their beliefs in a court of law if they wanted to receive the bequests.

The criminal prosecution of the Ballards and the contested will of Supple illustrate the difficulty of adjudicating claims of fraud in the solicitation of funds by purportedly religious organizations. In the light of the constitutional guarantee of freedom of religious exercise, Justice Jackson's solution is administratively the simplest and politically the wisest: a rule of caveat emptor between buyers and sellers of religious doctrines. As Jackson pointed out, it is difficult to distinguish between religious sincerity and religious truth, and the main loss to consumers deceived by religious frauds is psychological rather than financial. The issue is more complicated when the interest of a third party is at stake, as when Supple's grandnephew was effectively disinherited by the alleged fraud influencing Supple's testamentary dispositions. But even in that case, the grandnephew had no vested right to inherit, and the issue of fraud was essentially one of buyer and seller between Supple and the religious organizations he chose to benefit.

8. *In re Supple's Estate*, 55 Cal. Rptr. 542 (1966).

Local governments may also wish, for reasons of safety and convenience, to limit the places and times of religious groups selling literature and soliciting funds. For example, a Minnesota state fair restricted the distribution and sale of religious literature, along with fundraising, to assigned booths. The Hare Krishna sect objected to the restrictions because they suppressed proselytizing activities that it claimed to be religiously obligatory. In *Heffron v. International Society*,[9] the Court unanimously ruled in 1981 that the state could, for the safety and convenience of the public, limit the opportunity of religious sects to sell literature and solicit funds. But the Court divided five to four on the constitutionality of restricting the sect to booths to distribute literature without monetary recompense or contributions. The majority thought that the safety and convenience of the public justified restricting even the free distribution of literature to booths. The minority disagreed, arguing that potential danger and inconvenience to the public did not justify the sweep of the restriction.

One method whereby local governments attempt to prevent fraud in the solicitation of funds is to require reports on the funds' distribution. In *Larson v. Valente*,[10] the Court reviewed a Minnesota statute that required certain religious organizations to register with the state as charitable organizations and to report in detail their distribution of contributed funds. Minnesota required only religious organizations that received 50 or more percent of their funds from nonmembers to register and file a report on their distribution of the funds collected. The state notified the Unification Church, popularly known as the Moonies, that the church was required to register as a charitable organization and report its distribution of contributed funds. The church then asked a federal district court to declare the Minnesota statute unconstitutional and to enjoin the law's enforcement against the church.

9. *Heffron v. International Society*, 452 U.S. 640 (1981).
10. *Larson v. Valente*, 456 U.S. 228 (1982).

Justice Brennan, speaking for five justices, ruled that the Minnesota statute impermissibly preferred some religions over others, specifically older, well-established religions over newer, less structured ones. Against Minnesota's defense of the statute as a reasonable method to prevent fraud, Brennan made three points. First, there was no evidence that members supervised distribution of the funds of religious organizations more effectively than nonmembers did. Second, there was no greater incentive for members to control religious organizations' distribution of funds where members contribute more of the funds than nonmembers do. Third, there was no evidence that a rising proportion of contributions by nonmembers increased the need for state supervision. Although Brennan might have concluded from his analysis that the Minnesota statute had a primary effect of advancing some religions and inhibiting others, and thereby failed the second prong of the Schempp-Lemon test, he chose to rest the decision on the third prong of that test, which prohibits excessive entanglement between religion and government. In addition, the 50 percent rule regulating some but not other religious organizations' solicitation of funds, in his view, impermissibly fomented political factionalism along religious lines.

Two justices, White and Rehnquist, dissented on the merits. (They and two other justices, Burger and O'Connor, dissented on the threshold question regarding the Unification Church's standing to object to the 50 percent rule before it was established that the church was a religious organization.) White made four points. First, the 50 percent rule did not manifestly distinguish among religions on the basis of their institutional characteristics. Second, the consequences of the rule for well-established as opposed to less structured religions were conjectural. Third, it was reasonable to fear fraud more when outsiders contributed funds than when insiders contributed them. Fourth, there was more secular reason to distinguish religious organizations on the basis of the relative contributions by members and nonmembers than to exempt all religious organizations from requirements imposed on other charitable organizations.

White argued more realistically on the substantive issue than Brennan. The Minnesota statute plausibly assumed fraud to be more likely when religious organizations collect funds from outsiders than when they collect funds from insiders. Outsiders contribute only once or occasionally, while members contribute regularly. If church administrators are responsible to members, members supervise the distribution of funds, and if church administrators are not responsible to members, members can address their complaints to higher authorities or discontinue contributions. But nonmembers have no such potential impact on the distribution of funds by religious organizations.

The majority, with reason, perceived the 50 percent rule as one aimed at religions like the Unification Church. But the rule, on its face, supervised only the distribution of funds, not their solicitation. The Minnesota legislators, whatever their hostility to the doctrines or practices of the Unification Church, acted to protect contributing nonmembers from potential fraud. The legislature identified one area of potential fraud, deemed it more needful of regulation than other areas, and fashioned the 50 percent rule to define the religious organizations to be regulated.

Brennan took note that the legislators explicitly drafted the 50 percent rule so as to include the Unification Church and to exclude the hierarchically organized Catholic Church. This result, according to him, constituted politicization of religion in the matter of preventing fraudulent solicitation of funds. But there may be solid, nonpolitical reasons for the legislative decision not to supervise the distribution of funds contributed to hierarchically organized churches like the Catholic Church. As indicated previously, dissatisfied member contributors to hierarchically organized churches can complain to higher authorities or cease to contribute. Moreover, there is no evidence of widespread fraud, present or past, on the part of administrators of the Catholic Church or other hierarchically organized churches, which have their own internal auditing systems. One might also ask how any legislative decision on regulating funds contributed to religious organizations could avoid political consequences. If the funds contributed to hierarchically organized religions but not to religions otherwise organized are supervised, then members of the regulated religions may be politically disaffected. If the funds contributed to all religions are supervised, then members of every church may be disaffected. And if the funds of no religion are supervised, then the unaffiliated and agnostics may be politically disaffected.

In *Maryland v. Munson*,[11] the Court ruled that states may not impose limits on the amount of money charities spend on fundraising. Maryland had set a limit of 25 percent of charities' gross income for fundraising, and about half the states have similar laws. Maryland had a waiver provision for charities that could demonstrate the reasonableness of higher solicitation costs. The law applied to all charities, including those of religious organizations. Justice Blackmun, joined by four other justices, thought the limits on fundraising costs were a direct restriction on free speech, and that the goal of preventing fraud did not justify the limits. In his view, high fundraising costs are not an accurate index of fraud. Nor was he satisfied with the waiver provision, which he regarded as a licensing control over the dissemination of ideas. Four justices dissented. In their view, the Maryland law was merely an economic regulation. The decision leaves open the possibility that states may in the public interest require disclosure of fundraising costs to potential donors or state governments.

11. *Maryland v. Munson*, 467 U.S. 947 (1984).

TAX LIABILITY

Claims to tax-exempt status as religious organizations have not gone unchallenged by the Internal Revenue Service. A leading case involved Dr. Merle E. Parker and the Foundation of Divine Meditation that he sponsored and directed. In addition to conducting religious services and sponsoring recreational activities, Parker published tracts and a newspaper, the *National Christian Crusader,* which promoted the other publications. Some of his publications promised the readers financial profit if they invested in such projects as growing Ysabel Ming trees and raising earthworms. Parker and the foundation did a thriving business, grossing $207,000 one year and $290,000 another. In the light of these and other facts, the U.S. court of appeals held that the foundation was engaged in activities that were substantially not tax-exempt (*Parker v. Commissioner*).[12] The court of appeals admitted that religious organizations need not lose their tax-exempt status simply because they offered literature for sale, and that the worship services and associated recreational activities were religious. Nonetheless, the court of appeals ruled that Parker's organization evidenced substantial nonreligious purposes by the breadth and scope of its profit-making activities, its method of promotion, the generally nonreligious subject matter of some publications, its large annual earnings, its substantial accumulation of assets, and Dr. Parker's own statements.

Although the Internal Revenue Service alleged no fraud by Dr. Parker or the foundation, it did challenge the foundation's right to tax-exempt status as a religious organization—that is, the religious character of many foundation activities. Such challenges are inevitable, and the courts have to rule on them on an individual case-by-case basis. In the Parker case, the court of appeals

12. *Parker v. Commissioner,* 365 F.2d. 813 (1964).

made volume of commercial activity the measure of ineligibility for tax-exempt status. That criterion harmonizes with the purpose of the statutory exemption and involves no determination of the truth or falsity of religious beliefs.

The Supreme Court ruled unanimously in 1981 that church-run schools—that is, schools without a corporate identity separate from that of a church—are not obliged to pay federal unemployment compensation taxes on their employees (*St. Martin's Evangelical Lutheran Church v. South Dakota*).[13] The Court reached the result entirely on statutory grounds without deciding whether the religious clauses of the First Amendment would permit Congress to impose taxes on church-run schools. If, as I think, the secular and religious functions of church-run schools can be separately identified, then there is no reason the government may not impose taxes related to secular employment (e.g., teachers of secular subjects, administrative staff, janitors).

In 1982 the Court ruled unanimously that Amish employers were not entitled to a constitutional exemption from the legal duty to pay employers' Social Security taxes and to withhold employees' Social Security taxes for their Amish employees (*U.S. v. Lee*).[14] The Amish believe that they have a religious duty to provide for their relatives (cf. 1 Tim. 5:8), and Lee, an Amish employer, had not paid unemployment compensation and Social Security taxes on his Amish employees for several years. In 1978 the I.R.S. sought payment of $27,000 in back taxes from Lee. Lee paid $91 for the first quarter of 1973 under protest and sued for a refund of the tax and an injunction against past and future taxes.

All the justices accepted that Lee's objection to paying the taxes was one based on religious conviction. Chief Justice Burger, joined by the other justices except Stevens, likewise accepted the

---

13. *St. Martin's Evangelical Lutheran Church v. South Dakota,* 101 S.Ct. 2142 (1981).

14. *U.S. v. Lee,* 102 S.Ct. 1051 (1982).

proposition that only an overriding governmental interest could constitutionally justify restricting the freedom of religious exercise claimed by Lee. But Burger held that the government had such an overriding interest in restricting Lee's religious exercise because there is no principled way to distinguish Amish claims to exemption from Social Security taxes from religiously based claims to exemption from other taxes, such as taxes to support the armed forces.

Justice Stevens rejected the overriding governmental interest standard that Burger applied to the cases. He would not require exemption of religious objectors to valid laws of general applicability if the government fails to demonstrate substantial adverse interests, but would rather place the burden on religious objectors to show unique reasons for exemption. According to him, the government could easily exempt the Amish from Social Security taxes, since the government would gain as much from benefits not paid out under the programs as it would lose from the taxes not paid into the programs. In the view of the difficulty of processing religious objections to other taxes, however, Stevens found it minimally rational for the government to deny Amish employers' claims to exemption from Social Security taxes.

The Amish unquestionably believe as a matter of religious conviction that they should provide for relatives in need, but the Court seems to have accepted without examination the further representation of Lee's lawyers that Amish belief extended to nonpayment of Social Security taxes. The Court might have inquired further into the nature of the Amish objection to the taxes. Did the Amish object to paying the taxes as immoral on their part or as unjust on the part of the government? The question is not purely speculative, since Lee *did* pay the tax for the first quarter of 1973, albeit under protest. Independently of the fact that Lee paid part of the Social Security taxes levied by the government, however, it is by no means self-evident how Lee or any religious objector could sincerely believe that *compulsory* payment of taxes, however unjust on the part of the government, would constitute an immoral act on the part of the objector. Moreover, compulsory payment of the taxes would leave Lee and his Amish employees legally free, if less financially able, both to reject Social Security benefits and to provide for needy relatives.

REGULATION OF EMPLOYMENT

In a major decision affecting church-related schools, the Court in 1979 ruled that the National Labor Relations Board had no statutory jurisdiction over the union organization of lay teachers in the parochial schools of two Catholic dioceses (*National Labor Relations Board v. Catholic Bishop of Chicago*).[15] The NLRB had argued that schools religiously associated but not completely religious were subject to its jurisdiction. Chief Justice Burger, joined by four justices, however, in order to avoid the constitutional issue of possibly impermissible entanglement of church and state, interpreted an absence of specific inclusion of church-related schools in the coverage of the National Labor Relations Act to mean that Congress intended to exclude them. Justice Brennan, joined by three justices, objected to both Burger's method of statutory construction and his conclusion about Congress' intent.

Burger's statutory analysis was disingenuous, to say the least, for an avowed strict constructionist. Why should not Congress be presumed to intend general language to apply to all areas of labor relations not specifically excluded? Moreover, as Brennan pointed out, the Senate in 1947 specifically rejected an exclusion of religious organizations other than hospitals from coverage of the Taft-Hartley Act. Had the Court ruled that Congress intended to include church-related schools in the jurisdiction of the NLRB, one may wonder what the Court would have done

15. *National Labor Relations Board v. Catholic Bishop of Chicago*, 99 S. Ct. 1313 (1979).

with the constitutional question. For my part, I think that governmental regulation of labor relations regarding lay teachers in church-related schools is a secular matter that can be separately identified. And if secular and religious functions can be separately identified in the matter of government regulation of church-related schools, why can't those different functions be separately identified in the matter of government aid to such schools?

As already indicated in chapter 6, the Supreme Court in 1987 held that the exemption of religious organizations from the prohibition of religious discrimination by employers under Title VII of the Civil Rights Act of 1964 is compatible with the religious establishment clause.[16] As also indicated in chapter 6, the Supreme Court in 2012 held that the establishment clause prohibits the government from appointing ministers and that the free-exercise clause prohibits it from interfering with religious groups' freedom to select them.[17]

METHODS OF RECRUITING AND
RETAINING MEMBERS

Some newer religious sects may rely on emotional appeal to win members and an emotional environment to retain them. Competent adults, of course, have a constitutional right to join any religious sect they choose. But legal questions arise about the rights of minors to adhere to religious sects, or cults, against their parents' or guardians' wishes, and the competency of individuals, especially youths, to make a rational and free choice in the emotional atmosphere of religious communes.

Young people may be the focus of cult recruitment, and parents and guardians may disapprove of the commitments that cults demand from offspring and wards. While parents and guardians

16. *Corporation v. Amos,* 107 S.Ct. 2862 (1987).
17. *Hosanna-Tabor Evangelical Lutheran Church v. Equal Employment Opportunity Commission* 132 S. Ct. 694 (2012).

generally have legal authority—and also legal responsibility—to decide what is in the best interest for the welfare of their off-spring and wards, post-Roe decisions have upheld the right of minors demonstrating sufficient maturity to elect to have abortions against the wishes of their parents.[18] These decisions rest on the theory that mature minors have a constitutional right to abortions. That line of reasoning suggests that mature minors have a constitutional right to join religious cults and communes.

Parents frequently claim that their offspring who have joined religious cults and communes have been "brainwashed" to act against their best interests. But parents have no legal authority or responsibility for youths over eighteen years of age. Young adults will be presumed to be mature enough to make decisions in their own best interests, and so, in the event of legal action by relatives, courts will inquire only into the question of the competency of young adults to make a rational and free decision to join a religious cult or commune.

Thus the legal obstacles to parents obtaining custody of their children living in religious communes are formidable. This is why parents in this situation often turn to professional "deprogrammers" to abduct their children, whether minors or young adults, from those communes. Such abductions of young adults, absent exigent circumstances, are illegal for the simple reason that all civilized societies restrict the legitimate use of force to the government. Admittedly, parents may be caught between a rock and a hard place. If they go to court, they are likely to lose the case, and if they hire "deprogrammers," they act illegally.

Where cults use physical force to retain the adherence of members, the legal situation is different. Courts can order an end to individuals' detention against their will, prosecutors can prose-

---

18. *Planned Parenthood Association v. Danforth*, 428 U.S. 52 (1976); *Bellotti v. Baird*, 442 U.S. 622 (1979); *H. L. v. Matheson*, 450 U.S. 398 (1981).

cute cult leaders for the offense, and private parties may use force in sufficiently exigent circumstances to rescue those detained against their wishes.

In other situations, the legal remedies available to anxious parents are quite limited, but that is the price society pays for the premium it puts on individual freedom.

10

WESTERN TRADITIONS
OF CONSCIENCE

The purpose of this chapter is twofold: to survey the history of the term *conscience* in Western thought and to indicate prominent theories on the rights and duties of conscience in relation to political authority. No culture without some idea of moral conscience has yet been discovered. Primitive societies did not speak of conscience, but they did appeal to the heart and loins to distinguish morally good from morally bad behavior. From the perspective of Western civilization, the Bible and Paul of Tarsus were important influences on the history of conscience.

THE HEBREW BIBLE

In the first book of the Hebrew Bible, the writer described how "the man and his wife hid themselves from the presence of the Lord God among the trees of the garden" after they had eaten the forbidden fruit (Gen. 3:8).[1] Thus the writer of Genesis attributed to Adam and Eve a sense of moral guilt subsequent to their act of disobedience. Although worship of God and upright

---

1. The scriptural citations are from the Revised Standard Version.

action were more associated in the early history of the Jewish people with the observance of ritual than with interior dispositions, a profound change was introduced into the religious and moral life of the people under the influence of the prophets. Jeremiah, for example, spoke of God as a searcher of mind and heart who judges human beings' actions as good or bad at the very moment of their performance (Jer. 11:20). The prophets did not challenge the claims of the Mosaic Law, but insisted on the primacy of interior dispositions in its observance.

But the efforts of the prophets were not generally crowned with success, and at the time of Jesus, the Jewish religion, at least as represented in the Gospels by the Pharisees, was still more absorbed with the performance of external actions than with internal dispositions in the achievement of religious and moral virtue. In the Sermon on the Mount, Jesus echoed the prophets and called blessed the pure in heart (Mt. 5:8). Thus, like the prophets, Jesus stressed the primacy of interior dispositions over external actions.

The word *conscience* appears only once in the Hebrew Bible, in which the Book of Wisdom, adopting Semitic thought to the Greek language and categories, declares that "wickedness … is condemned by its own testimony," and that "distressed by conscience, it has always exaggerated the difficulties" (Wis. 17:11). In this way the writer of Wisdom used the word *conscience* in the sense of moral, as distinguished from psychological, consciousness, but only to describe the consciousness of guilt subsequent to a human being's morally bad action.

In the context of the Israelite theocracy, there was no doubt about the general religious duty of citizens to obey God's anointed. Even in the case of the kings of the northern kingdom, all of whom the writers of the Hebrew Bible condemned for rebelling against David's descendants, subjects were not to claim a general right or duty to disobey their rulers. Moreover, although the prophets indicted both kings of the North and kings of the South for their infidelities to Yahweh, they threatened the kings with retribution by him rather than revolution by their subjects. But Israelites were obliged to obey Yahweh's commands when his commands conflicted with those of the kings, absolutely regarding the prohibition against the worship of idols, and as circumstances permitted regarding the positive prescriptions of the Mosaic Law.

THE NEW TESTAMENT AND PAUL

The Greek word for conscience, *syneidesis,* appears nowhere in the Gospels. Paul used the word infrequently, but it does appear twenty times in the letters attributed to him and ten times elsewhere in the New Testament. (Paul probably adopted the term from contemporary Stoic philosophy.) According to him, conscience fulfills in pagans the purpose that the Mosaic Law serves for Jews, since "what the Law requires is written in their hearts, while their conscience also bears witness, and their conflicting thoughts accuse or perhaps excuse them when ... God judges the secrets of men by Christ Jesus" (Rom. 2:15–16). But conscience also pertains to Christians: "The aim of our charge is love that issues from a pure heart and a good conscience and sincere faith" (1 Tim. 1:5.). Indeed, Paul urged Christians to obey secular governing authorities "not only to avoid God's wrath but also for the sake of conscience"—that is, as a matter of moral principle (Rom. 13:5). He appealed to his own good conscience in preaching the gospel: "I am speaking the truth in Christ, I am not lying; my conscience bears me witness in the Holy Spirit" (Rom. 9:1). He also claimed a good conscience regarding his past preaching: "I have lived before God in all good conscience up to this day" (Acts 23:10), and "our boast is this, the testimony of our conscience that we have behaved in the world and still more toward you with holiness and godly sincerity" (Rom. 14:14).

Of the twenty references to conscience in the letters attributed to Paul, eight appear in the First Letter to the Corinthians in connection with the controversy over eating meat that had been used in pagan sacrifice. There and in Romans, Paul indicated clearly his view that even an incorrect conscience is morally binding for the individual. He considered it no sin for Christians to eat such meat, but he recognized the moral obligation of scrupulous members of the Roman and Corinthian communities not to do so. "I know and am fully persuaded that nothing is unclean in itself, but it is unclean for anyone who thinks it unclean" (Rom. 14:14). He therefore cautioned other members of those communities to respect the consciences of their scrupulous brethren to the extent of not eating such meat themselves. "If anyone sees you ... at table in an idol's temple, might he not be encouraged, if his conscience is weak, to eat meat offered to idols? ... Thus, sinning against your brethren and weakening their conscience when they are weak, you sin against Christ" (1 Cor. 8:10, 12).

Many of Paul's uses of the word *conscience* seem to have been limited to negative, legal, and rule-oriented contexts (thou shalt not). But his central theme of the supremacy of a living faith over external works indicates that his moral doctrine was broader than those citations of conscience (e.g., Rom. 4). There are in the New Testament, as in the Old, two strands in the biblical traditions of morality: one negative, legal, and rule-oriented; the other positive, prophetic, and oriented toward the realization of ideals of justice and love. At any rate, Paul's writings were probably more influential than any other source in the popularization of the concept of conscience in the Western world.

The Israelites never accepted the legitimacy of foreign rulers or the corresponding obligation to obey them, whatever accommodations the Israelites had to accept in those circumstances. Because the religious aspirations of the New Testament were ethnically and territorially universal, however, Jesus urged obedience to Caesar—except for "things that belong to God" (Mt. 22:21; cf. Rom. 13:1–7). The spread of Christianity, the hierarchical structure of the church, and the power of the papacy were to make that exception almost the rule.

THE GREEKS AND ROMANS

In the ancient Greek world, Democritus of Abdera used the word *conscience* (*synderesis*) in the sense of moral, as opposed to psychological, consciousness.[2] Later, when Greek ethical thought probed the relation of nature (*physis*) to law (*nomos*), Socrates appealed to a divine monitor (*daimonion*) to justify his actions:[3] "I am subject to a divine or supernatural experience [*theion kai daimonion*] ... a sort of voice that comes to me." Moreover, "when it comes, it always dissuades me from what I am proposing to do and never urges me on."[4] But elsewhere Socrates refers to a positive moral mandate communicated to him in a recurring dream:[5] "In the course of my life, I have often had the same dream, appearing in different forms at different times but always saying the same thing: 'Socrates, practice and cultivate the arts.'" Without appeal to mythical language or mystical experience, Aristotle stated summarily the Socratic position on the centrality of reason in moral action:[6] "Practical wisdom [*phronesis*] issues commands; its end is to tell us what we ought to do and what we ought not to do."

While Socrates was convinced of the wrongfulness of the Athenian law court's sentence of death against him for following his voice, he refused to escape the penalty. In an ingenious dialogue with the laws before his death,[7] he argued that a refusal to accept the penalty of the court would undermine the rule of law

---

2. Hermann Diels, *Die Fragmente der Vorsocatiker*, ed. Walter Kranz, 10th ed. (Berlin: Weidmann, 1960), 2:206–7.

3. Plato, *Apology* 31C, D.   4. Plato, *Apology* 31C, D.

5. Plato, *Phaedo* 60E.

6. Aristotle, *Nicomachean Ethics* 1143a.

7. Plato, *Crito* 50A–54B.

and the political community itself. Second, legal regulation of marriage and education conferred the benefits of life and human fulfillment on citizens and made them contractually responsible to obey the laws, even when disagreeable. Third, Socrates himself had ratified the contract by choosing to live in Athens when he was free to leave. Fourth, his fellow citizens, not the laws, had done the wrong to him. Socrates' arguments were historically conditioned by the identification of society with the city-state, the *polis,* and the city-state with its laws, but they were echoed in the controversies surrounding civil disobedience in this country. Martin Luther King, for example, proclaimed his willingness to accept the penalty for his disobedience of existing laws, but his opponents rejoined that civil disobedience itself, in pursuit of whatever ideals, is a violation of law and threatens the foundations of organized society.

Neither Plato nor Aristotle used the word *conscience,* but philosophers influenced by Stoicism did. Cicero, for example, wrote that "the moral consciousness [*conscientia*] of living well and the record of many deeds done well is most pleasing,"[8] and Seneca expressed the idea of conscience as "a sacred spirit in man," which is "an observer and guardian of good and evil in us."[9]

But the Roman interpreters of Stoic philosophy modified the Greek idea of moral judgment in one important respect. More legally oriented than the Greeks, the Roman Stoics identified reason with natural law and moral consciousness with legal obligation. Medieval theologians adopted this concept of conscience as law in the theocentric context of a divine legislator.

THOMAS AQUINAS

One of the most developed theories of conscience is that of Thomas Aquinas. In the first part of his *Summa Theologica,* in the treatise on human beings and the section on human beings'

8. Cicero, *De Senectute* 3:9.   9. Seneca, *Epistulae* 41, 1.

intellectual powers, Aquinas spoke of *synderesis* and conscience. He claimed that *synderesis* is a disposition (*habitus*) of the soul, not a special power. "Human reasoning, since it is a movement, progresses from an understanding of some things, namely, things known by nature without inquiry by reason, as from a fixed source. And human reasoning also terminates in understanding, since it is by naturally self-evident principles that we judge about those things that we discovered in the process of reasoning."[10] From this analysis, Aquinas says that *syndereis* "incites to good and complains about evil."[11]

In the article following the one on *synderesis*, Aquinas argued that conscience is not a power, but rather an act, a judgment of practical reason regarding a particular action.[12] He appealed to the proper meaning of the word *conscience* as signifying the relation of knowledge to something else (*cum alio scientia*) and indicated that "acts connect knowledge to something else."[13] According to Aquinas, this relation of knowledge to action occurs in three ways. First, it occurs insofar as we recognize that we have or have not done something, and conscience is accordingly said to witness. Second, it occurs insofar as we judge through conscience that something should or should not be done, and conscience is accordingly said to judge. Third, it occurs insofar as we acknowledge that something has been done well or ill, and conscience is accordingly said to approve or accuse. Since a disposition (*habitus*) is the source of the act, however, Aquinas admitted that the word *conscience* is sometimes applied to the disposition for first principles of practical reason, *synderesis*, rather than to the act of judgment itself.

10. Thomas Aquinas, *ST* I, Q. 79, A. 12; the translation is from Aquinas, *On Law, Morality, and Politics*, ed. William P. Baumgarth and Richard J. Regan (Indianapolis: Hackett, 2002), 2.

11. *ST* I, Q. 79, A. 12

12. *ST* I, Q. 79, A. 13.

13. *ST* I, Q. 79, A. 13, from *On Law, Morality, and Politics*, 4.

The relation of knowledge to action in the first way described by Aquinas would seem to have identified conscience with psychological consciousness, reflecting the root meaning of the Latin word (*con-scientia*) and the Greek equivalent (*syn-eidesis*). The second way, though called judicial by Aquinas, perhaps better deserves to be called legislative, since he regarded this function of conscience as morally authoritative for, and legally binding on, the individual. The third way, in which knowledge is applied to past action, perhaps better deserves to be called judicial. In any case, it is the second way with which Aquinas was principally concerned in his treatment of conscience.

When Aquinas dealt in the first part of the second part of the *Summa Theologica* with the qualities of specifically human acts—that is, acts involving reason and the will—he asked whether the will is evil when it acts contrary to an erroneous judgment of reason.[14] If conscience erroneously judges that the one is obliged to do something in itself morally wrong (e.g., polygamy), one is morally obliged to do it. If conscience erroneously judges that one is obliged not to do something in itself morally good (e.g., drink a little wine at dinner), one is morally obliged not to do it. And if conscience erroneously judges that one should or should not do something in itself morally indifferent (e.g., go for a walk), one is morally obliged to do or not to do it. "Without qualification, every will that wills contrary to reason, whether reason be correct or erroneous, is always evil."[15]

In the next article Aquinas asked whether the will is good when it wills in accord with an erroneous reason—that is, whether an erroneous reason excuses persons.[16] The answer, according to Aquinas, depends on whether the ignorance is voluntary. "The ignorance that causes things to be involuntary takes away

14. *ST* I-II, Q. 19, A. 5.
15. *ST* I-II, Q. 19, A. 5, from *On Law, Morality, and Politics*, 7.
16. *ST* I-II, Q. 19, A. 6.

the character of moral good and evil," but "ignorance that is in any way voluntary, whether directly or indirectly does not cause things to be involuntary."[17] (One wills ignorance directly by willing not to know, and one wills ignorance indirectly by negligence.) Invincible ignorance of circumstantial facts excuses the will of one who acts in accord with erroneous conscience. But ignorance of God's law, the natural and also the divine law of the New Testament in the case of Christians, does not excuse the will of one who acts in accord with erroneous reason.

The natural law is God's plan for human beings as communicated to them by human reason.[18] The first principle of the natural law is that human beings should seek what is good for them as such and avoid what is evil for them as such, and that principle is innately self-evident to all human beings having the use of reason.[19] The precepts of the natural law are based on that principle.[20] Reason understands that everything for which human beings have a natural inclination is good for human beings and to be sought, and everything contrary to a natural inclination is evil for them and to be avoided. (Natural inclinations are the inclinations of *human*, that is, *rational*, nature, and so the inclinations are only natural insofar as they are in accord with reason.) The primary precepts reflect the natural inclinations. First, human beings as substances have a natural inclination to preserve their lives, and so they should take *reasonable* means to do so. Second, human beings as animals have a natural inclination to mate and raise children, and so they should do so in *reasonable* ways. Third, human beings as such have natural inclinations to seek truth and live cooperatively with others in society, and so they should do so in *reasonable* ways.

Secondary precepts are conclusions from the primary pre-

17. *ST* I-II, Q. 19, A. 6, from *On Law, Morality, and Politics*, 8.
18. *ST* I-II, Q. 91, A. 2.   19. *ST* I-II, Q. 94, A. 2.
20. *ST* I-II, Q. 94, A. 2.

cepts.[21] Proximate secondary precepts are conclusions that follow with little reflection and roughly correspond with the second tablet of the Decalogue (e.g., thou shalt not kill).[22] It is these precepts that human beings cannot fail to know without fault. Remote secondary precepts are conclusions that require greater reflection and instruction from wiser persons (e.g., respect the elderly).[23] These precepts human beings can fail to know and may have exceptions (e.g., goods should be returned to their owner, but not a gun to a homicidal maniac).[24] Since force and fear are necessary to restrain the wicked, at least so that they leave others in peace, and human beings need instruction and training, human laws are necessary in order that human beings may live in peace and attain virtue.[25] The laws impose moral obligation insofar as they are just, and things are just insofar as they are in accord with reason, whose primary rule is the natural law.[26] And so every human law has the character of law insofar as it is from the natural law.[27] Some human laws are conclusions from the general precepts of the natural law (e.g., murder is a punishable crime), and other human laws are further specifications of the general precepts (e.g., specific punishments for specific crimes).[28]

From the forgoing sketch of Aquinas' doctrine on conscience and law, several points are evident. First, moral judgments are founded on an innate disposition of the soul toward moral goodness and away from moral evil. Second, conscience in the strict sense is a judgment of reason that a contemplated action should or should not be done. Third, one should not act contrary to conscience, even in the case of erroneous reason. Fourth, ignorance of proximate secondary precepts is inexcusable. Fifth, there is an objective moral order that constitutes the natural law, which reason communicates to human beings.

21. *ST* I-II, Q. 94, A. 4.   22. *ST* I-II, Q. 100, AA. 1 and 3.
23. *ST* I-II, Q. 100, A. 3.   24. *ST* I-II, Q. 94, A. 4.
25. *ST* I-II, Q. 95, A. 1.   26. *ST* I-II, Q. 96, A. 4.
27. *ST* I-II, Q. 96, A. 2.   28. *ST* I-II, Q. 96, A. 2.

Aquinas held that the individual's conscience is bound to obey legitimate political authority, since that authority derives from God, the author of the human nature that requires it. But when political authority is defective in title or excessive in exercise, there is no obligation to obey. Thus neither a usurper nor a legitimate ruler abusing his authority by unjust commands can bind the conscience of citizens to obey him. Indeed, if the ruler contravenes the very purpose of his authority by commanding a sinful action, the subject is under an obligation not to obey him. In the case of a usurper, Aquinas allowed active resistance if no other recourse was open to the citizen, but in the case of an abuse of legitimate authority, he endorsed nothing more than passive resistance.[29]

LUTHER AND THE REFORMATION

Martin Luther and other Protestant Reformers appealed prominently to conscience to justify their break with Rome. They accepted the authority of Scripture as normative, but stressed the necessity of private interpretation. Their appeals to conscience were to prophetic witness rather than to legal rules, and to experience rather than to reason. Reacting to the Reformers' rejection of the church's authority, post-Tridentine Catholic theologians stressed the objective, rational, and legal bases of conscience, but also, unlike Aquinas, attempted to codify rules of conscience by means of comprehensive legal casuistry.

The political consequences of the Reformation's appeals to private judgment were enormous. Within the context of the then-existing sacral societies, fragmentation of religious unity meant a fragmentation of political unity. To confront this challenge, two radically different approaches were available: (1) to secularize religion; and (2) to secularize government. The first approach would

29. Aquinas, CS II, dist. 44, Q. 2, A. 2; cf. Richard J. Regan, "Aquinas on Politics, Obedience and Disobedience," *Thought* 56 (March 1981): 77–88.

require subordination of religion to the state and the restriction of religious freedom (*cujus regio, ejus religio*). The second would require a regime of religious toleration. Thomas Hobbes and John Locke were, respectively, articulate spokesmen for these two approaches.

HOBBES

To meet the political disunity resulting from the religious dissidence of the Reformation, Hobbes consciously elaborated a theory that would allow no claim of private judgment or religious belief against the command of the sovereign. In the state of nature, in which every human being wars against every other one, nothing can be called just or unjust. But "reason suggests convenient articles of peace upon which men may be drawn to agreement," and these articles are "laws of nature."[30] Hobbes' laws of nature are thus dictates of a calculating, self-interested reason. They are the conditions for the rational pursuit of self-preservation and the rules that a calculating human being would observe in pursuing one's own advantage if one were conscious of the human predicament in a universe ruled by passion. These laws are not given by God or ordered to a natural whole, except in the sense that God, howsoever Hobbes understood him or it, is the sovereign of the universe, and that human beings are endowed with a calculating reason. Indeed, the laws oblige only "*in foro interno,* that is to say, they bind to a desire that they should take place, but *in foro externo,* that is, to the putting them into act, not always."[31]

The science of the laws of nature is "the true and only moral philosophy,"[32] since moral philosophy studies what is good and evil, "names that signify our appetites and aversions."[33] Human beings differ in their judgment not only of what is pleasant or un-

---

30. Thomas Hobbes, *Leviathan* (New York: Dutton, 1950), chap. 13, 105.
31. Hobbes, *Leviathan,* chap. 15, 131.   32. Hobbes, *Leviathan,* 132.
33. Hobbes, *Leviathan,* 132.

pleasant, but even of what is conformable to reason or disagree-able to reason. "Nay, the same man in diverse times differs from himself" on what is good or evil.[34] Hence there are "disputes, controversies, and at last war."[35] So long as human beings are in the condition of nature alone, which is the condition of war, "private appetite is the measure of good and evil."[36] The laws of nature, therefore, are only improperly called laws, "for they are but conclusions or theorems concerning what conduces to the conservation and defense of [individuals] themselves, whereas law properly is the word of him that by right has command over others."[37]

Hobbes' theory on the relation of conscience to the laws of the commonwealth is quite different from his theory of the individual's obligations to the laws of nature. By the covenants of every individual with every other individual, the multitude is united in one person, "that great Leviathan or ... mortal God."[38] And "he that carries this person is called sovereign and said to have sovereign power."[39] Among the prerogatives of the sovereign, for all practical purposes unlimited, Hobbes included the power to judge what doctrines are fit to be taught. "It belongs ... to him that has sovereign power to be judge, or constitute all judges of, opinions and doctrines, as a thing necessary to peace [and] thereby to prevent discord and civil war."[40] This broad prerogative of the sovereign, of course, is as much a limitation on thought and speech generally as on religious expression specifically.

When Hobbes discussed the things that weaken the commonwealth, he clearly indicated what doctrines he considered most dangerous to the peace of the commonwealth. First, he condemned as seditious the doctrine that "every private man is judge of good and evil actions."[41] Although "this is true ... where there are no civil laws, and also under civil government in such

34. Hobbes, *Leviathan*, 132.　　35. Hobbes, *Leviathan*, 132.
36. Hobbes, *Leviathan*, 132.　　37. Hobbes, *Leviathan*, 133.
38. Hobbes, *Leviathan*, chap. 17, 143.　　39. Hobbes, *Leviathan*, chap. 17, 144.
40. Hobbes, *Leviathan*, chap. 18, 148.　　41. Hobbes, *Leviathan*, chap. 29, 277.

cases as are not determined by the law," it is otherwise manifest that "from this false doctrine men are disposed to debate with themselves and dispute the commands of the commonwealth, and afterwards to obey or disobey them as in their private judgment they think fit."[42] Thereby, "the commonwealth is distracted and weakened."[43] Hobbes then related the latter position to appeals to conscience. "Another doctrine repugnant to civil society is that whatsoever a man does against his conscience is sin, and it depends on the presumption of making himself judge of good and evil."[44] Indeed, "the law is the public conscience by which he has already undertaken to be guided."[45] Otherwise, "the commonwealth must needs be distracted, and no man dare to obey the sovereign power farther than it shall seem good in his own eyes."[46]

Hobbes' severe strictures against private judgment and individual responsibility to conscience reflect in part the political consequences of religious dissension in seventeenth-century England. But they are also consequences of his philosophical view of nature and reason. For him, nature is simply the sum total of material elements and their motion, and reason is simply the faculty of human beings that calculates what is to their individual self-interest or loss. There is in his theory no finality in nature and no faculty of reason to take its measure. Hence, since nature and reason are so conceived, Hobbes logically concluded that individual judgment and conscience are both irrelevant and harmful to society.

According to Hobbes, sin is "nothing but the transgression of the [civil] law."[47] When spiritual authorities claim the right to declare what is sin, they "challenge by consequence to declare what is law."[48] As in his discussion of the diseases of the com-

---

42. Hobbes, *Leviathan*, 277–78.
43. Hobbes, *Leviathan*, 278.
44. Hobbes, *Leviathan*, 278.
45. Hobbes, *Leviathan*, 278.
46. Hobbes, *Leviathan*, 278.
47. Hobbes, *Leviathan*, 283.
48. Hobbes, *Leviathan*, 282–83.

monwealth, he argued that "if men were at liberty to take for God's commandments their own dreams and fancies, … scarce two men would agree upon what is God's commandment, and … every man would despise the commandments of the commonwealth."[49] He concluded, therefore, "that in all things not contrary to the moral law (that is to say, to the law of nature), all subjects are bound to obey that for divine law which is declared to be so by the laws of the commonwealth."[50]

Hobbes did admit that it is "equity … that every man equally enjoy his liberty" in anything not regulated by the commonwealth.[51] This limited idea of religious freedom accords perfectly with his general concept of the liberty of subjects, which lies "only in those things … the sovereign has pretermitted."[52] Hobbes gave no examples of the religious freedom that he thinks the sovereign should pretermit, but one may be inferred from his general definition of the liberty of private opinion. Indeed, he expressly said in another place that no sovereign can command or forbid belief in Christ, since "belief and unbelief" never follow the commands of human beings.[53]

LOCKE

Locke drew heavily on Hobbes' theory of the construction of civil society, and he, like Hobbes, started with the idea of a prepolitical state of nature. This state is one of perfect freedom for individuals "to order their actions and dispose of their possessions and persons as they think fit, within the bounds of the law of nature [and] without asking leave or depending on the will of any other man."[54] The state of nature is also one of equality, which is "the foundation of that obligation to mutual love among men on

---

49. Hobbes, *Leviathan*, chap. 26, 246.   50. Hobbes, *Leviathan*, 246–47.
51. Hobbes, *Leviathan*, 247.   52. Hobbes, *Leviathan*, chap. 21, 180.
53. Hobbes, *Leviathan*, chap. 42, 435.
54. John Locke, *The Second Treatise of Government*, ed. Thomas P. Peardon (New York: Liberal Arts Press, 1952), chap. 2, 4.

which ... the duties we owe to one another and ... the great maxims of justice and charity" are derived.[55] Although the state of nature is a state of liberty, it is not a state of license. "The state of nature has a law of nature to govern it which obliges everyone, and reason, which is that law, teaches all mankind who will but consult it that, being all equal and independent, no one ought to harm another in his life, health, or possessions."[56] All human beings have in the state of nature the right to restrain another from invading their rights, but "only to retribute to him as far as calm reason and conscience dictate, which is proportionate to his transgression."[57] Locke also held that "truth and keeping of faith belongs to men as men and not as members of society."[58]

Natural law, therefore, seems to have meant something quite different for Locke than it did for Hobbes. For Hobbes, it meant a rule of reason calculated to help to preserve one's life and insure one's security. For Locke, it meant a moral law promulgated by human reason and obligatory on all human beings as they reflect on their fundamental equality. But Locke's treatment of the construction of political or civil society indicates that the state of nature giving rise to society is in fact a state of war quite similar to Hobbes' model. Civil society is instituted "to avoid and remedy these circumstances of the state of nature which necessarily follow from every man being judge in his own case."[59] In the state of nature, one's enjoyment of one's freedom is "constantly exposed to the invasions of others."[60] Indeed, "were it not for the corruption and viciousness of degenerate man," there would be no need of civil society.[61] It is a state of war that makes human beings "willing to quit a condition which, however free, is full of fears and continual dangers."[62]

---

55. Locke, *Second Treatise*, 4–5.
56. Locke, *Second Treatise*, 5.
57. Locke, *Second Treatise*, 6.
58. Locke, *Second Treatise*, 10.
59. Locke, *Second Treatise*, chap. 7, 50.
60. Locke, *Second Treatise*, chap. 9, 70.
61. Locke, *Second Treatise*, 72.
62. Locke, *Second Treatise*, 72.

But Locke differed from Hobbes on the function of government in his own construction of political society, a difference that
is of central importance for the relation of government to religious
freedom and individual conscience. Where Hobbes' contract created a Leviathan, a mortal God, which possessed absolute power
and constituted the font of all morality, Locke's contract created
a government limited to securing the physical integrity of persons
and property from violence. From this framework of *gendarme*
government, Locke declared in his *Letter Concerning Toleration*
that he esteemed it "above all things necessary to distinguish exactly the business of civil government from that of religion and to
settle the just bounds that lie between the one and the other."[63]

The commonwealth, said Locke, is a "society of men constituted only for the procuring, preserving, and advancing their own
civil interests," which he enumerated as "life, liberty, ... indo-
lency of body, and the possession of outward things."[64] "All civil
power, right, and dominion is bounded and confined to the only
care of promoting these things," and "it neither can nor ought in
any manner to be extended to the salvation of souls."[65] Among
other reasons, Locke argued that "the care of souls cannot belong
to the civil magistrate because his power consists only in outward
force," while "true and saving religion consists in the inward persuasion of the mind."[66] Locke concluded that "all power of civil
government relates only to men's civil interests, is confined to the
case of the things of this world, and has nothing to do with the
world to come."[67]

Again unlike Hobbes, Locke clearly affirmed the role of an
individual's conscience in moral decisions. "No way whatsoever

63. Locke, *A Letter Concerning Toleration*, in *The Works of John Locke*, 12th ed.
(London: Rivington, 1824), 5:9.
64. Locke, *Letter Concerning Toleration*, 10.
65. Locke, *Letter Concerning Toleration*, 10.
66. Locke, *Letter Concerning Toleration*, 1.
67. Locke, *Letter Concerning Toleration*, 13.

that I shall walk in against the dictates of conscience will ever bring me to the mansions of the blessed."[68] Citing approvingly Dr. Sharp, an archbishop of York, and echoing Aquinas, he expanded on the duty to follow conscience in his *Third Letter for Toleration:*[69]

Where a man is mistaken in his judgment, even in that case it is always a sin to act against it. Though we should take for a duty that which is really a sin, yet so long as we are thus persuaded, it will be highly criminal in us to act in contradiction to this persuasion, and the reason for this is evident because, by so doing, we willfully act against the best light which we at present have for direction of our actions.

But Locke was aware of the possibility of conflicts between dictates of conscience and commands of government:[70]

A good life, in which consists not the least part of religion and true piety, concerns also the civil government, and in it lies the safety both of men's souls and of the commonwealth. Moral actions belong, therefore, to the jurisdiction both of the outward and inward court, both of the civil and domestic governor, I mean both of the magistrate and conscience.

Locke asked what the result should be if the magistrate enjoins something that the conscience of an individual judges to be unlawful. Although he deemed the case unlikely if the government was faithfully administered, he allowed that in such a case "a private person is to abstain from the actions that he judges unlawful."[71] But the individual is "to undergo the punishment, which is not unlawful for him to bear, for the private judgment of any person concerning a law enacted in political matters for the public good does not take away the obligation of that law nor deserve a dispensation."[72]

68. Locke, *Letter Concerning Toleration*, 28.
69. Locke, *A Third Letter for Toleration*, in *The Works of John Locke*, 5:146–47.
70. Locke, *Letter Concerning Toleration*, 41.
71. Locke, *Letter Concerning Toleration*, 43.
72. Locke, *Letter Concerning Toleration*, 43.

Locke was thus circumspect on the rights of conscientious objectors to the commands of government. In his view, an individual who judges a command of government to be contrary to the dictate of one's conscience is morally justified, even obliged, to refuse to perform the command, but the individual is also morally obliged to submit to punishment for the disobedience. The individual may, of course, be physically obliged to submit to such punishment, but why should one consider oneself *morally* obliged to undergo punishment for following the dictates of one's conscience? Perhaps Locke thought submission to punishment necessary to distinguish morally motivated opposition to government policy from politically motivated opposition. Or perhaps Locke thought that conscientious objectors owed submission to punishment because of their general duty to the organized society in which they lived. In any case, he did not elaborate his reasons. From the perspective of the dissenting individual, his admission of the right and duty of conscientious objectors to disobey a command of the government seems oddly joined with a prescription of moral duty to accept punishment for such refusal to obey, but his position has both ancient models (e.g., Socrates), and modern disciples (e.g., Mahatma Gandhi and Martin Luther King).

Locke's dictum on conscientious objection invites a comparison to the American civil disobedience in the 1960s and 1970s. Although there is agreement between Locke and many civil disobedience theorists on the duty to submit to punishment, there is one important difference regarding some practitioners of civil disobedience at the time. Locke allowed disobedience only to a specific command of government, the performance of which is contrary to an individual's conscience. Some later practitioners of civil disobedience, however, claim a right and duty to disobey laws other than the specific laws and policies they consider unjust or immoral, a claim that Locke would have regarded as quasi-revolutionary in nature.

But whatever the complexity of potential conflicts between the commands of civil government and the dictates of individual conscience in political matters, Locke clearly declared his view that civil governments have no competence to legislate purely religious matters, such as "that the people or any party amongst them should be compelled to embrace a strange religion and join in the worship and ceremonies of another church."[73] In such cases, human beings are not "obliged by that law against their consciences, for political society is instituted for no other end than but only to secure every man's possession of the things of this life."[74] Thus legislation of purely religious matters concerns "things that lie not within the verge of the magistrate's authority."[75]

Locke's views rather than Hobbes' prevailed in most of the Western world and are reflected in the First Amendment of the United States Constitution. Locke was able to envision a harmonious world of religious tolerance largely because he limited the functions of both government and religion. According to him, government exists to secure the physical well-being of person and property, while religion is a matter of internal, psychological conviction. Government is concerned with this world and religion with the next. He agreed with Aquinas that conscience is a judgment of reason and should be followed even when erroneous, and he conceived conscience in a theocentric and legal context of human responsibility to divine and natural law, although these laws, in the last analysis, were only matters of opinion morally binding on individuals. He accordingly disagreed with Aquinas about the accessibility of these laws to human intelligence. Like Aquinas, Locke's treatment of conscience emphasized the observance of negative rules rather than any positive function of reli-

73. Locke, *Letter Concerning Toleration*, 43.
74. Locke, *Letter Concerning Toleration*, 43.
75. Locke, *Letter Concerning Toleration*, 43.

gious prophecy. He thus restricted the operation of conscience, at least for the most part, to negative judgments of reason from religious premises that were only opinions. In this respect he was a forerunner not only of the modern Western settlement in favor of religious tolerance, but of modern subjectivist interpretations of conscience, as well.

LATER PHILOSOPHERS

Conscience played no role in the moral philosophy of David Hume. In fact, he claimed that "reason is, and only ought to be, the slave of the passions [emotions] and can never pretend to any other office than to serve and obey them."[76] This strong anti-rational proposition, of course, must be understood within the framework of Hume's general philosophical system. Hume used *passion* to signify emotion or affection in general, not unregulated or violent emotion, and he argued that reason could pave the way for the operation of the moral sense of approbation or disapproval by showing the utility or futility of particular modes of human behavior. But Hume allowed reason only two functions: "the comparing of ideas and the inferring of matters of fact."[77] He said that moral distinctions were not to be derived from reason as concerned with mathematical demonstrations, and that they were not to be derived from matters of fact, since values are not objective facts governed by the association of ideas. Thus Hume concluded that morality "is a matter of fact, but it is the object of feeling, not of reason."[78]

Hume's moral philosophy, lacking the classical and medieval conception of practical moral reason and its mode of operation, rested ultimately on feeling, and this emphasis is reflected today in the emotive ethical theories of modern empiricists. The function that Hume assigned to reason—namely, to determine the utility

76. David Hume, *A Treatise of Human Nature*, ed. L. A. Selby-Bigge (Oxford: Clarendon Press, 1951), book 2, part 3, sec. 3, 415.

77. Hume, *Treatise of Human Nature*, book 3, part 1, sec. 1, 469.

78. Hume, *Treatise of Human Nature*, book 3, part 1, sec. 1, 463.

of particular behavior for oneself or others—was later more fully developed by Jeremy Bentham and the two Mills (James and John Stuart). Contemporary empiricists and utilitarians follow Hume's narrower conception of human reason, and it is no accident that the idea of conscience does not feature in their respective theories.

Jean-Jacques Rousseau stressed the primacy of feeling in his moral philosophy, and his Savoyard vicar tells Emile:[79]

To exist is to feel. Our feeling is undoubtedly earlier than our intelligence, and we had feelings before we had ideas.... To know good is not to love it. This knowledge is not innate to man. But as soon as his reason leads him to perceive it, his conscience impels him to love it. It is this feeling that is innate.

Although reason and reflection play a part in the development of morality, ultimately "what I feel to be right is right, [and] what I feel to be wrong is wrong."[80] Feeling may have signified for Rousseau immediate apprehension or intuition, but its subjective emphasis is clear enough.

In his *Social Contract,* Rousseau claims that human beings pass at once from an amoral to a moral state through the institution of political society. "The passage from the state of nature to the civil state produces a very remarkable change in man by substituting justice for instinct in his conduct and giving his actions the morality which they had formerly lacked."[81] Indeed, "the mere impulse to appetite is slavery, while obedience to a law which we prescribe to ourselves is liberty."[82] Nature itself has directed the will of human beings to the good, but individuals, even when gathered in assembly, may form erroneous ideas of it. Only the general will is always right, and it is the business of the legislator

79. Jean-Jacques Rousseau, *Emile,* ed. Barbara Foxley (London: Dent, 1911), 253.

80. Rousseau, *Emile,* 249.

81. Rousseau, *The Social Contract and Discourses,* ed. G. D. H. Cole (London: Dent, 1913), 18.

82. Rousseau, *Social Contract and Discourses,* 19.

to interpret this will and bring the laws into conformity with it.

There are undeniably incompatible elements in the nature and source of the moral order. On the one hand, the moral law is written in human hearts and individual conscience, and the collective legislative voice may fail to express the collective will. On the other, individuals should conform to the will of the sovereign people and, if necessary, even be forced to be free. Rousseau's problem in this respect was not his alone. Plato faced a similar dilemma, but the Enlightenment's tendency to make an artificial construct of human society radically complicated it.

Although Immanuel Kant is celebrated for the rational and formal character of his moral philosophy, certain subjective emphases of his system are particularly relevant to modern concepts of conscience. Kant acknowledged morality as an imperative instinct, and he made subjective intention the absolute moral good. "Nothing can possibly be conceived in the world, or even out of it, which can be called good without qualification except a good will."[83] Moreover, he divorced this moral good from any consideration of results or purposes. "A good will is good simply by virtue of the volition, not because of what it performs or effects, not by its aptness for attaining some proposed end."[84] Even the formal a priori principle of morality, the categorical imperative, contains the idea of a radically autonomous will. *"Act as if the maxim of your action is good simply by the volition, not because of what it performs or effects."*[85] A human being is subject *"only to his own general laws,"*[86] and this autonomy of the will, "the supreme moral principle,"[87] is opposed to all "false principles of morality,"[88] which are not the

---

83. Immanuel Kant, *Metaphysical Foundations of Morals*, in *The Philosophy of Kant*, ed. and trans. Carl J. Friedrich (New York: Random House, 1949), 140.

84. Kant, *Metaphysical Foundations*, 141.

85. Kant, *Metaphysical Foundations*, 170 (italics in original).

86. Kant, *Metaphysical Foundations*, 181 (italics in original).

87. Kant, *Metaphysical Foundations*, 187.

88. Kant, *Metaphysical Foundations*, 188.

result of the individual will's own legislation. In this sense Kant rejected both the biblical moral norm of the will of God and the classical moral norm of the order of nature.

Where eighteenth-century philosophers were individually and ahistorically oriented in their treatment of conscience, many nineteenth-century philosophers responded to the burgeoning development of modern science by concentrating on the social and historical bases of conscience. In the wake of the Darwinian theory of evolution and the data on comparative religion, Herbert Spencer and Emile Durkheim stressed the social conditioning of conscience by particular cultures.[89] Karl Marx socially conditioned conscience on economic factors, for example, on class-consciousness.[90] Moreover, adopting the model of the Hegelian dialectic of history, he made conscience—that is, class-consciousness—not only a product of history, but also a determining factor in its evolution.[91] Friedrich Nietzsche distinguished two primary types of morality, the master or superman morality, which creates its own values out of life forces, and the slave or herd morality, which, out of resentment, imposes a uniform system to the benefit of the weak and the powerless.[92] In his view, the first type is the morality of modern human beings, and the second the morality of classical philosophy and Judeo-Christian theology. Thus both Marx and Nietzsche made conscience a function of class, although Marx emphasized purely economic factors in the context of a historical dialectic in favor of what Nietzsche called "slave morality." Sigmund Freud, in his turn, socially conditioned

89. See, for example, Herbert Spencer, *The Principles of Ethics* (New York: Appleton, 1892), especially part 4; and Emile Durkheim, *Moral Education*, trans. Herman Schauer (New York: Free Press, 1961).

90. See, for example, Karl Marx, *A Contribution to the Critique of Political Economy*, trans. N. I. Stone (Chicago: Kerr, 1911), 11–12.

91. See, for example, Marx, *Theses on Feuerbach*, in *Karl Marx and Friedrich Engels on Religion* (Moscow: Foreign Language Publications House, 1957), 72.

92. Friedrich Nietzsche, *Beyond Good and Evil*, in *The Complete Works of Friedrich Nietzsche*, trans. Helen Zimmern (New York: Russell and Russell, 1964), 12:227.

conscience in terms of the suppression of primitive libido by a family-conditioned superego.[93]

On the other side of the spectrum, many nineteenth-century philosophers and theologians stressed the autonomous value of conscience. Johann Gottlieb Fichte, following Kant, advises human beings to "act according … to conscience"—that is, according to the "immediate conscience of … determinate duty."[94] Thus conscience was for him a feeling, although the immediate feeling in question expressed agreement or harmony between "our empirical ego and the pure ego."[95] From the Christian perspective, the existentialist Søren Kierkegaard, John Henry Newman, and Lord John Acton insisted on the authenticity and primacy of conscience.[96]

Twentieth-century philosophy reflected the nineteenth-century division between scientific and instinctive interpretations of conscience. Scientifically, logical positivists pointed out that moral propositions are not verifiable, and early spokespersons of linguistic analysis called them emotive.[97] Later linguistic analysts accepted the usage of moral language as such and sought the utilitarian grounds for it in various forms of self-interest.[98] On the other hand, existentialists, phenomenologists, and value philosophers stressed the centrality of instinctive moral commitment.

Like Luther, religious dissenters in America appealed prominently to the role of conscience in the moral life of the individual.

93. Sigmund Freud, *Taboos and the Ambivalence of Emotions,* in *The Basic Works of Sigmund Freud,* ed. A. A. Brill (New York: Random House, 1938), 821–64.

94. Johann Gottlieb Fichte, *Sämmlichte Werke,* ed. I. H. Fichte (Berlin: Veit, 1846) 4:173–74.

95. Fichte, *Sämmlichte Werke,* 169.

96. See, for example, Søren Kierkegaard, *Purity of Heart,* trans. Douglas V. Steere (New York: Harper, 1948); John Henry Newman, *A Letter to His Grace, the Duke of Norfolk* (London: Pickering, 1875); John Emmerich, Lord Acton, *Essays on Church and State,* ed. Douglas Woodruff (London: Hollis and Carter, 1952).

97. See, for example, A. J. Ayer, *Language, Truth, and Logic,* 2nd ed. (New York: Dover, 1946), 107ff.

98. See, for example, P. H. Nowell-Smith, *Ethics* (Oxford: Blackwell, 1957).

But Henry David Thoreau in the mid-nineteenth century made the most unique American contribution to Western traditions of conscience. Convinced that he should not cooperate with the United States government's war against Mexico in 1847 or with its tolerance and acceptance of slavery, he held that a person of moral principle should do more than stand aside. Thoreau meant to affect his society by breaking its laws, and he was willing to pay the price of going to prison for doing so. "Under a government which imprisons any unjustly, the true place for a just man is also in prison."[99] At the end of his life, Thoreau defended John Brown's raid on Harper's Ferry and accepted the principle of violence. "I do not wish to kill or be killed, but I can foresee circumstances in which these things would be by me unavoidable."[100] Against the evil of four million Negroes in slavery, "the Sharps rifles and the revolvers were employed in a righteous cause."[101] Thoreau linked individual conscience with social revolution and became an exemplar for many advocates of civil disobedience in the twentieth century.

SUMMARY

There were two strands of morality in the biblical tradition: one positively oriented toward religious witness and actions according to justice and love, and the other negatively oriented regarding the observance of rules and obedience of divine law. The Platonic and Aristotelian view of morality was concerned with practical reason rather than prophetic action, with self-mastery and perfection rather than social reform, with habitual behavior rather than particular acts. The Stoics modified the classical Greek view of morality insofar as they identified reason with natural law and moral consciousness with legal obligation. Accord-

99. Henry David Thoreau, *Essay on Civil Disobedience in Walden and Other Essays,* ed. Brooks Atkinson (New York: Random House, 1950), 646.

100. Thoreau, *A Plea for Captain John Brown,* in *Thoreau: People, Principles, and Politics,* ed. Milton Meltzer (New York: Hill and Wang, 1963), 187.

101. Thoreau, *A Plea for Captain John Brown,* 187.

ingly, the Stoic model of conscience was more rule-oriented than the Platonic and Aristotelian model of practical reason. Aquinas adopted features of the biblical, classical, and Stoic views of morality. He founded moral judgment on a pre- or para-rational disposition of the soul toward moral good, but he considered conscience itself a judgment of reason with respect to a particular action. He conceived the operation of conscience in a theocentric context of natural and divine law and directed toward the observance of rules more than the fulfillment of prophetic witness.

Like biblical prophets, Luther's appeals to conscience were to witness rather than rules, and to experience rather than reason, but he isolated private individuals from religious community judgment. Modern philosophers emphasized the subjective bases of conscience. Although both Hobbes and Locke viewed individual conscience largely as a religious product, Hobbes condemned it as a threat, and Locke allowed it a private normative value for the individual. With the exception of theologians like Kierkegaard and Newman, most other modern spokespersons secularized conscience. Hume founded his moral philosophy on a moral sense of feeling of approbation or disapprobation, but he also accorded utilitarian considerations of enlightened self-interest an ancillary role. Rousseau and Fichte identified conscience with feeling, and Kant also made conscience autonomous, although in the context of a rational categorical imperative. Spencer, Durkheim, Marx, Nietzsche, and Freud conditioned conscience on social, economic, historical, or psychological factors.

On the American scene, Thoreau stands in the tradition of biblical prophecy, although his view was more socially and politically oriented than most religious prophets of premodern times. More recently, some have appealed to conscience as justification for disobedience of public law in the cause of peace and social justice, sometimes without regard to its consequences for the rule of law or the effects on third parties.

A TYPOLOGY OF CONFLICTS
BETWEEN INDIVIDUAL CONSCIENCE
AND PUBLIC LAW

I have in the course of commenting on Supreme Court cases involving the free exercise clause implicitly used a typology of conflicts between individual conscience and public law. I shall here made the typology explicit.

First, there are moral imperatives that are recognized as prohibitions (e.g., don't work on the Sabbath). This class of negative moral imperatives is not necessarily identified with a code of ethical absolutes. Some, perhaps most, negative moral imperatives are based on codes of ethical absolutes, as is the case with Orthodox Jews, who feel morally obliged to refrain from working on the Sabbath. But other negative moral imperatives apply only to specific situations, as is the case with selective conscientious objectors to a particular war.

In the case of negative moral imperatives, when an individual considers them important, the individual cannot perform the prohibited acts without conscious loss of moral integrity and respect for oneself as a personal agent. Of course, to the extent that an individual does not consider that a negative moral imperative obliges in particular circumstances, in which case there is no operative negative prohibition at all, the individual will not feel any loss of moral integrity. Or to the extent that an individual is not responsible for a prohibited act, the individual will also not feel a loss of moral integrity. But when one does consider a serious moral prohibition applicable and oneself a free agent, one cannot perform the act prohibited without a consciousness of serious moral fault, since applicable negative moral imperatives are absolutely specific.

Second, there are moral imperatives that mandate actions (e.g., practice polygamy, preach the gospel). These affirmative moral imperatives are divisible into two classes according to their relative degree of specificity. One class, as in the case of the Mormons who practiced polygamy in response to their perception of divine revelation, was based on a relatively specific prescription. Circumstances may not be favorable to executing such prescriptions for one reason or another (e.g., the unavailability of eligible spouses in the case of polygamy), and a psychologically adult individual would not feel under such conditions that the individual has in any way compromised the individual's religious or moral integrity if the individual is unable to carry out the religious or moral prescription. But if circumstances are favorable, and if the individual perceives the prescription to be of sufficient importance, then one is likely to feel at least a sense of religious or moral incompleteness, if not moral fault, for failing to carry out the prescription.

The other class of affirmative moral imperatives, as in the case of Jehovah's Witnesses' evangelism on the streets or from door to door, is based on general prescriptions. The individual determines the time, place, and means of implementing the prescriptions, and if a specific mode of implementation (e.g., door-to-door canvassing) is unavailable to the individual, alternate means are (e.g., assemblies, parades, telephones, the mails). Accordingly, an individual prevented by law or other circumstances from using particular means to fulfill a general duty is not likely to feel any sense of religious or moral failure or fault for that reason alone, however unjust the individual may perceive the legal prohibition to be.

This typology of moral obligation is, I submit, both introspectively verifiable and logically consistent, and conforms to the psychological evidence of a greater sense of guilt for violating what an individual perceives as a negative religious or moral imperative than for failing to implement what an individual perceives as a positive religious or moral duty.[1] But since the typology is purely formal and does not take into consideration varieties of subject matter, the question arises whether it is sufficient. Critics of American policies on race and war might argue that such a typology reflects an individualist bias and does not accurately reflect the highest moral obligation of human beings to involve themselves in the quest for social justice and world peace. The point may be well taken to the extent that it criticizes preoccupation of moral consciousness with the individual rather than with society, and with abstinence from doing wrong rather than with activity doing good. But the argument should be properly addressed to the formation of conscience, not the ultimate judgments of conscience itself.

An individual who condemned the Vietnamese War as immoral, for example, could have distinguished between the individual's moral obligation not to fight in that war and the moral obligation to engage in specific modes of protest against the war. The conscientious objector to the war could not have participated in it without a sense of serious moral fault,[2] although the objector could have refrained from a particular act of protest without such a sense. If the objector did nothing to protest the war over a long enough period of time, of course, the objector might have felt a profound sense of moral failure, but the objector would not have felt this sense unless the objector perceived the particular act of protest as a relatively specific duty.

Insofar as the individual perceived the war as gravely unjust and was unable to alter the government's course of action or persuade most other citizens, at least in the short run, by ordinary means of political advocacy, the individual might have been led to perceive various degrees of coercion (nonviolent to violent) as a morally obligatory pattern of action. What might otherwise have been perceived as only a general moral duty to oppose the war might have been transformed into the perception of a relatively specific moral duty to oppose the

1. Cf. Edmund Bergler, *The Battle of Conscience* (Washington, D.C.: Washington Institute of Medicine, 1948), 7–13.

2. Cf. *Gillette v. U.S.*, 401 U.S. 437 (1971).

war by coercion. If so, such a claim of moral obligation would have been similar to the classical justification of revolution, although the claim was explicitly only directed against a particular governmental activity—namely, the war, not the legitimacy of the government itself. Thus the suggested typology of conscience can take account of the moral consciousness professed by anti-war and social activists, but it classifies the end product of perceived moral obligation rather than the objective issues involved.

The individual's interest in moral integrity also serves society's interest. Plato and Aristotle, for example, identified the development of moral virtue as the highest function of politics and the practice of citizenship as the highest function of morals. The former thesis was essentially Socrates' defense against the charges that he was undermining belief in the gods, and that he was corrupting the youth of Athens—namely, that his inquiries were aimed at the discovery of wisdom, that genuine wisdom constituted moral virtue, and that the acquisition of moral virtue would foster good citizens. Thomas Aquinas and medieval theologians similarly maintained the supremacy of the moral purposes of human society, but, since they believed that human beings had a destiny that transcended their earthly lives and that the church was the supreme teacher of the way to salvation in the next life, they could not accept political life as the highest object of moral virtue.

At least as a practical matter, John Locke stood for the principle that the public interest in the peace and unity of pluralist societies would be best served by wide deference to individual perceptions of religious and moral duties. This principle does not depend on the validity of the Greek and medieval concept of an objective moral order and the relation of political goals to it, but on the empirical evidence that most individuals recognize moral imperatives as subjectively important to them for religious or humanist reasons, and that these imperatives diverge widely. Moreover, society as a whole shares an interest in the freedom of individuals to act according to their conscience, since the freedom of all is intimately linked to the freedom of each. Furthermore, individuals who habitually behave according to their perception of religious or moral duties are more likely to internalize their legal duties as citizens than individuals who habitually act contrary to their perception of religious or moral duties.

Thus we may say that following one's conscience has a value for society as well as for the individual, whether that value is grounded on normative or empirical considerations. But if acting according to individual conscience is one public interest, other public interests may run counter to it. In the broadest sense every public law declares a public interest and rests on a perception of one or more societal values to be secured by the law. From this perspective, conflicts between individual conscience and public law represent not simply conflicts between morality on the one hand and law on the other, but also conflicts between the perception of moral value by individuals and the perception of moral values by society. Such conflicts, therefore, are in part between competing moral claims.

There are other viewpoints on the relation of private morality to public law. Latter-day disciples of Hobbes, for example, would argue that whatever is illegal is immoral—that is, that public law governs individual moral judgment. This analysis in effect denies the reality or relevance of one element in the conflictual situation—namely, a moral consciousness on the part of the individual in any way autonomous from that of public law. Since, however, many or most individuals do not regard public law as the source of all moral obligations, and since the First Amendment specifically disavows such a position, the Hobbesian analysis is not realistic about conflicts between individual conscience and public law. Individuals do perceive moral obligations that apparently conflict with law, and the Constitution does take this into account, at least as a general policy.

Legal positivists offer an alternate analysis of the relation of morality to law. According to their analysis, what is illegal is simply illegal, and laws impose penalties on those who disobey them. Thus the individual who challenges the morality of a law is entitled to no different treatment than any other individual who disobeys the law. Like the Hobbesian analysis, legal positivism is subject to the objections that individuals do in fact judge whether public laws conform to moral laws, and that the First Amendment gives legal recognition to individual duties higher than those owed to the government. The legal positivist discounts both the empirical evidence that individuals do assess the morality of public laws and that there is potentially a legal status under the Constitution for the moral claims of individuals. Moreover, legal positivists do not satisfactorily refute the argument that laws themselves are essentially based on the perception of moral values by public authorities.

Both the Hobbesian and the legal positivist analyses are frequently linked to an argument based on the common consent implicit in democratic government. The Hobbesian democrat would argue that the individual, by giving consent to majority rule, implicitly accepts the morality of society's laws as applied to the individual. But this type of argument does not answer the objections against the Hobbesian and legal positivist analyses. Indeed, the argument for conformity to democratically enacted law under all circumstances not only is deadening to moral sensitivity, but may also reflect a bias in favor of dominant community values.

Since the First Amendment guarantees freedom of religious, and by implication moral, exercise, conflicts between individual conscience and public law involve competing moral and legal claims. It is the professional task of philosophers, theologians, and jurists to assess them. Accordingly, it will be necessary to integrate the degrees of moral obligation perceived by individuals into a legal frame of reference—that is, to relate them to the prescriptions of public law with which they conflict.

First, a law may under the threat of imprisonment command what the conscience of an individual forbids absolutely (e.g., when state and local governments required that Jehovah's Witness pupils in public schools salute the flag).[3] Since public laws in such cases directly coerce individuals to act contrary to religious or moral duties perceived as important and absolutely obligatory, these claims of conscience should be rated the highest.

Second, a public law may forbid under threat of severe economic penalties what the conscience of an individual perceives as a right in-

---

3. Cf. *Minersville v. Gobitis*, 310 U.S. 586 (1940); *West Virginia v. Barnette*, 319 U.S. 624 (1943).

strumental to an absolute duty imposed by a negative moral imperative (e.g., when state and local laws prohibit Sabbatarians from engaging in business on Sundays).[4] Since the public laws at stake in such a case conflict only indirectly with religious or moral duties perceived by individuals as absolute, and since the laws conflict less severely with their religious or moral duties than direct coercion, these claims of individual conscience should be rated lower than the first class of conscientious objectors.

Third, a public law may forbid what an individual conscience specifically commands (e.g., when the federal government prohibited the practice of polygamy by Mormons).[5] Since, however, individuals perceive even such specific religious or moral duties as obligatory only if circumstances permit their performance—that is, the duties are relative to that extent—these claims of individual conscience should also be rated moderate in relation to the first class of conscientious objectors.

Fourth, a public law may forbid what the conscience of an individual commands as a means of implementing a general religious or moral duty (e.g., when a local government forbids itinerant evangelists from canvassing private residences without invitation from occupants to do so).[6] Since individuals perceive such duties to evangelize as religiously or morally obligatory only in general rather than specific terms, and individuals choose the time, place, and means of implementing them, these claims of conscience should be rated lowest in relation to the first three classes of conscientious objectors.

Respect for the moral dilemma of an individual forced to choose between obedience to conscience and obedience to a public law is an important value at stake in such conflicts. Therefore, the most pressing legal claim of conscience to exemption from the law should be based on a negative moral imperative that an individual perceives as so important that the individual cannot without loss of moral integrity perform the contrary act commanded by the law. And the lowest legal

---

4. Cf. *Braunfeld v. Brown*, 366 U.S. 599 (1961).
5. Cf. *Reynolds v. U.S.*, 98 U.S. 145 (1878); *Davis v. Beason*, 133 U.S. 333 (1890).
6. Cf. *Martin v. Struthers*, 319 U.S. 141 (1943).

claim of conscience to exemption from a public law should be based on an affirmative general moral imperative, an imperative that allows the individual discretion regarding its implementation. In between the two extremes are claims of conscience that assert rights substantially related to obligations imposed by negative moral imperatives and claims based on relatively specific affirmative moral imperatives.

When individuals challenge the validity of public laws, the putative public interests in support of the laws are at stake. When individuals claim exemption or immunity in the name of conscience from public laws whose validity they do not otherwise challenge, however, the public interests opposed to exemption of those individuals are at stake rather than the general purposes of the laws. Exemptions for conscientious objectors, of course, may threaten the general purposes of a law, but this need not be the case. If other citizens are not significantly affected by exempting individuals with conscientious objections from performing legally mandated acts, for example, then exceptions for conscientious objectors may be compatible with the general public interests served by the law. Mandated acts may not impose burdens on other citizens if individuals with conscientious objection are exempted from performing the acts, or if the number of conscientious objectors is relatively small. But the exemption of conscientious objectors is likely to be incompatible with the general purpose of legal prohibitions of acts regarded as contrary to substantial public interests.

TABLE OF CASES

271

Table of Cases

Table of Cases

Table of Cases

INDEX OF NAMES

Index of Names

INDEX OF SUBJECTS

The American Constitution and Religion was designed and typeset in Caslon by Kachergis Book Design of Pittsboro, North Carolina. It was printed on 60-pound Natures Book and bound by Thomson-Shore of Dexter, Michigan.